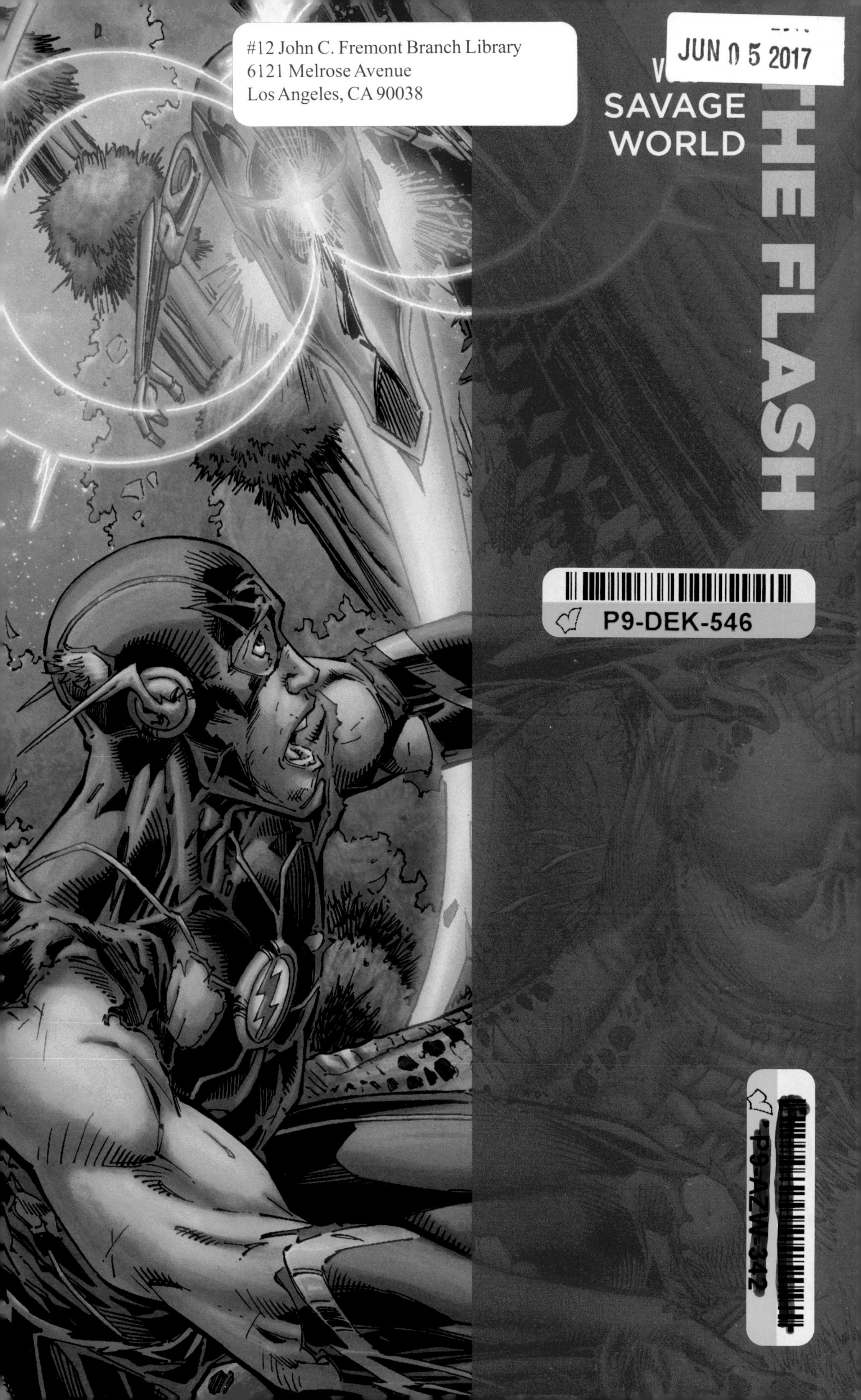
SAVAGE
WORLD
THE FLASH

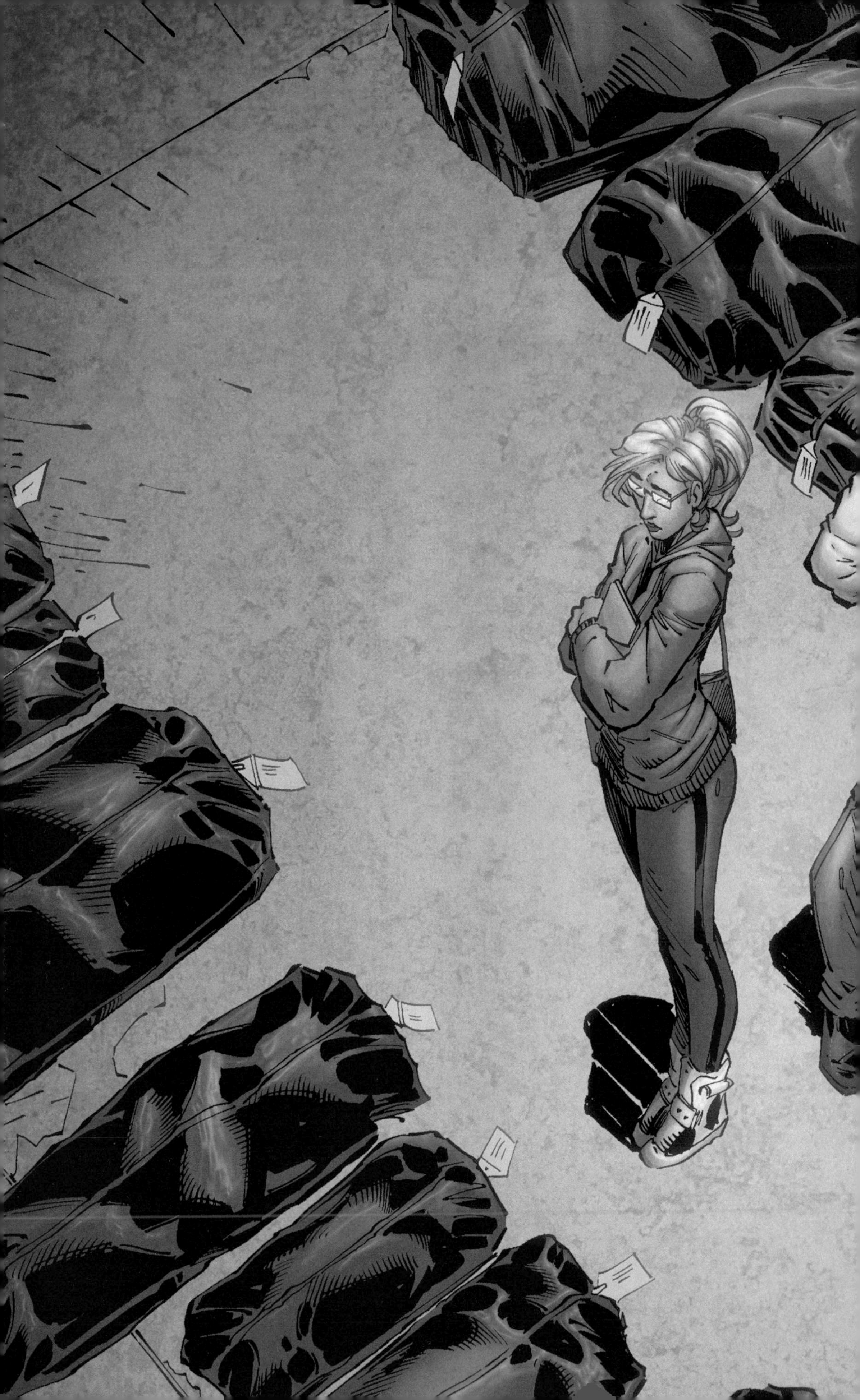

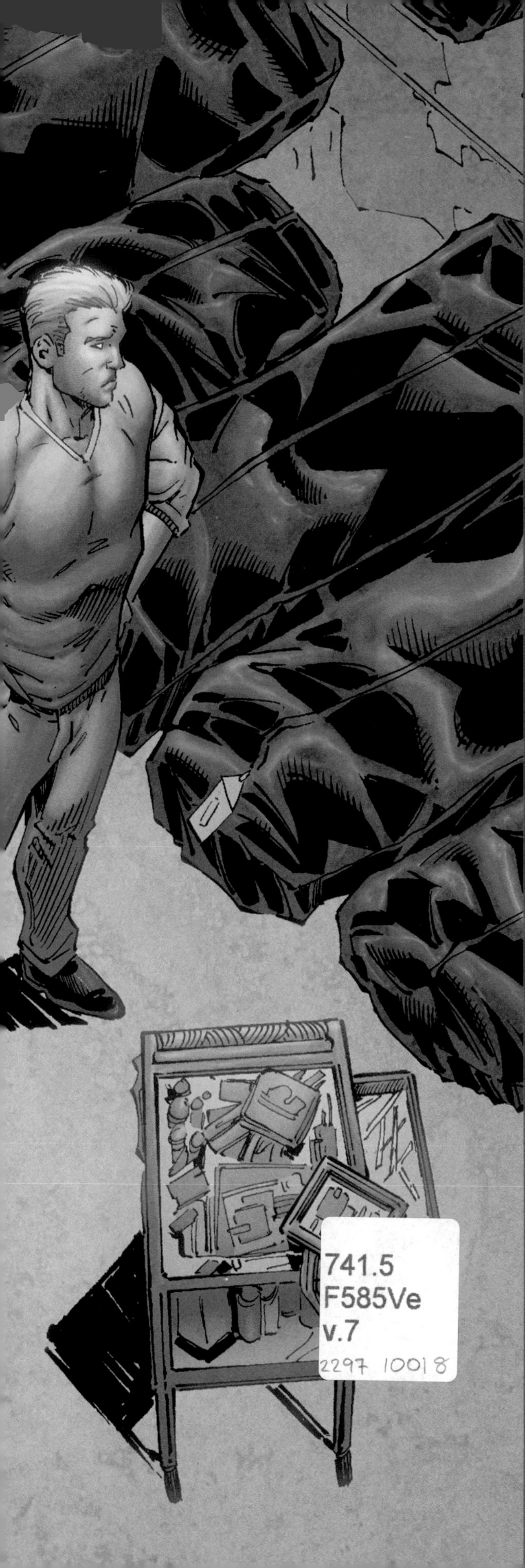

THE FLASH

VOLUME 7
SAVAGE WORLD

WRITTEN BY
ROBERT VENDITTI
VAN JENSEN

PENCILS BY
BRETT BOOTH
ANDRÉ COELHO
MIGUEL SEPULVEDA

INKS BY
NORM RAPMUND
SCOTT HANNA

COLOR BY
ANDREW DALHOUSE

LETTERS BY
TAYLOR ESPOSITO
DEZI SIENTY
PAT BROSSEAU

COLLECTION COVER ART BY
BRETT BOOTH,
NORM RAPMUND
& ANDREW DALHOUSE

BRIAN CUNNINGHAM Editor – Original Series
AMEDEO TURTURRO Assistant Editor – Original Series
JEB WOODARD Group Editor – Collected Editions
STEVE COOK Design Director – Books
DAMIAN RYLAND Publication Design

BOB HARRAS Senior VP – Editor-in-Chief, DC Comics

DIANE NELSON President
DAN DIDIO and JIM LEE Co-Publishers
GEOFF JOHNS Chief Creative Officer
AMIT DESAI Senior VP – Marketing & Global Franchise Management
NAIRI GARDINER Senior VP – Finance
SAM ADES VP – Digital Marketing
BOBBIE CHASE VP –Talent Development
MARK CHIARELLO Senior VP – Art, Design & Collected Editions
JOHN CUNNINGHAM VP – Content Strategy
ANNE DEPIES VP – Strategy Planning & Reporting
DON FALLETTI VP – Manufacturing Operations
LAWRENCE GANEM VP – Editorial Administration & Talent Relations
ALISON GILL Senior VP – Manufacturing & Operations
HANK KANALZ Senior VP – Editorial Strategy & Administration
JAY KOGAN VP – Legal Affairs
DEREK MADDALENA Senior VP – Sales & Business Development
JACK MAHAN VP – Business Affairs
DAN MIRON VP – Sales Planning & Trade Development
NICK NAPOLITANO VP – Manufacturing Administration
CAROL ROEDER VP – Marketing
EDDIE SCANNELL VP – Mass Account & Digital Sales
COURTNEY SIMMONS Senior VP – Publicity & Communications
JIM (SKI) SOKOLOWSKI VP – Comic Book Specialty & Newsstand Sales
SANDY YI Senior VP – Global Franchise Management

THE FLASH VOL. 7: SAVAGE WORLD

DC Comics, 2900 West Alameda Ave., Burbank, CA 91505
Printed by RR Donnelley, Owensville, MO, USA. 7/1/16. First Printing.
ISBN: 978-1-4012-6365-2

Library of Congress Cataloging-in-Publication Data

Venditti, Robert, author.
The Flash. Volume 7 / Robert Venditti, Van Jensen, writers ; Brett Booth, artist.
pages cm — (The New 52!)
ISBN 978-1-4012-6365-2
1. Graphic novels. I. Jensen, Van, author.. II. Booth, Brett, illustrator. III. Title.
PN6728.F53V46 2016
741.5'973—dc23
2015033156

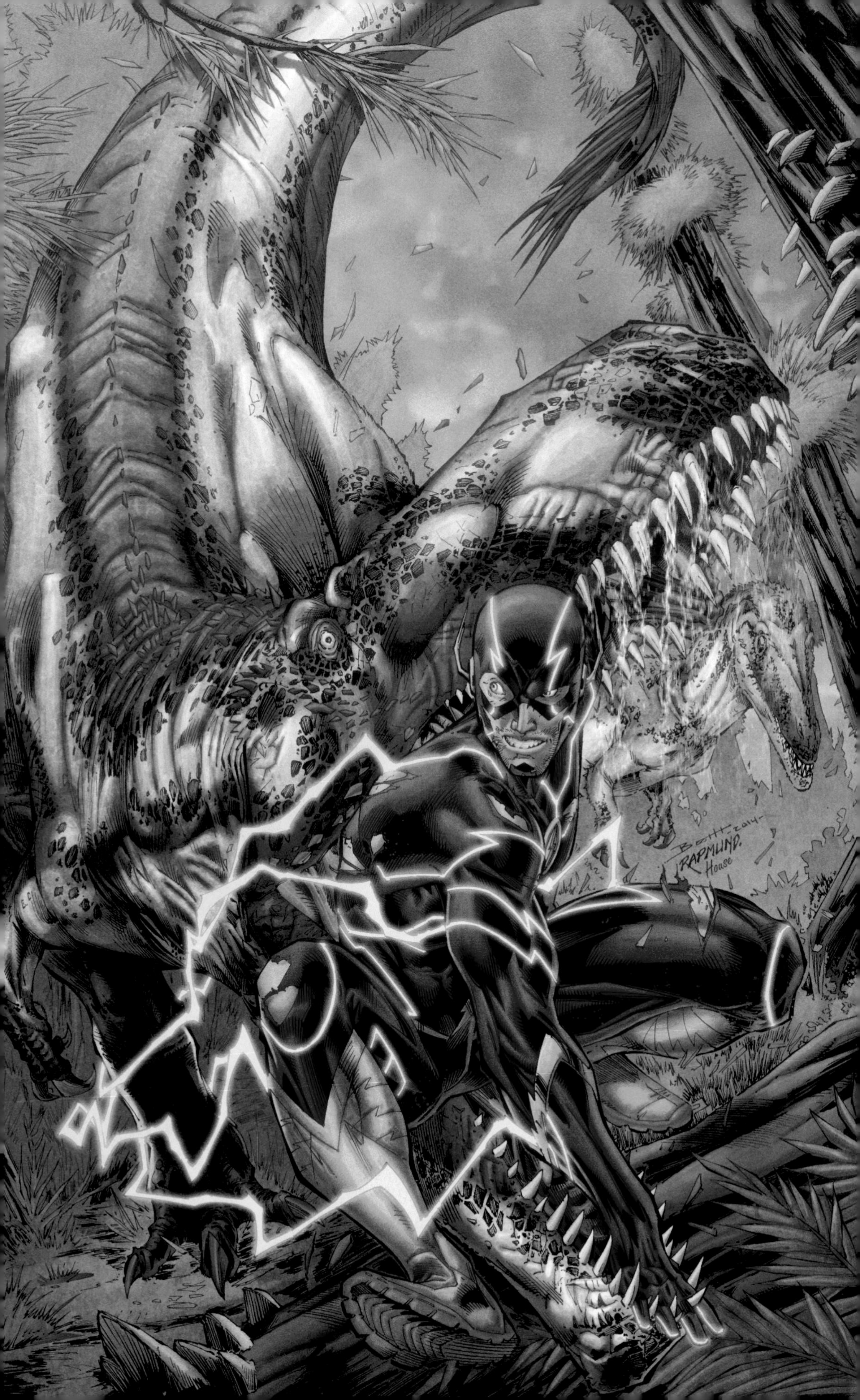
RAPMUND.
House

CASTAWAYS

ROBERT VENDITTI & VAN JENSEN writers BRETT BOOTH & ANDRÉ COELHO pencillers NORM RAPMUND inker ANDREW DALHOUSE colorist TAYLOR ESPOSITO letterer
cover by BRETT BOOTH, NORM RAPMUND & ANDREW DALHOUSE

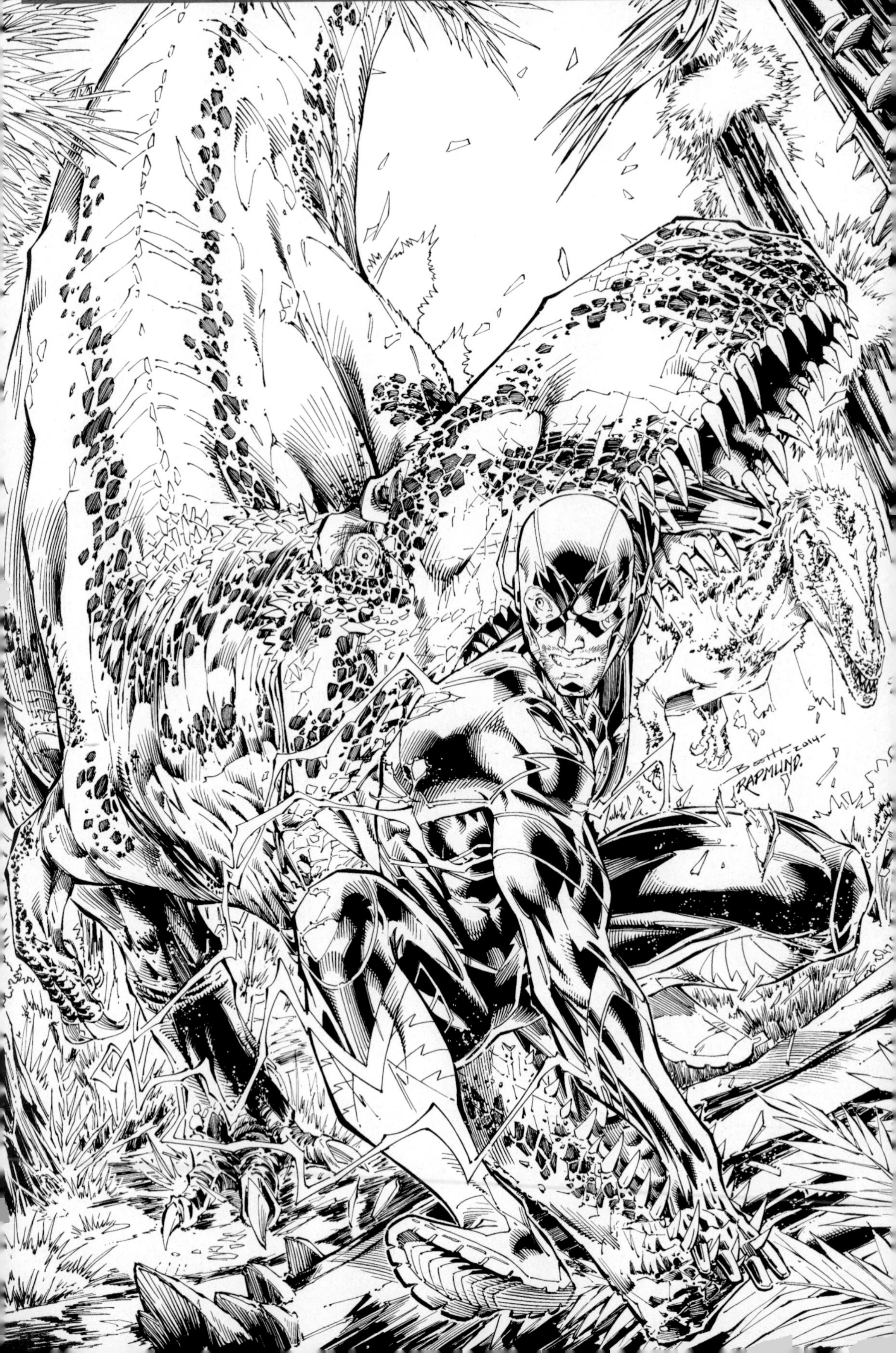

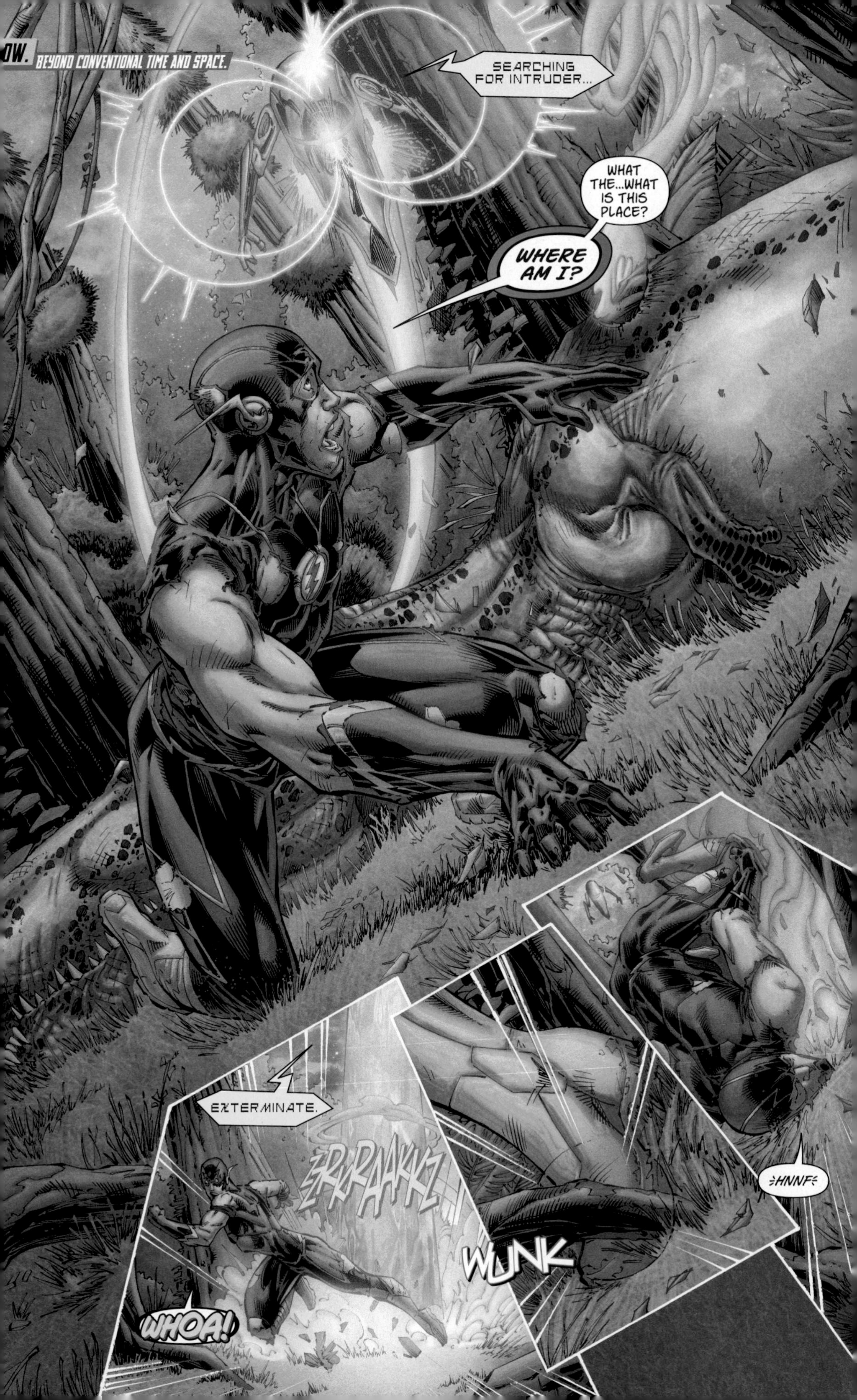
OW. BEYOND CONVENTIONAL TIME AND SPACE.
SEARCHING FOR INTRUDER...
WHAT THE...WHAT IS THIS PLACE?
WHERE AM I?
EXTERMINATE.
ZZRRAAKKZ
WHOA!
WUNK
HNNF

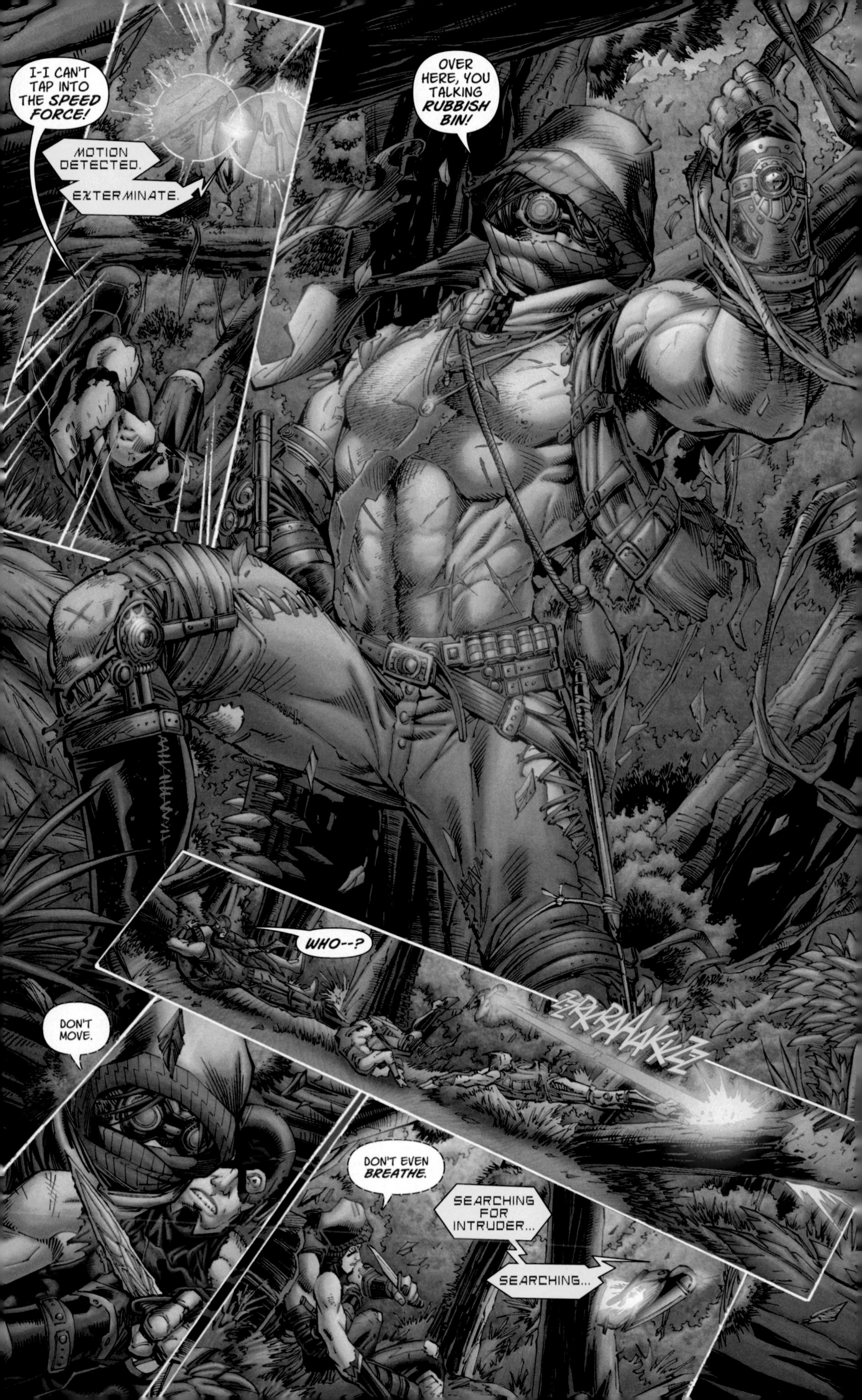

I-I CAN'T TAP INTO THE *SPEED FORCE!*
MOTION DETECTED.
EXTERMINATE.
OVER HERE, YOU TALKING *RUBBISH BIN!*
WHO--?
ZRAKRAKAKAKZZZ
DON'T MOVE.
DON'T EVEN *BREATHE.*
SEARCHING FOR INTRUDER...
SEARCHING...

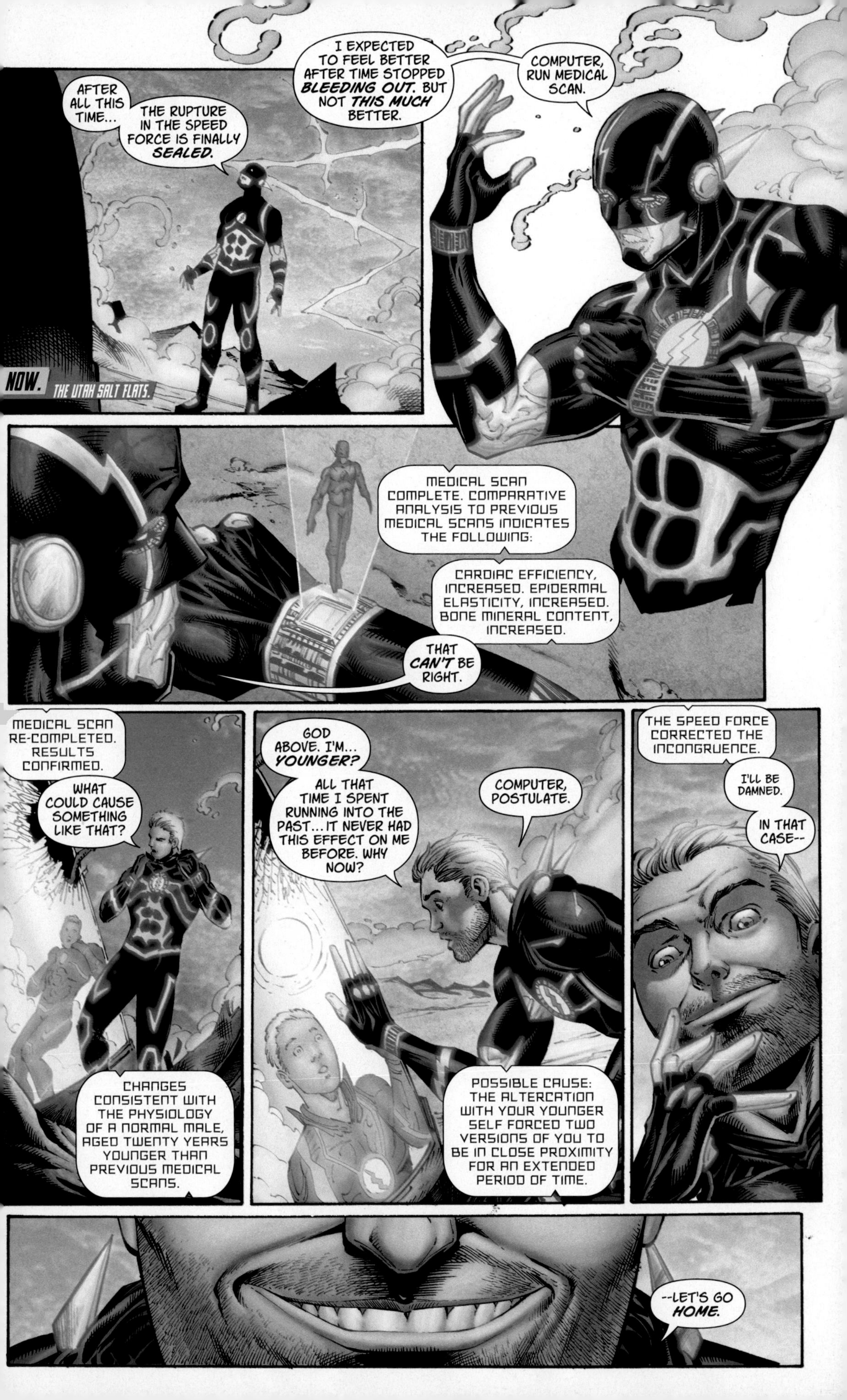
AFTER ALL THIS TIME...
THE RUPTURE IN THE SPEED FORCE IS FINALLY SEALED.
NOW.
THE UTAH SALT FLATS.
I EXPECTED TO FEEL BETTER AFTER TIME STOPPED BLEEDING OUT. BUT NOT THIS MUCH BETTER.
COMPUTER, RUN MEDICAL SCAN.
MEDICAL SCAN COMPLETE. COMPARATIVE ANALYSIS TO PREVIOUS MEDICAL SCANS INDICATES THE FOLLOWING:
CARDIAC EFFICIENCY, INCREASED. EPIDERMAL ELASTICITY, INCREASED. BONE MINERAL CONTENT, INCREASED.
THAT CAN'T BE RIGHT.
MEDICAL SCAN RE-COMPLETED. RESULTS CONFIRMED.
WHAT COULD CAUSE SOMETHING LIKE THAT?
CHANGES CONSISTENT WITH THE PHYSIOLOGY OF A NORMAL MALE, AGED TWENTY YEARS YOUNGER THAN PREVIOUS MEDICAL SCANS.
GOD ABOVE. I'M... YOUNGER?
ALL THAT TIME I SPENT RUNNING INTO THE PAST... IT NEVER HAD THIS EFFECT ON ME BEFORE. WHY NOW?
COMPUTER, POSTULATE.
POSSIBLE CAUSE: THE ALTERCATION WITH YOUR YOUNGER SELF FORCED TWO VERSIONS OF YOU TO BE IN CLOSE PROXIMITY FOR AN EXTENDED PERIOD OF TIME.
THE SPEED FORCE CORRECTED THE INCONGRUENCE.
I'LL BE DAMNED.
IN THAT CASE--
--LET'S GO HOME.

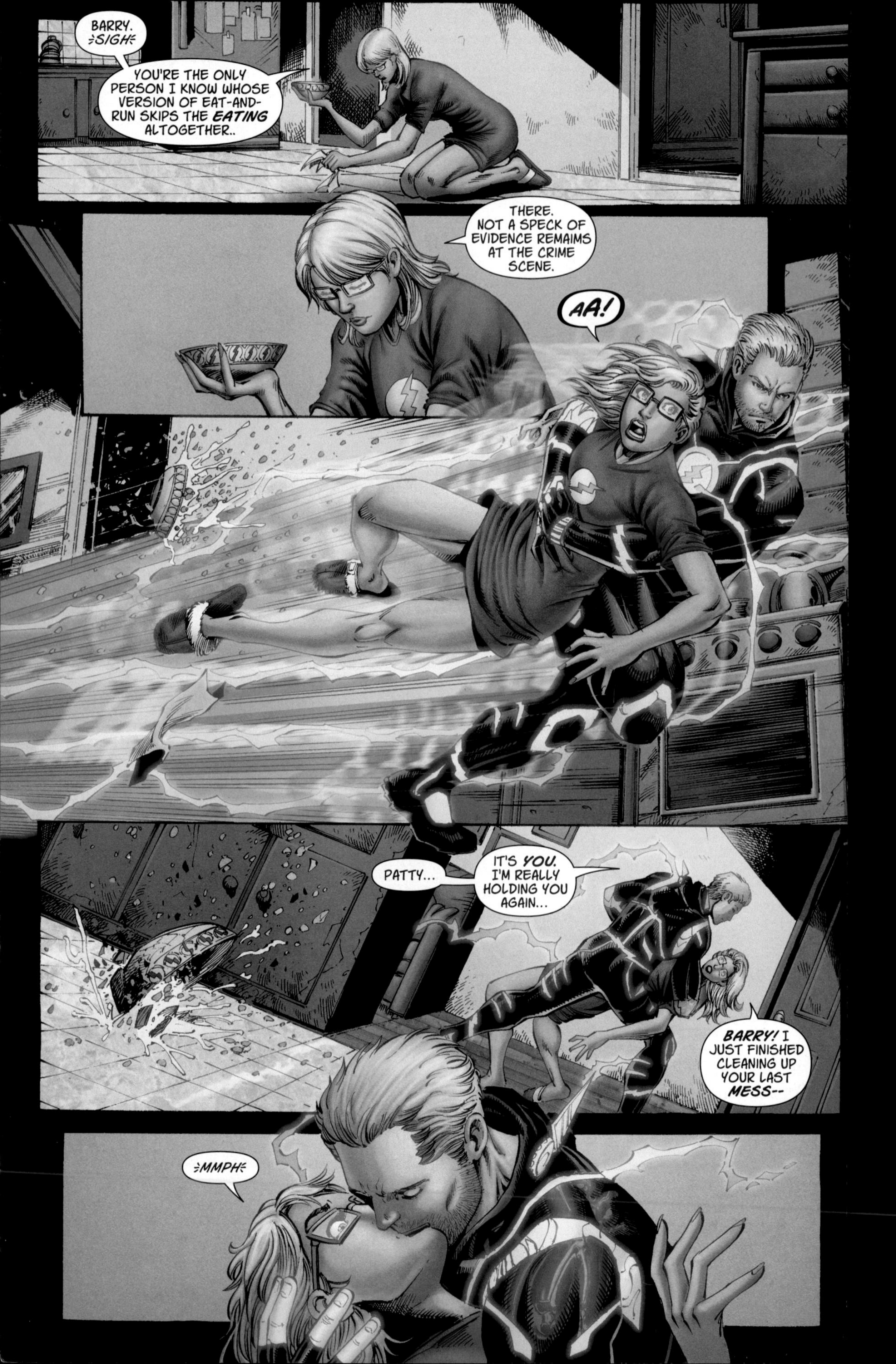
BARRY.
⋟SIGH⋞
YOU'RE THE ONLY PERSON I KNOW WHOSE VERSION OF EAT-AND-RUN SKIPS THE EATING ALTOGETHER..
THERE. NOT A SPECK OF EVIDENCE REMAIMS AT THE CRIME SCENE.
AA!
PATTY...
IT'S YOU. I'M REALLY HOLDING YOU AGAIN...
BARRY! I JUST FINISHED CLEANING UP YOUR LAST MESS--
⋟MMPH⋞

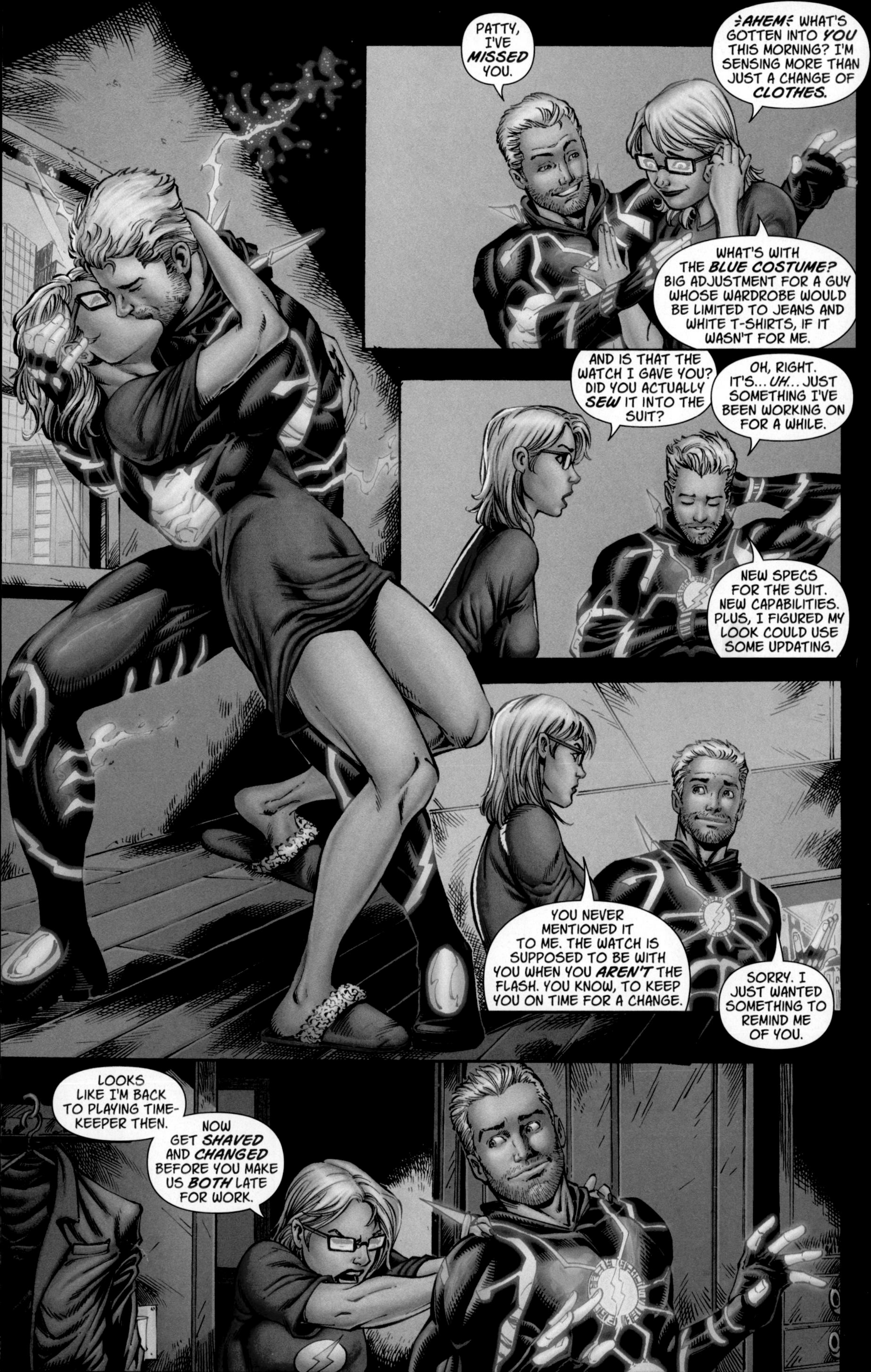
PATTY, I'VE MISSED YOU.
AHEM WHAT'S GOTTEN INTO YOU THIS MORNING? I'M SENSING MORE THAN JUST A CHANGE OF CLOTHES.
WHAT'S WITH THE BLUE COSTUME? BIG ADJUSTMENT FOR A GUY WHOSE WARDROBE WOULD BE LIMITED TO JEANS AND WHITE T-SHIRTS, IF IT WASN'T FOR ME.
AND IS THAT THE WATCH I GAVE YOU? DID YOU ACTUALLY SEW IT INTO THE SUIT?
OH, RIGHT. IT'S... UH... JUST SOMETHING I'VE BEEN WORKING ON FOR A WHILE.
NEW SPECS FOR THE SUIT. NEW CAPABILITIES. PLUS, I FIGURED MY LOOK COULD USE SOME UPDATING.
YOU NEVER MENTIONED IT TO ME. THE WATCH IS SUPPOSED TO BE WITH YOU WHEN YOU AREN'T THE FLASH. YOU KNOW, TO KEEP YOU ON TIME FOR A CHANGE.
SORRY. I JUST WANTED SOMETHING TO REMIND ME OF YOU.
LOOKS LIKE I'M BACK TO PLAYING TIME-KEEPER THEN.
NOW GET SHAVED AND CHANGED BEFORE YOU MAKE US BOTH LATE FOR WORK.

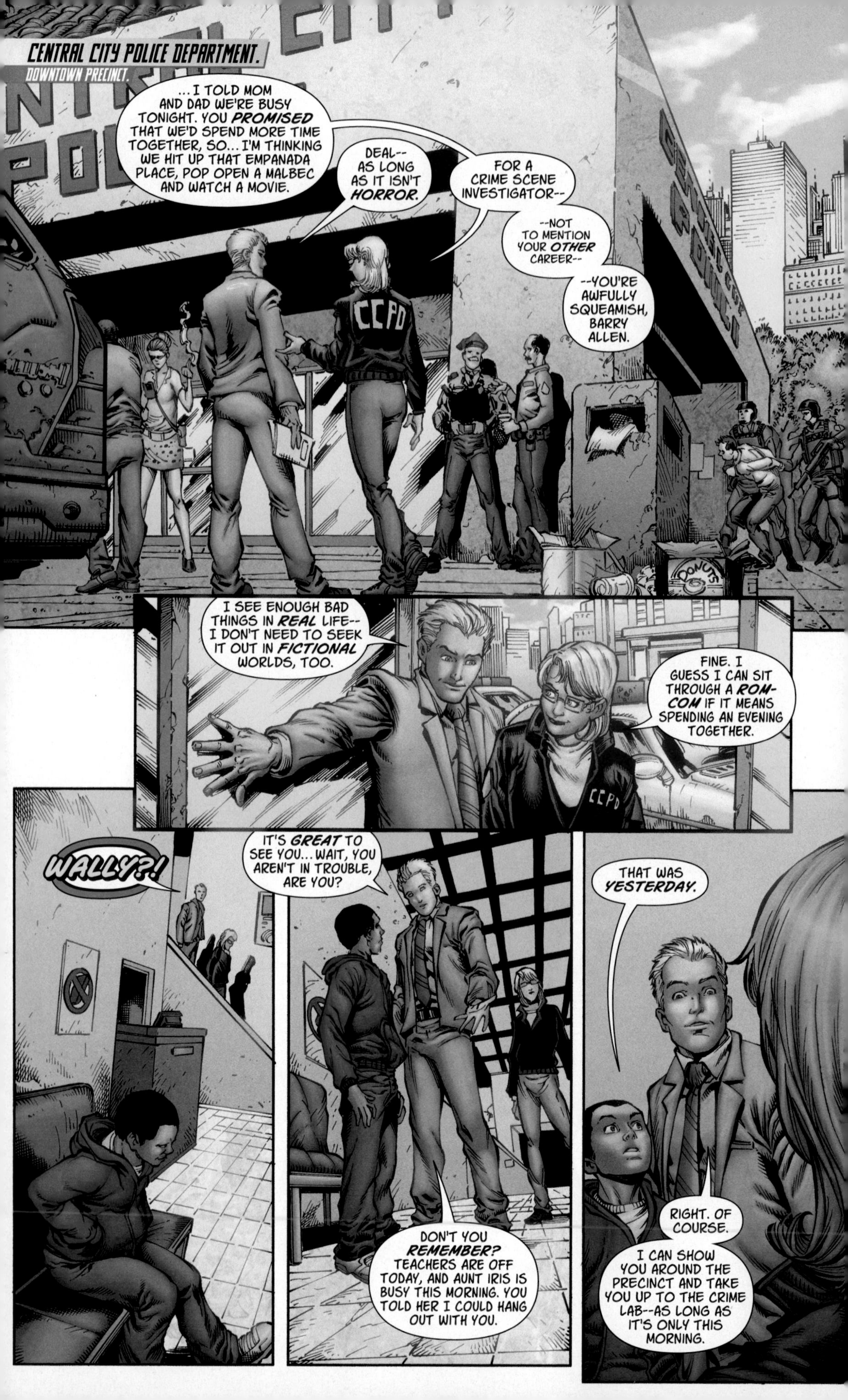
CENTRAL CITY POLICE DEPARTMENT.
DOWNTOWN PRECINCT.
...I TOLD MOM AND DAD WE'RE BUSY TONIGHT. YOU PROMISED THAT WE'D SPEND MORE TIME TOGETHER, SO... I'M THINKING WE HIT UP THAT EMPANADA PLACE, POP OPEN A MALBEC AND WATCH A MOVIE.
DEAL-- AS LONG AS IT ISN'T HORROR.
FOR A CRIME SCENE INVESTIGATOR--
--NOT TO MENTION YOUR OTHER CAREER--
--YOU'RE AWFULLY SQUEAMISH, BARRY ALLEN.
CCPD
DONUTS
I SEE ENOUGH BAD THINGS IN REAL LIFE-- I DON'T NEED TO SEEK IT OUT IN FICTIONAL WORLDS, TOO.
FINE. I GUESS I CAN SIT THROUGH A ROM-COM IF IT MEANS SPENDING AN EVENING TOGETHER.
CCPD
WALLY?!
IT'S GREAT TO SEE YOU... WAIT, YOU AREN'T IN TROUBLE, ARE YOU?
DON'T YOU REMEMBER? TEACHERS ARE OFF TODAY, AND AUNT IRIS IS BUSY THIS MORNING. YOU TOLD HER I COULD HANG OUT WITH YOU.
THAT WAS YESTERDAY.
RIGHT. OF COURSE.
I CAN SHOW YOU AROUND THE PRECINCT AND TAKE YOU UP TO THE CRIME LAB--AS LONG AS IT'S ONLY THIS MORNING.

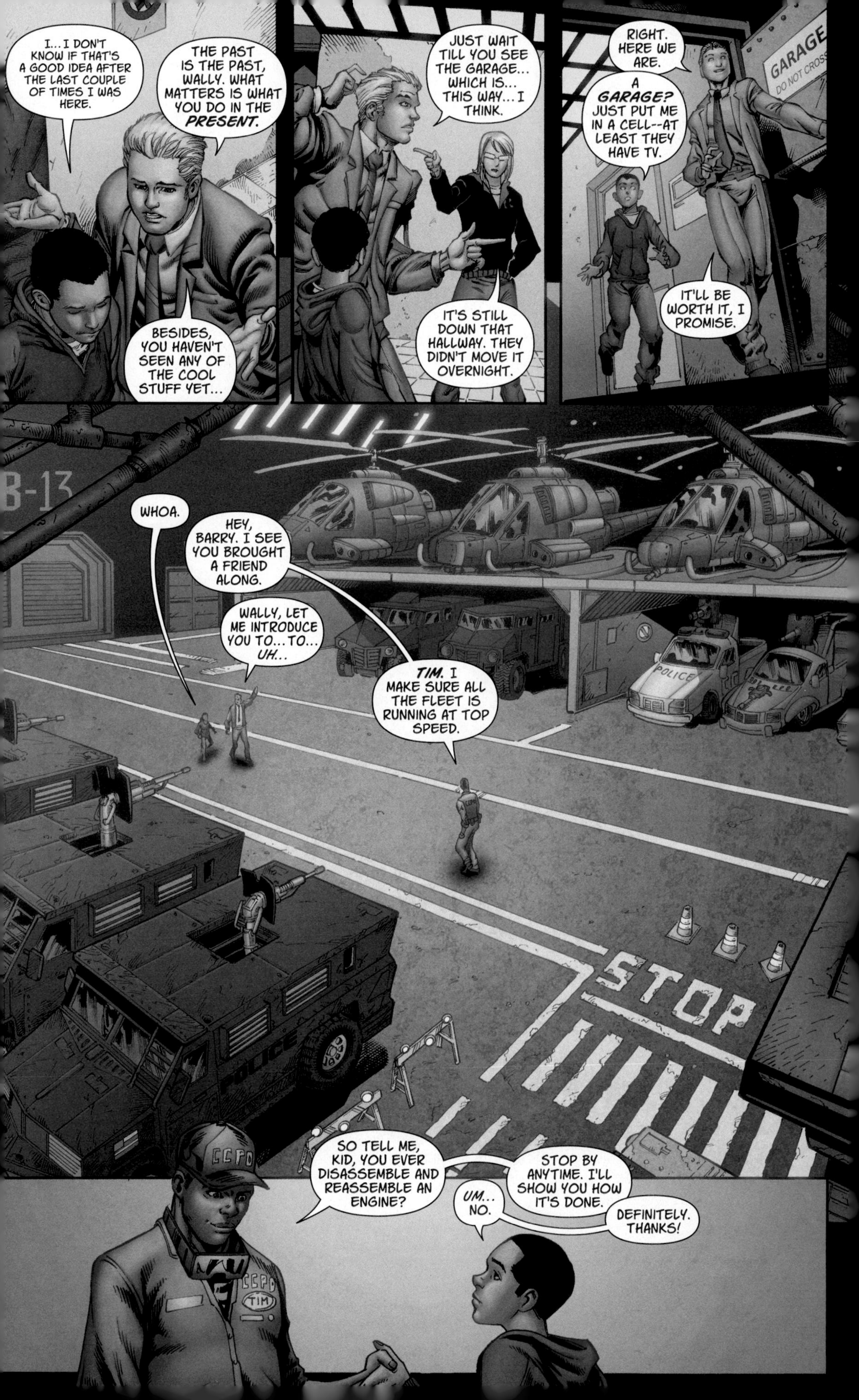
I... I DON'T KNOW IF THAT'S A GOOD IDEA AFTER THE LAST COUPLE OF TIMES I WAS HERE.
THE PAST IS THE PAST, WALLY. WHAT MATTERS IS WHAT YOU DO IN THE PRESENT.
BESIDES, YOU HAVEN'T SEEN ANY OF THE COOL STUFF YET...
JUST WAIT TILL YOU SEE THE GARAGE... WHICH IS... THIS WAY... I THINK.
IT'S STILL DOWN THAT HALLWAY. THEY DIDN'T MOVE IT OVERNIGHT.
GARAGE
DO NOT CROSS
RIGHT. HERE WE ARE.
A GARAGE? JUST PUT ME IN A CELL--AT LEAST THEY HAVE TV.
IT'LL BE WORTH IT, I PROMISE.
B-13
WHOA.
HEY, BARRY. I SEE YOU BROUGHT A FRIEND ALONG.
WALLY, LET ME INTRODUCE YOU TO... TO... UH...
TIM. I MAKE SURE ALL THE FLEET IS RUNNING AT TOP SPEED.
POLICE
STOP
SO TELL ME, KID, YOU EVER DISASSEMBLE AND REASSEMBLE AN ENGINE?
UM... NO.
STOP BY ANYTIME. I'LL SHOW YOU HOW IT'S DONE.
DEFINITELY. THANKS!
CCPD
TIM

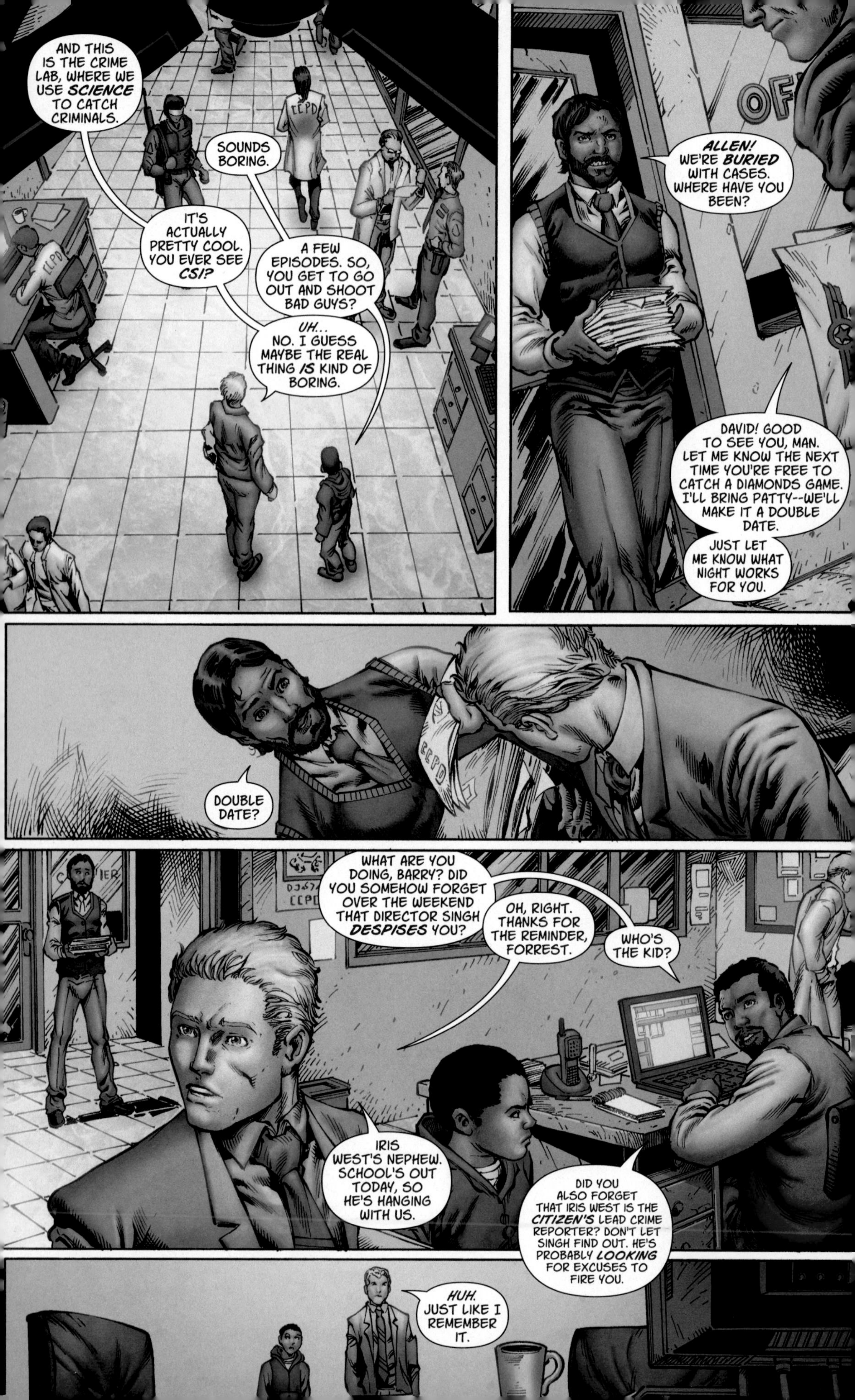
AND THIS IS THE CRIME LAB, WHERE WE USE SCIENCE TO CATCH CRIMINALS.
SOUNDS BORING.
IT'S ACTUALLY PRETTY COOL. YOU EVER SEE CSI?
A FEW EPISODES. SO, YOU GET TO GO OUT AND SHOOT BAD GUYS?
UH... NO. I GUESS MAYBE THE REAL THING IS KIND OF BORING.
ALLEN! WE'RE BURIED WITH CASES. WHERE HAVE YOU BEEN?
DAVID! GOOD TO SEE YOU, MAN. LET ME KNOW THE NEXT TIME YOU'RE FREE TO CATCH A DIAMONDS GAME. I'LL BRING PATTY--WE'LL MAKE IT A DOUBLE DATE.
JUST LET ME KNOW WHAT NIGHT WORKS FOR YOU.
DOUBLE DATE?
WHAT ARE YOU DOING, BARRY? DID YOU SOMEHOW FORGET OVER THE WEEKEND THAT DIRECTOR SINGH DESPISES YOU?
OH, RIGHT. THANKS FOR THE REMINDER, FORREST.
WHO'S THE KID?
IRIS WEST'S NEPHEW. SCHOOL'S OUT TODAY, SO HE'S HANGING WITH US.
DID YOU ALSO FORGET THAT IRIS WEST IS THE CITIZEN'S LEAD CRIME REPORTER? DON'T LET SINGH FIND OUT. HE'S PROBABLY LOOKING FOR EXCUSES TO FIRE YOU.
HUH. JUST LIKE I REMEMBER IT.

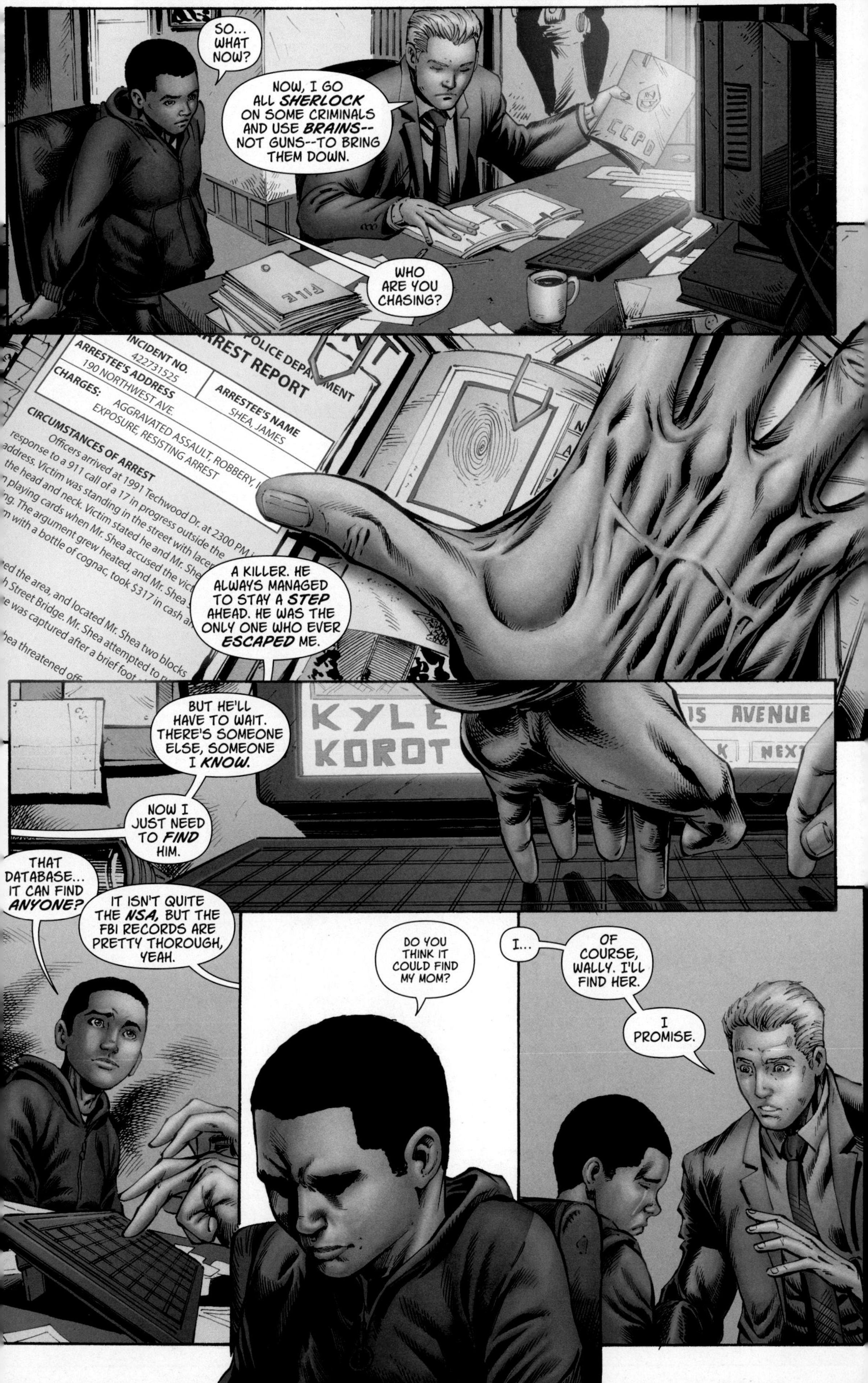
SO... WHAT NOW?
NOW, I GO ALL SHERLOCK ON SOME CRIMINALS AND USE BRAINS--NOT GUNS--TO BRING THEM DOWN.
WHO ARE YOU CHASING?
ARREST REPORT
INCIDENT NO.
422731525
ARRESTEE'S ADDRESS
190 NORTHWEST AVE.
ARRESTEE'S NAME
SHEA, JAMES
CHARGES:
AGGRAVATED ASSAULT, ROBBERY,
EXPOSURE, RESISTING ARREST
CIRCUMSTANCES OF ARREST
A KILLER. HE ALWAYS MANAGED TO STAY A STEP AHEAD. HE WAS THE ONLY ONE WHO EVER ESCAPED ME.
KYLE KOROT
AVENUE
BUT HE'LL HAVE TO WAIT. THERE'S SOMEONE ELSE, SOMEONE I KNOW.
NOW I JUST NEED TO FIND HIM.
THAT DATABASE... IT CAN FIND ANYONE?
IT ISN'T QUITE THE NSA, BUT THE FBI RECORDS ARE PRETTY THOROUGH, YEAH.
DO YOU THINK IT COULD FIND MY MOM?
I...
OF COURSE, WALLY. I'LL FIND HER.
I PROMISE.

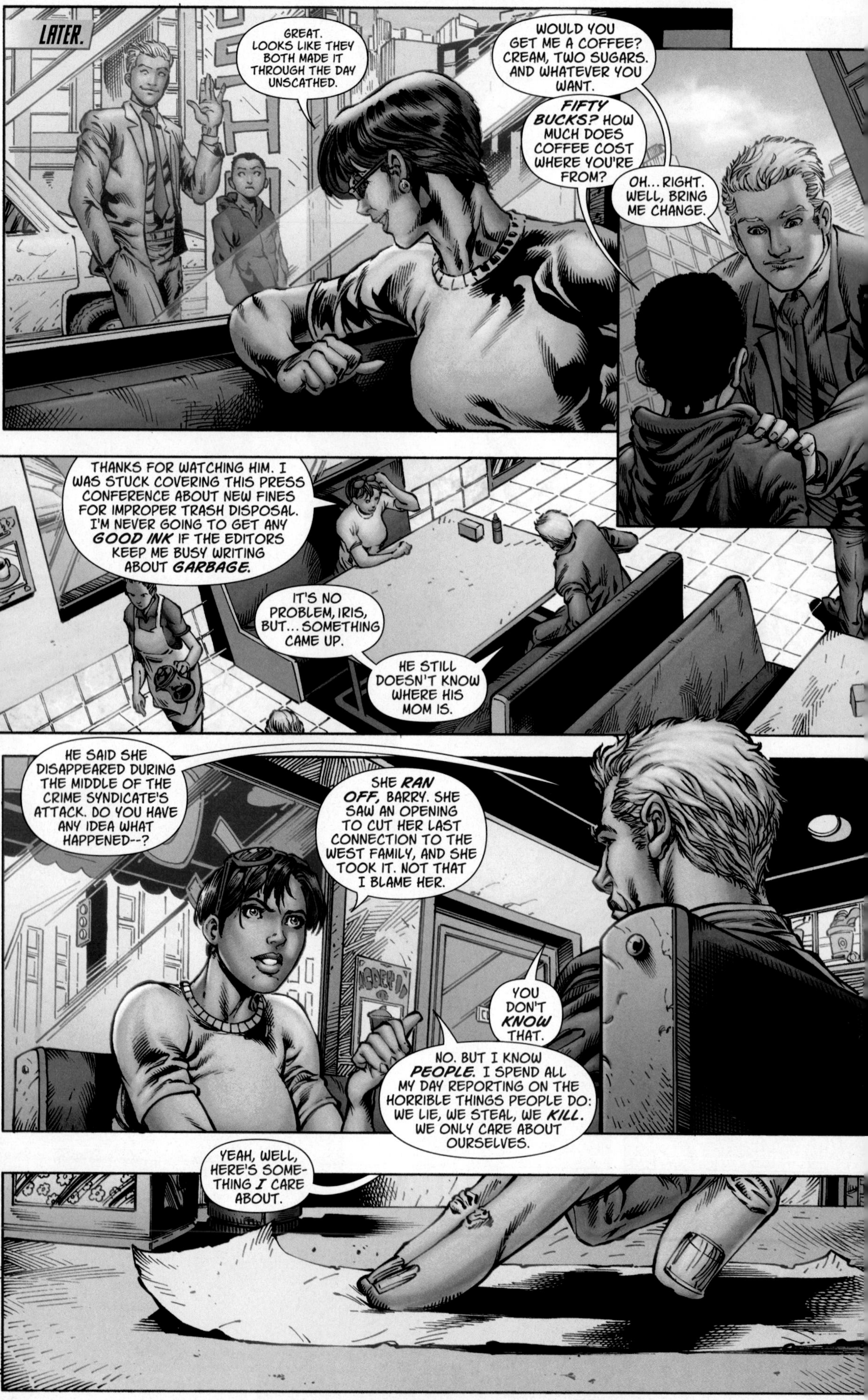
LATER.
GREAT. LOOKS LIKE THEY BOTH MADE IT THROUGH THE DAY UNSCATHED.
WOULD YOU GET ME A COFFEE? CREAM, TWO SUGARS. AND WHATEVER YOU WANT.
FIFTY BUCKS? HOW MUCH DOES COFFEE COST WHERE YOU'RE FROM?
OH... RIGHT. WELL, BRING ME CHANGE.
THANKS FOR WATCHING HIM. I WAS STUCK COVERING THIS PRESS CONFERENCE ABOUT NEW FINES FOR IMPROPER TRASH DISPOSAL. I'M NEVER GOING TO GET ANY GOOD INK IF THE EDITORS KEEP ME BUSY WRITING ABOUT GARBAGE.
IT'S NO PROBLEM, IRIS, BUT... SOMETHING CAME UP.
HE STILL DOESN'T KNOW WHERE HIS MOM IS.
HE SAID SHE DISAPPEARED DURING THE MIDDLE OF THE CRIME SYNDICATE'S ATTACK. DO YOU HAVE ANY IDEA WHAT HAPPENED--?
SHE RAN OFF, BARRY. SHE SAW AN OPENING TO CUT HER LAST CONNECTION TO THE WEST FAMILY, AND SHE TOOK IT. NOT THAT I BLAME HER.
YOU DON'T KNOW THAT.
NO. BUT I KNOW PEOPLE. I SPEND ALL MY DAY REPORTING ON THE HORRIBLE THINGS PEOPLE DO: WE LIE, WE STEAL, WE KILL. WE ONLY CARE ABOUT OURSELVES.
YEAH, WELL, HERE'S SOMETHING I CARE ABOUT.

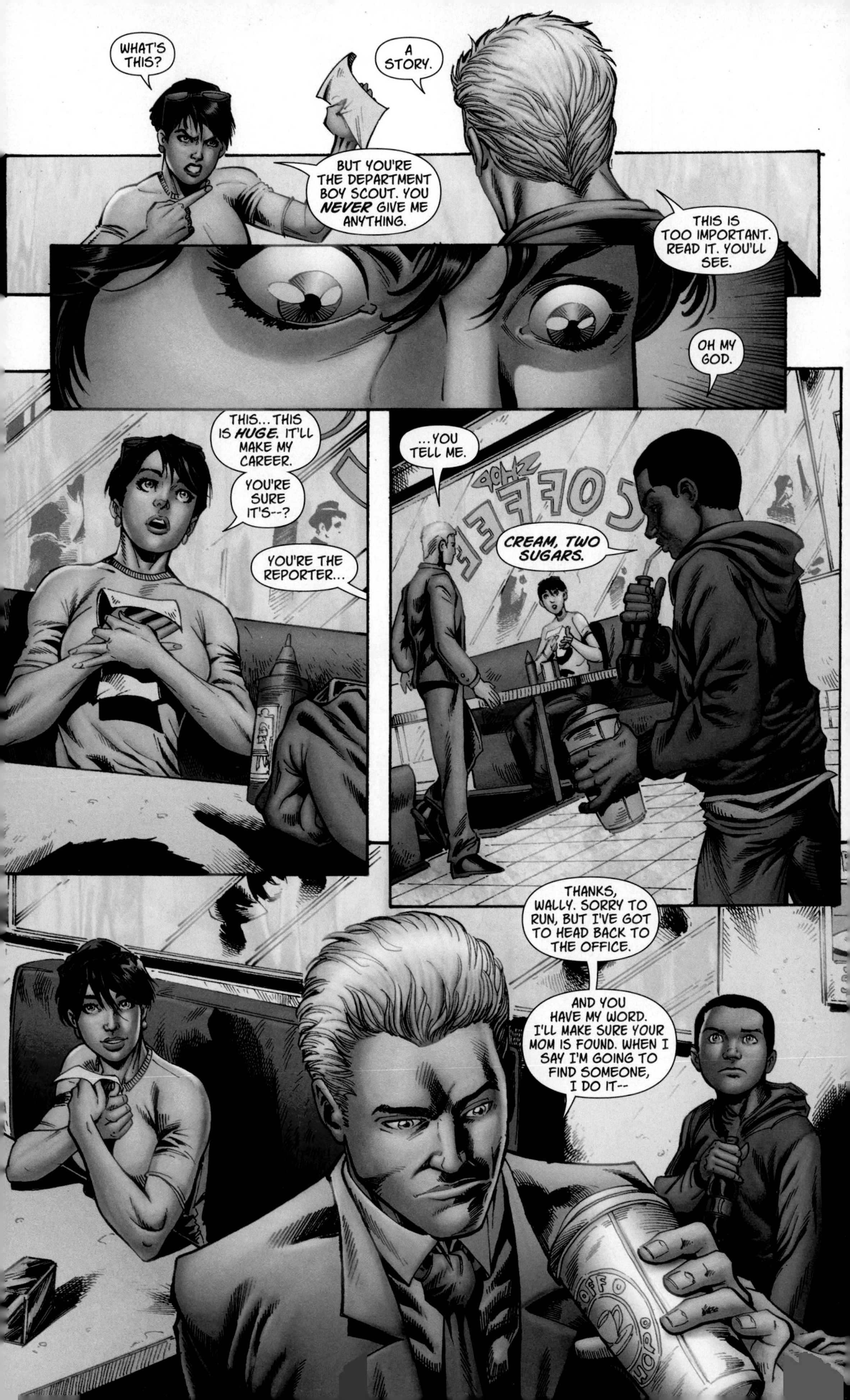
WHAT'S THIS?
A STORY.
BUT YOU'RE THE DEPARTMENT BOY SCOUT. YOU NEVER GIVE ME ANYTHING.
THIS IS TOO IMPORTANT. READ IT. YOU'LL SEE.
OH MY GOD.
THIS... THIS IS HUGE. IT'LL MAKE MY CAREER.
YOU'RE SURE IT'S--?
YOU'RE THE REPORTER...
...YOU TELL ME.
CREAM, TWO SUGARS.
THANKS, WALLY. SORRY TO RUN, BUT I'VE GOT TO HEAD BACK TO THE OFFICE.
AND YOU HAVE MY WORD. I'LL MAKE SURE YOUR MOM IS FOUND. WHEN I SAY I'M GOING TO FIND SOMEONE, I DO IT--

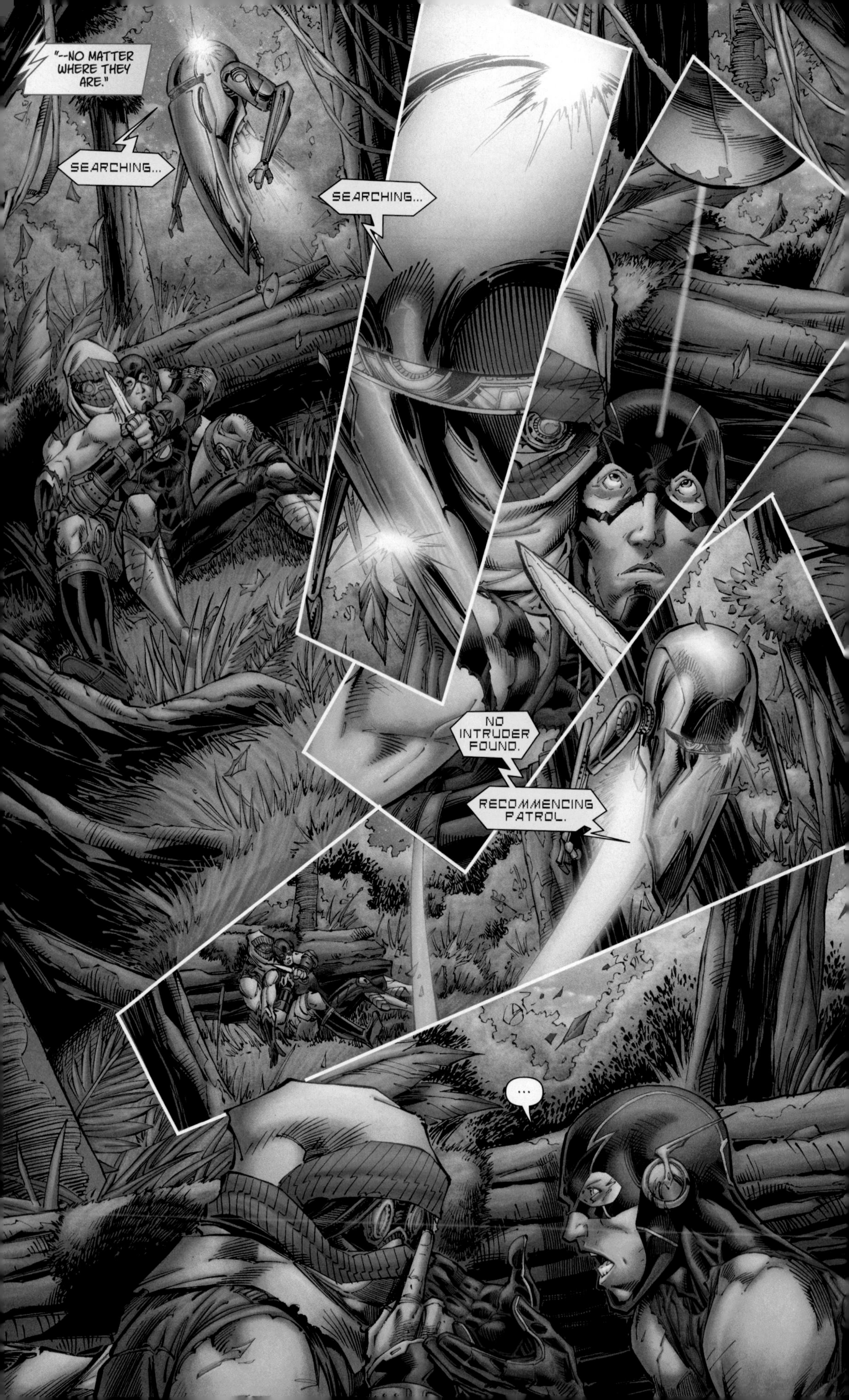
"--NO MATTER WHERE THEY ARE."
SEARCHING...
SEARCHING...
NO INTRUDER FOUND.
RECOMMENCING PATROL.
...

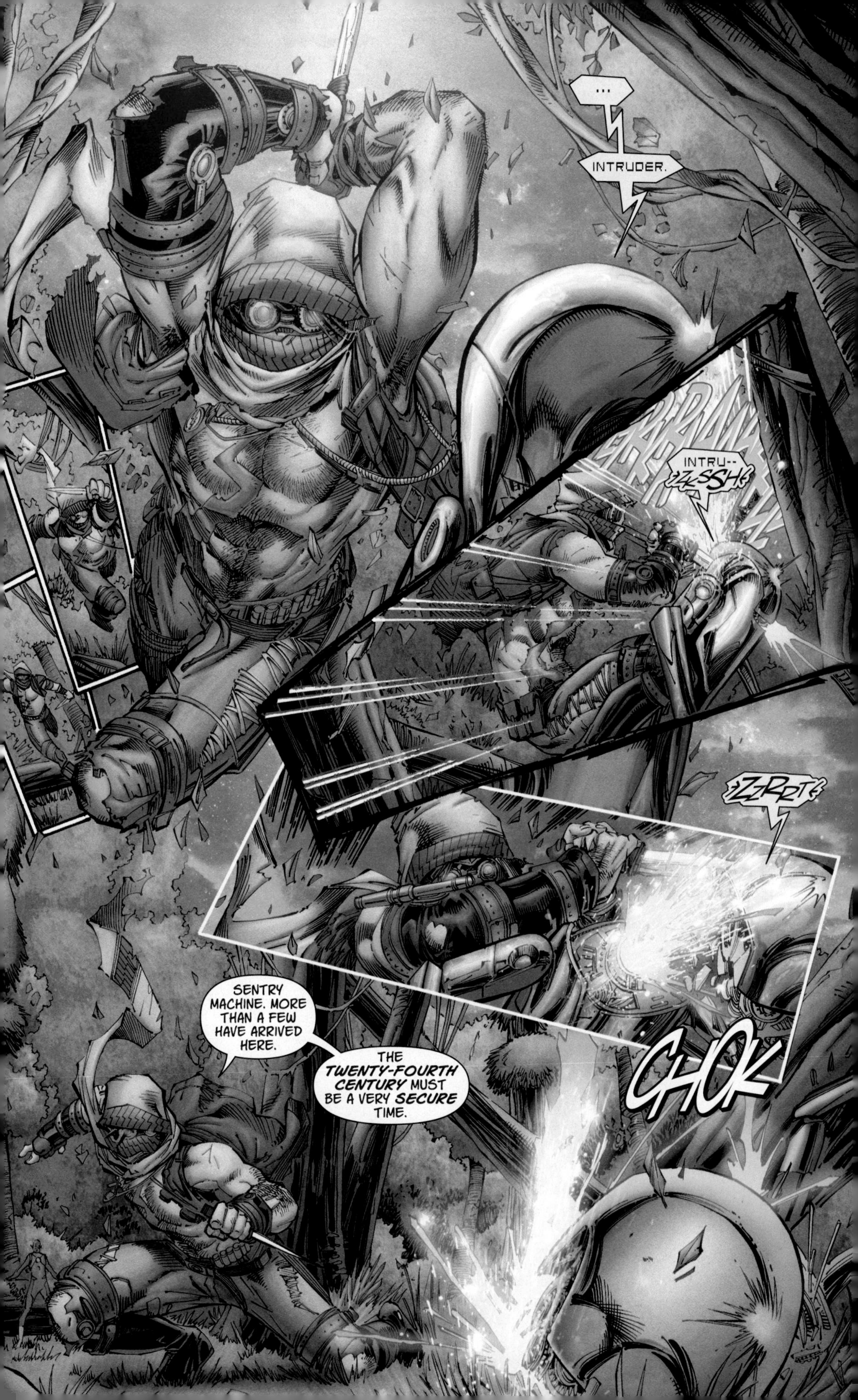
...
INTRUDER.
INTRU--
ZZSSH
ZZRRT
CHOK
SENTRY MACHINE. MORE THAN A FEW HAVE ARRIVED HERE.
THE TWENTY-FOURTH CENTURY MUST BE A VERY SECURE TIME.

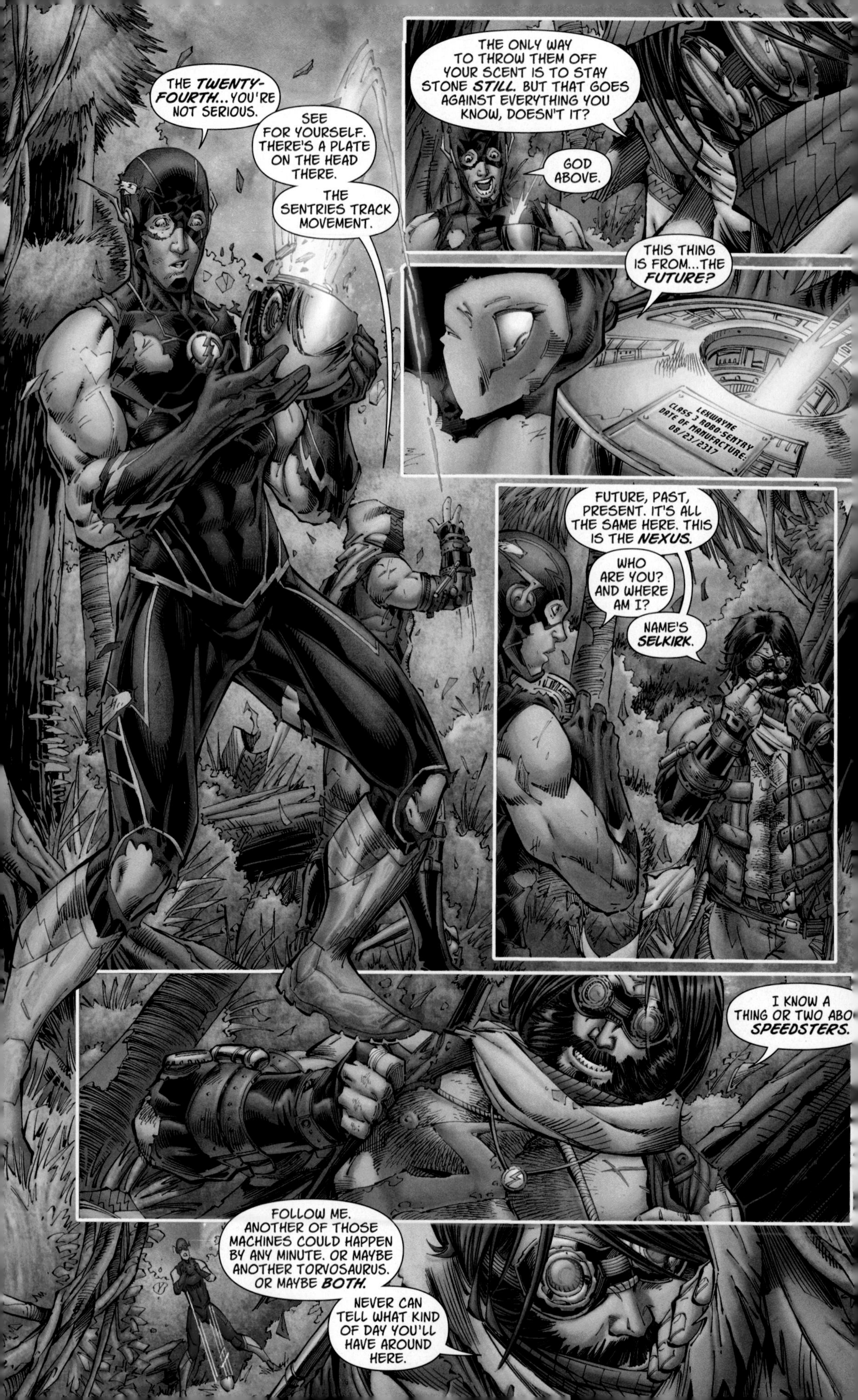

THE *TWENTY-FOURTH*...YOU'RE NOT SERIOUS.
SEE FOR YOURSELF. THERE'S A PLATE ON THE HEAD THERE.
THE SENTRIES TRACK MOVEMENT.
THE ONLY WAY TO THROW THEM OFF YOUR SCENT IS TO STAY STONE *STILL.* BUT THAT GOES AGAINST EVERYTHING YOU KNOW, DOESN'T IT?
GOD ABOVE.
THIS THING IS FROM...THE *FUTURE?*
LEXWAYNE
CLASS 3 ROBO-SENTRY
DATE OF MANUFACTURE:
08/23/2317
FUTURE, PAST, PRESENT. IT'S ALL THE SAME HERE. THIS IS THE *NEXUS.*
WHO ARE YOU? AND WHERE AM I?
NAME'S *SELKIRK.*
I KNOW A THING OR TWO ABO *SPEEDSTERS.*
FOLLOW ME. ANOTHER OF THOSE MACHINES COULD HAPPEN BY ANY MINUTE. OR MAYBE ANOTHER TORVOSAURUS. OR MAYBE *BOTH.*
NEVER CAN TELL WHAT KIND OF DAY YOU'LL HAVE AROUND HERE.

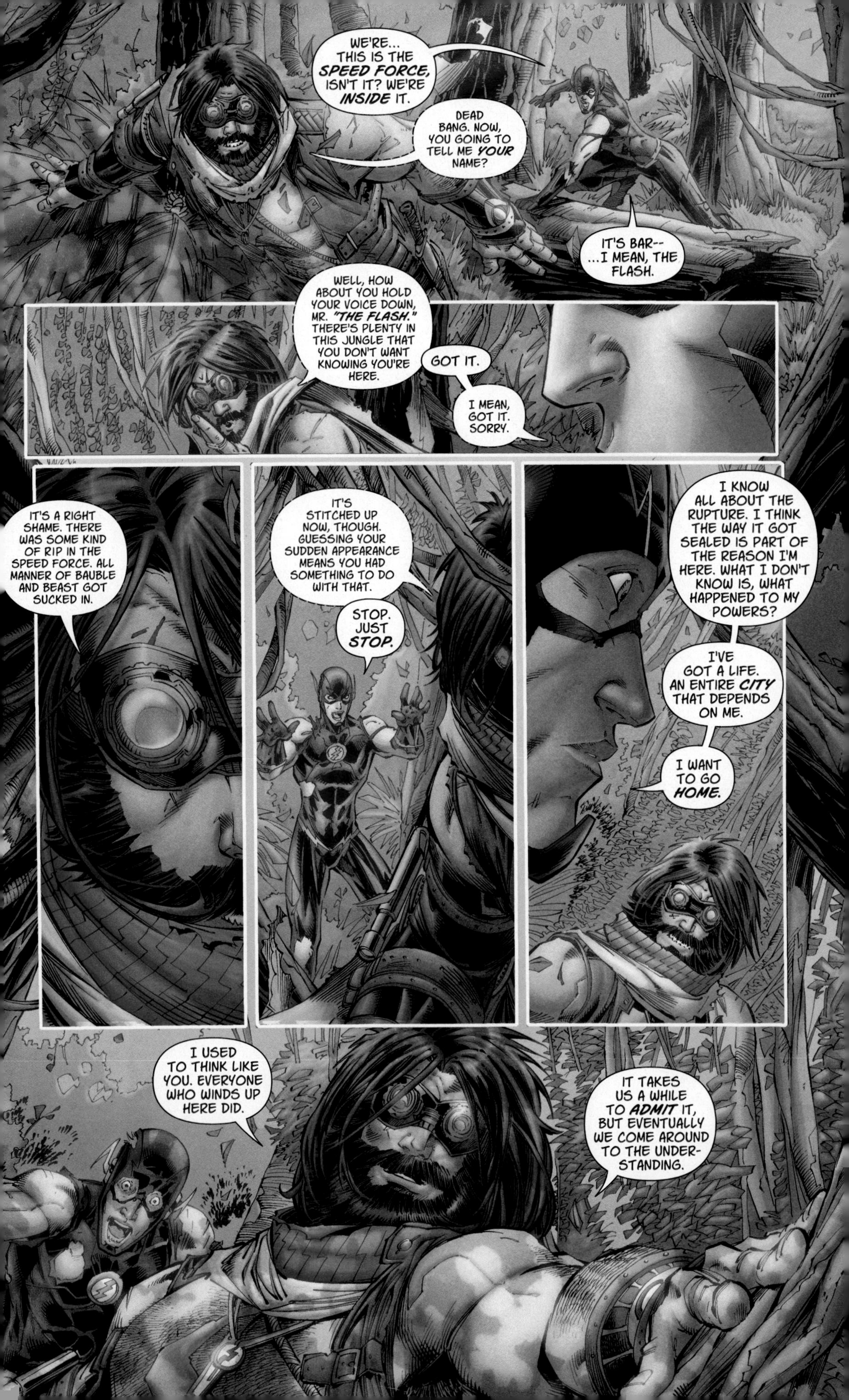
WE'RE... THIS IS THE SPEED FORCE, ISN'T IT? WE'RE INSIDE IT.
DEAD BANG. NOW, YOU GOING TO TELL ME YOUR NAME?
IT'S BAR-- ...I MEAN, THE FLASH.
WELL, HOW ABOUT YOU HOLD YOUR VOICE DOWN, MR. "THE FLASH." THERE'S PLENTY IN THIS JUNGLE THAT YOU DON'T WANT KNOWING YOU'RE HERE.
GOT IT.
I MEAN, GOT IT. SORRY.
IT'S A RIGHT SHAME. THERE WAS SOME KIND OF RIP IN THE SPEED FORCE. ALL MANNER OF BAUBLE AND BEAST GOT SUCKED IN.
IT'S STITCHED UP NOW, THOUGH. GUESSING YOUR SUDDEN APPEARANCE MEANS YOU HAD SOMETHING TO DO WITH THAT.
STOP. JUST STOP.
I KNOW ALL ABOUT THE RUPTURE. I THINK THE WAY IT GOT SEALED IS PART OF THE REASON I'M HERE. WHAT I DON'T KNOW IS, WHAT HAPPENED TO MY POWERS?
I'VE GOT A LIFE. AN ENTIRE CITY THAT DEPENDS ON ME.
I WANT TO GO HOME.
I USED TO THINK LIKE YOU. EVERYONE WHO WINDS UP HERE DID.
IT TAKES US A WHILE TO ADMIT IT, BUT EVENTUALLY WE COME AROUND TO THE UNDER-STANDING.

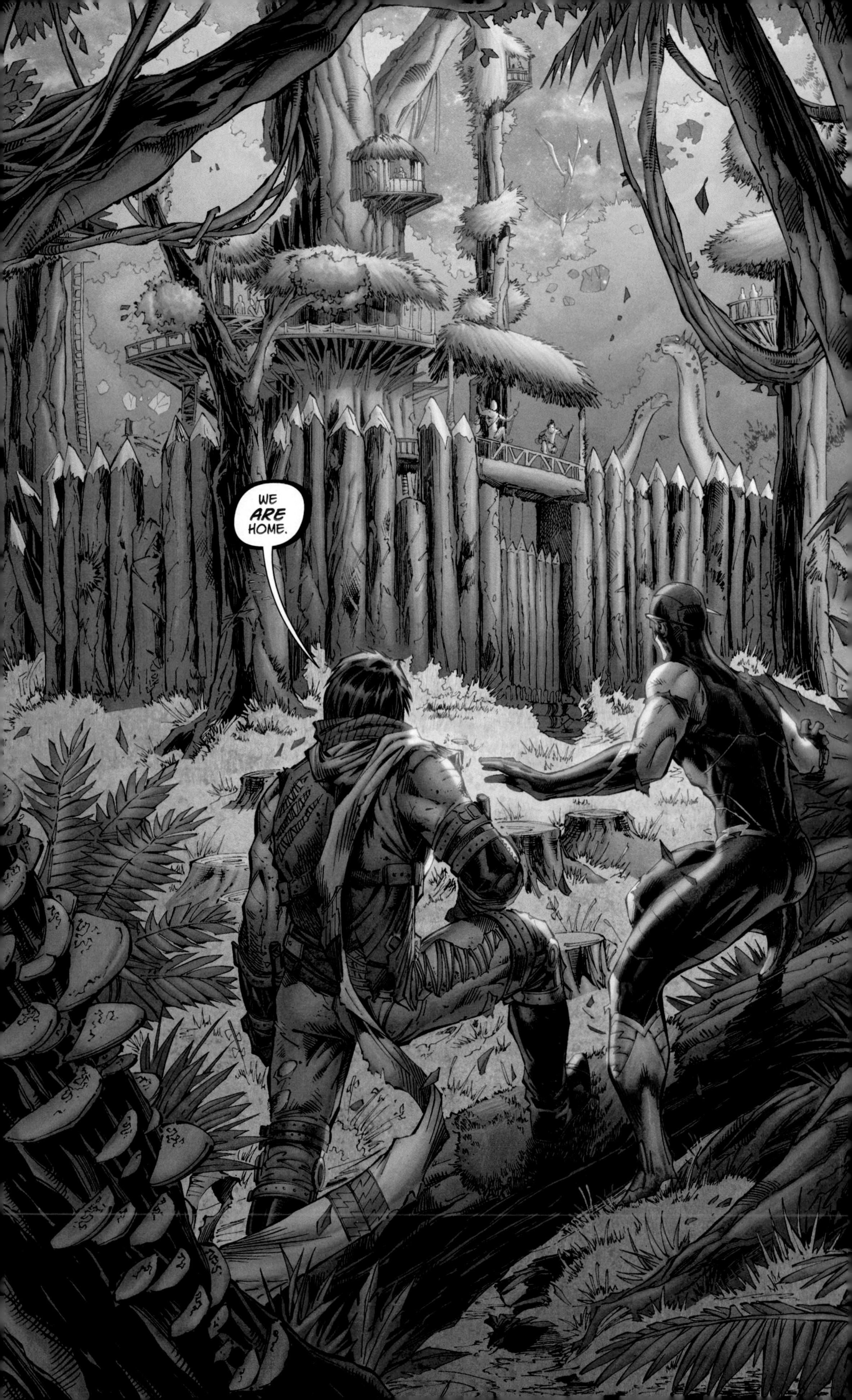
WE ARE HOME.

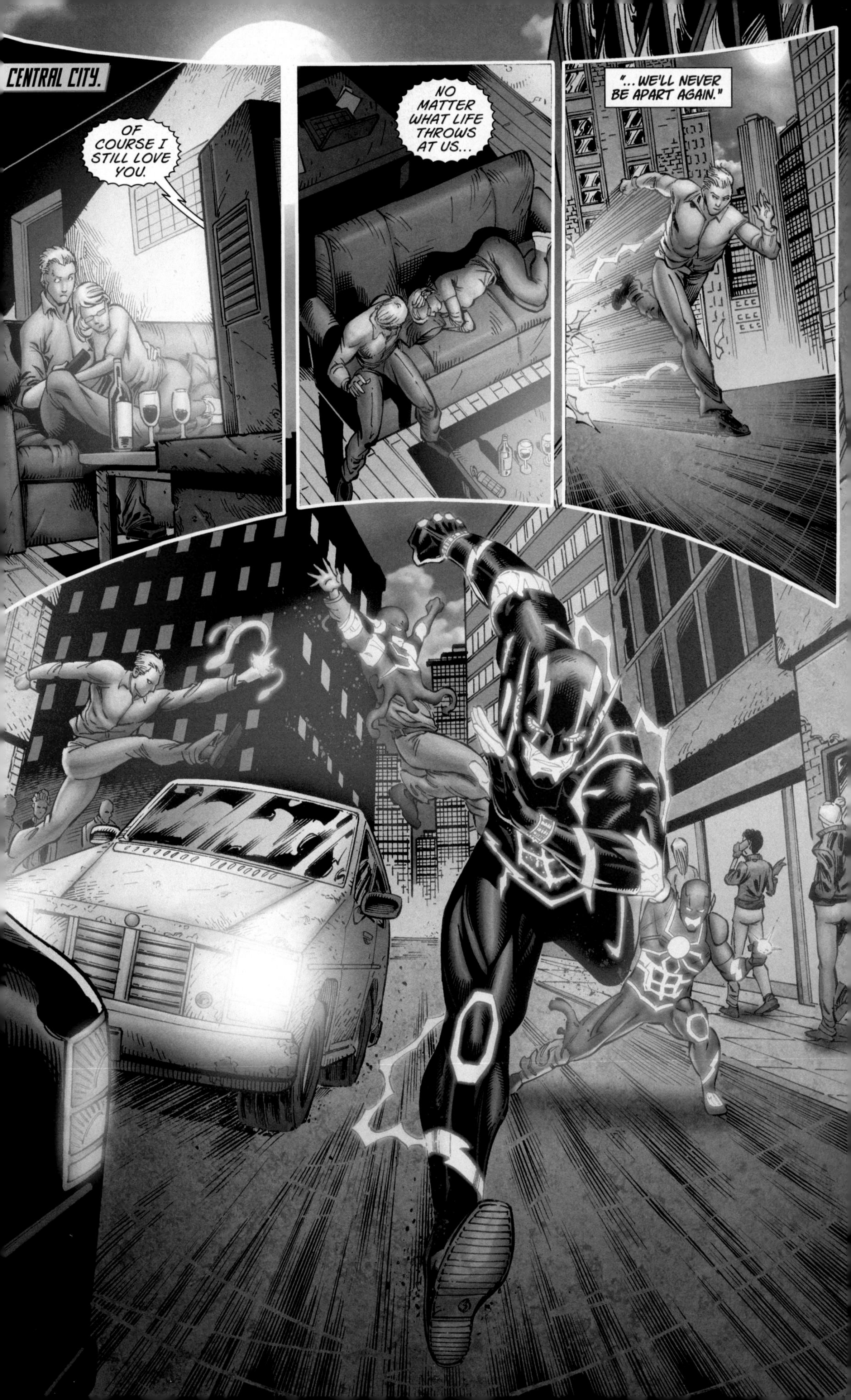
CENTRAL CITY.
OF COURSE I STILL LOVE YOU.
NO MATTER WHAT LIFE THROWS AT US...
"...WE'LL NEVER BE APART AGAIN."

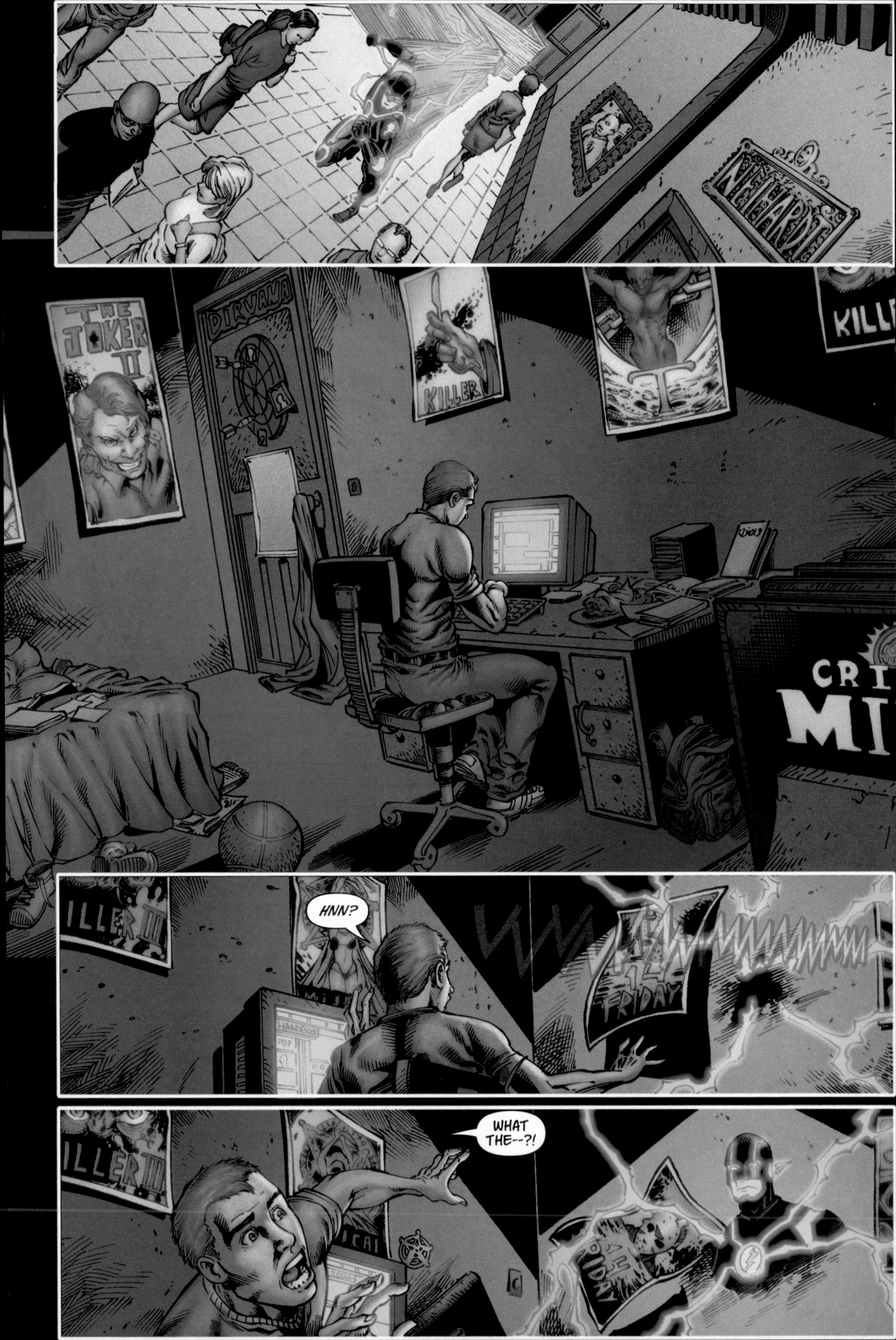
HNN?
WHAT THE--?!

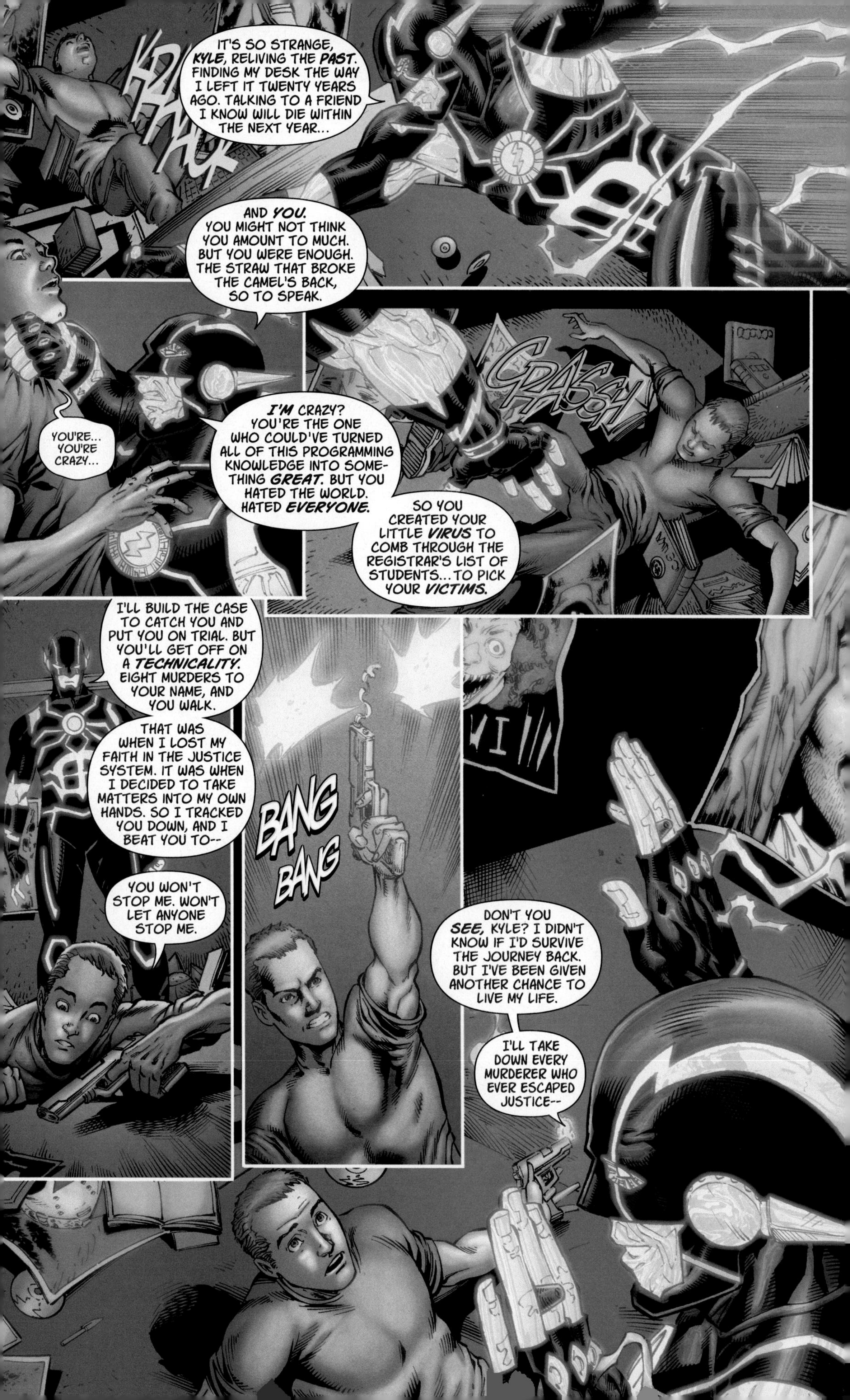
KRAKK
IT'S SO STRANGE, KYLE, RELIVING THE PAST. FINDING MY DESK THE WAY I LEFT IT TWENTY YEARS AGO. TALKING TO A FRIEND I KNOW WILL DIE WITHIN THE NEXT YEAR...
AND YOU. YOU MIGHT NOT THINK YOU AMOUNT TO MUCH. BUT YOU WERE ENOUGH. THE STRAW THAT BROKE THE CAMEL'S BACK, SO TO SPEAK.
YOU'RE... YOU'RE CRAZY...
I'M CRAZY? YOU'RE THE ONE WHO COULD'VE TURNED ALL OF THIS PROGRAMMING KNOWLEDGE INTO SOMETHING GREAT. BUT YOU HATED THE WORLD. HATED EVERYONE.
CRASSH
SO YOU CREATED YOUR LITTLE VIRUS TO COMB THROUGH THE REGISTRAR'S LIST OF STUDENTS...TO PICK YOUR VICTIMS.
I'LL BUILD THE CASE TO CATCH YOU AND PUT YOU ON TRIAL. BUT YOU'LL GET OFF ON A TECHNICALITY. EIGHT MURDERS TO YOUR NAME, AND YOU WALK.
THAT WAS WHEN I LOST MY FAITH IN THE JUSTICE SYSTEM. IT WAS WHEN I DECIDED TO TAKE MATTERS INTO MY OWN HANDS. SO I TRACKED YOU DOWN, AND I BEAT YOU TO--
YOU WON'T STOP ME. WON'T LET ANYONE STOP ME.
BANG
BANG
DON'T YOU SEE, KYLE? I DIDN'T KNOW IF I'D SURVIVE THE JOURNEY BACK. BUT I'VE BEEN GIVEN ANOTHER CHANCE TO LIVE MY LIFE.
I'LL TAKE DOWN EVERY MURDERER WHO EVER ESCAPED JUSTICE--

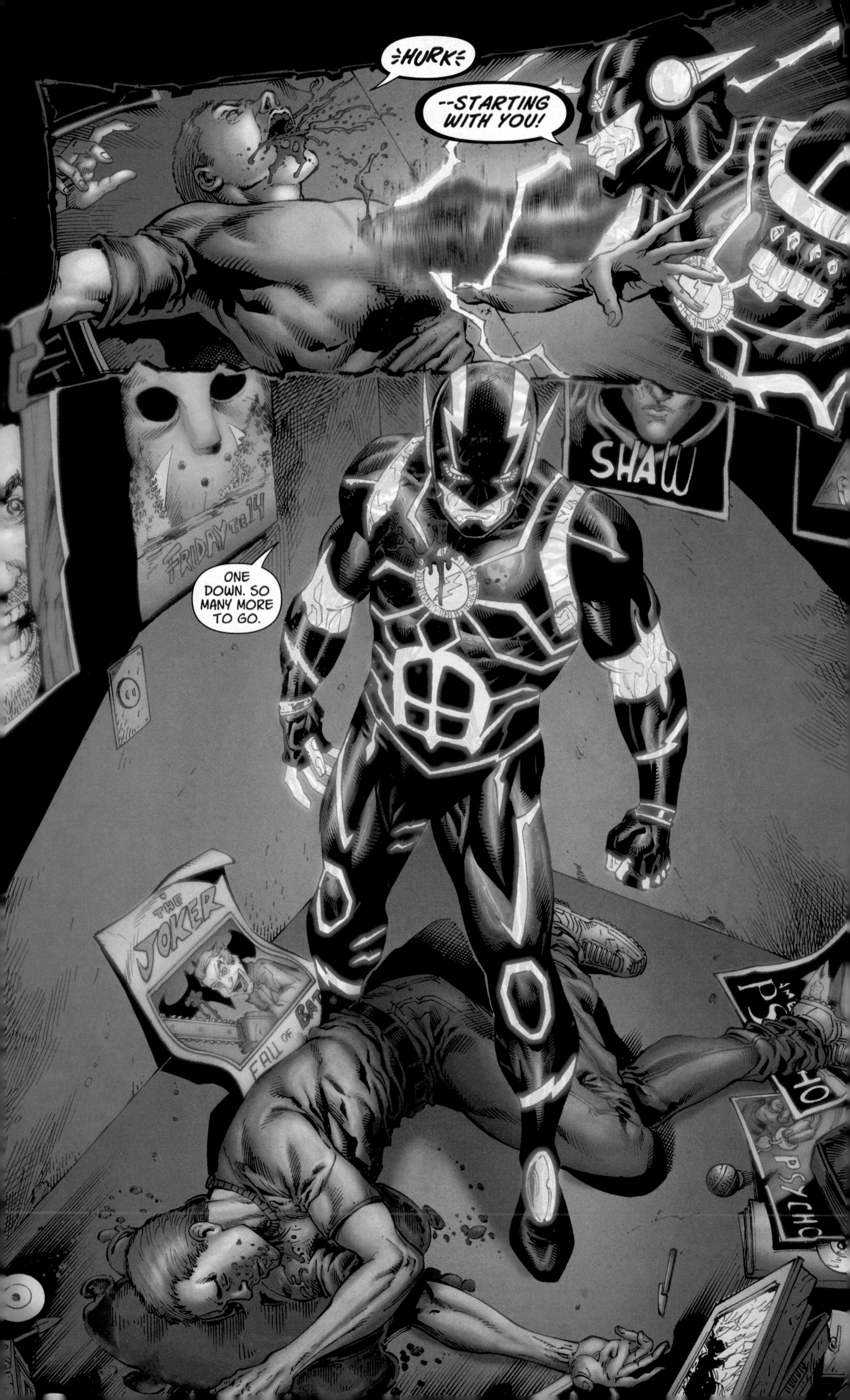

HURK
--STARTING WITH YOU!
SHAW
FRIDAY THE 14
ONE DOWN. SO MANY MORE TO GO.
THE JOKER
FALL OF BAT
PSYCHO
PSYCHO

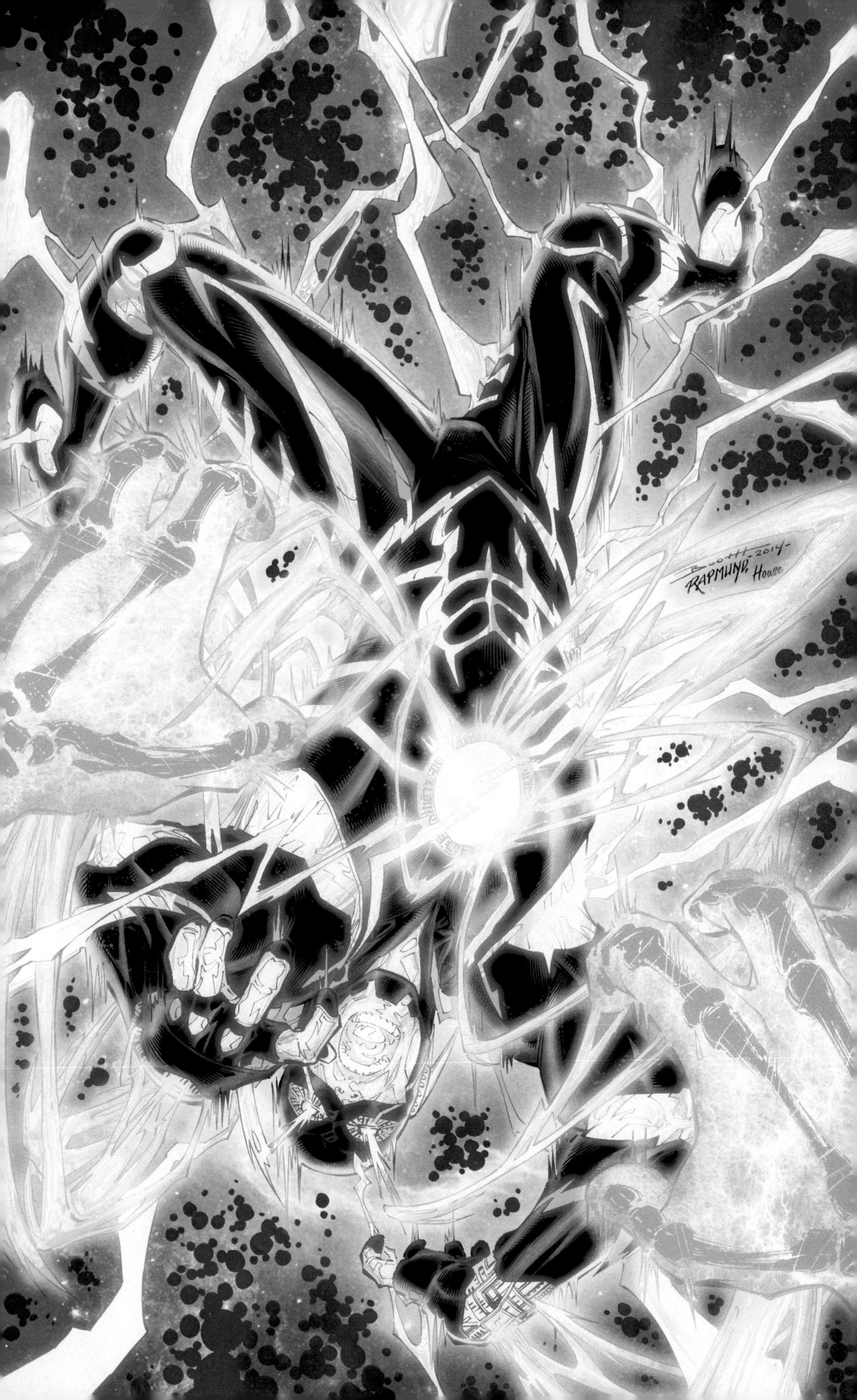
Booth 2014
RAPMUND, House

THE SAVAGE WORLD OF THE SPEED FORCE

ROBERT VENDITTI & VAN JENSEN writers BRETT BOOTH penciller NORM RAPMUND inker ANDREW DALHOUSE colorist DEZI SIENTY letterer
cover by BRETT BOOTH, NORM RAPMUND & ANDREW DALHOUSE

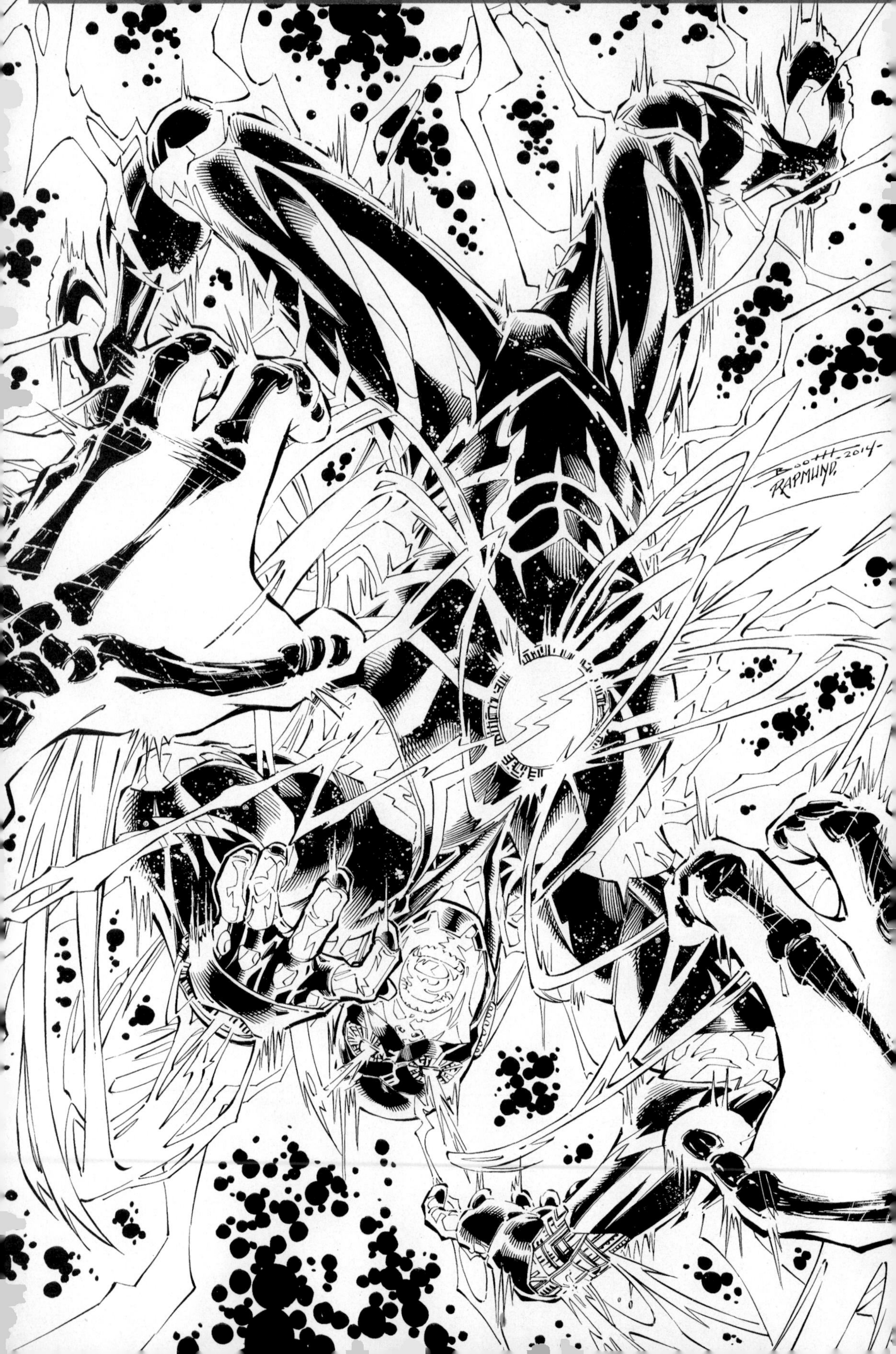
BOOTH -2014-
RAPMUND

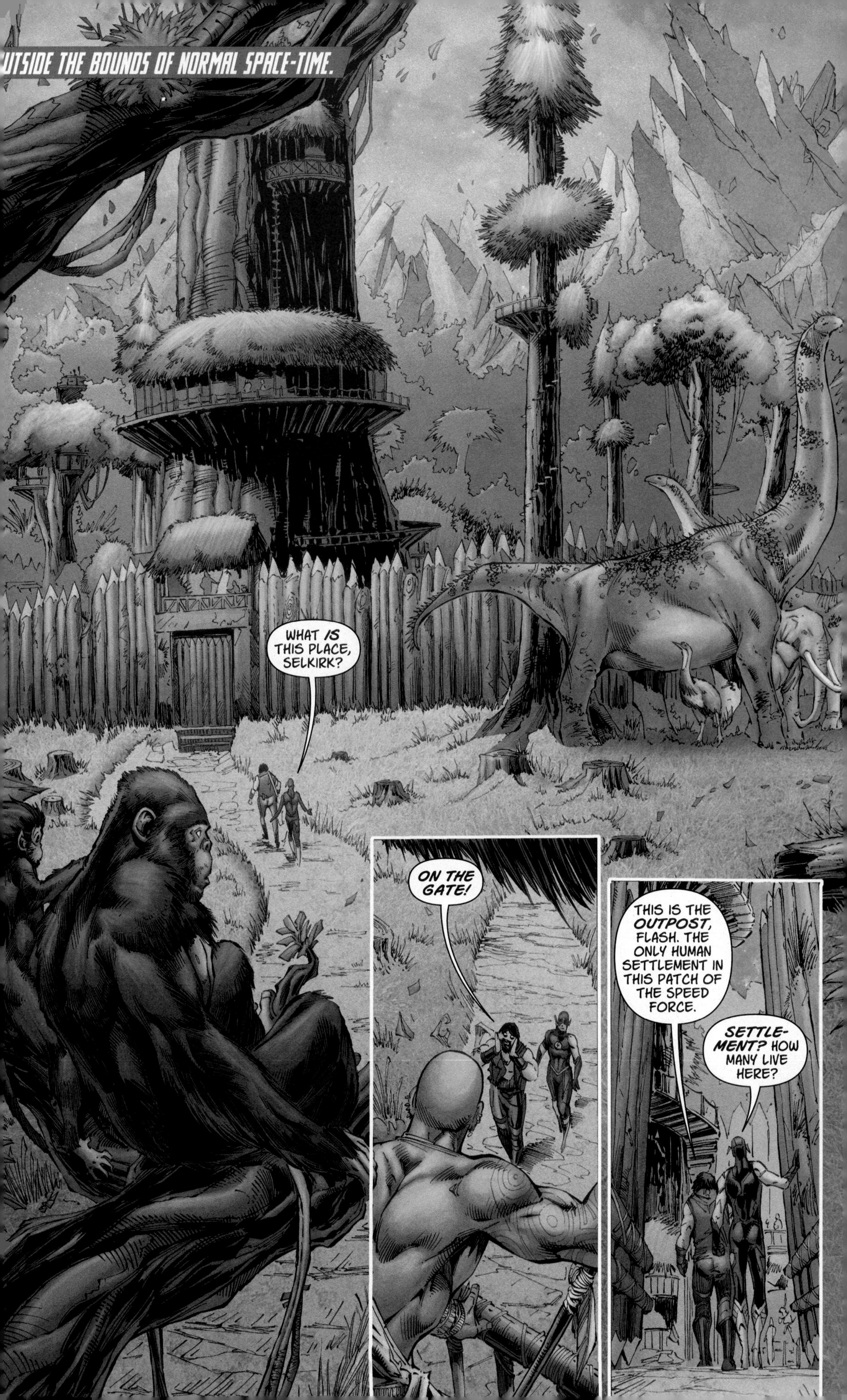

UTSIDE THE BOUNDS OF NORMAL SPACE-TIME.
WHAT IS THIS PLACE, SELKIRK?
ON THE GATE!
THIS IS THE OUTPOST, FLASH. THE ONLY HUMAN SETTLEMENT IN THIS PATCH OF THE SPEED FORCE.
SETTLEMENT? HOW MANY LIVE HERE?

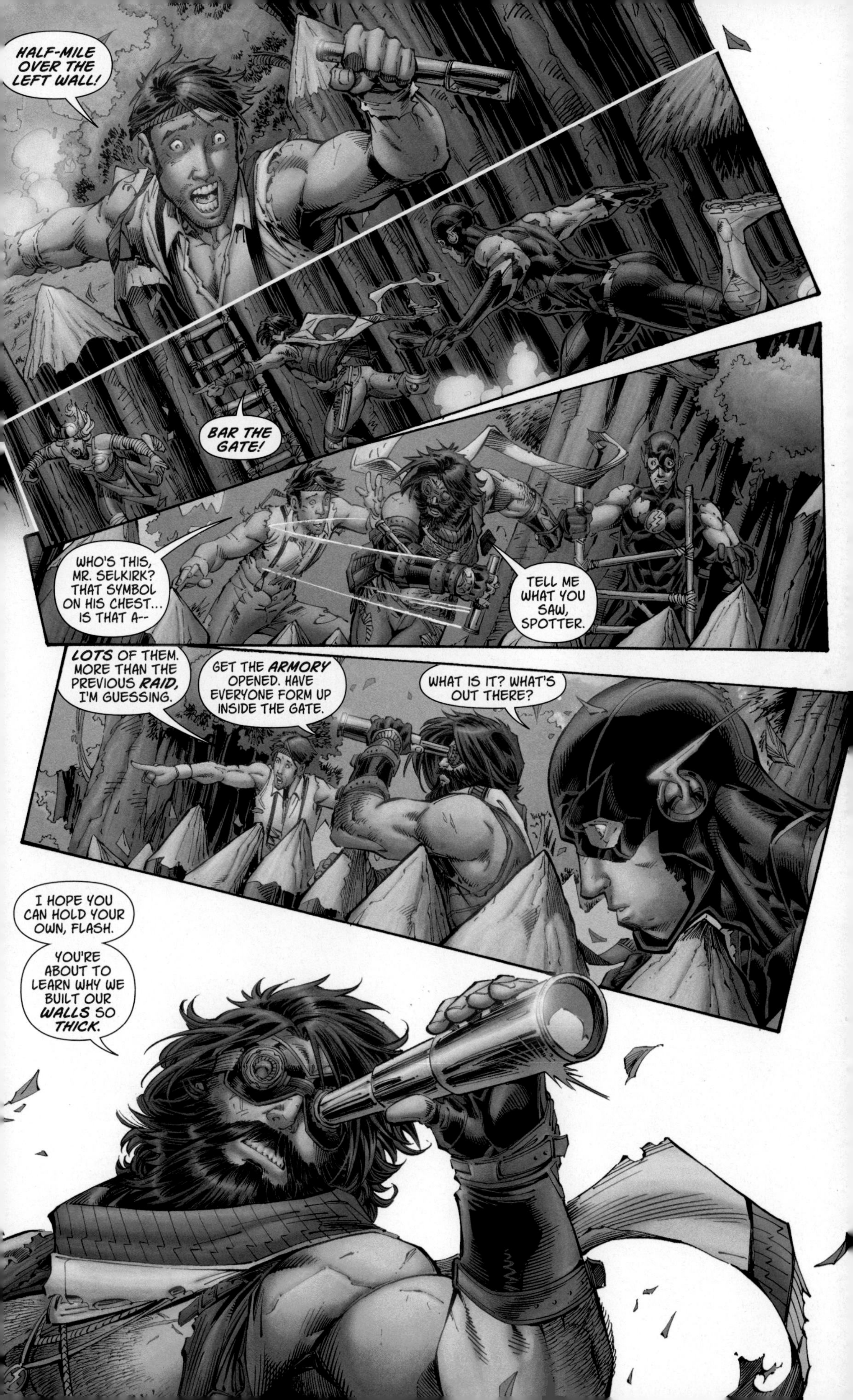
HALF-MILE OVER THE LEFT WALL!
BAR THE GATE!
WHO'S THIS, MR. SELKIRK? THAT SYMBOL ON HIS CHEST... IS THAT A--
TELL ME WHAT YOU SAW, SPOTTER.
LOTS OF THEM. MORE THAN THE PREVIOUS RAID, I'M GUESSING.
GET THE ARMORY OPENED. HAVE EVERYONE FORM UP INSIDE THE GATE.
WHAT IS IT? WHAT'S OUT THERE?
I HOPE YOU CAN HOLD YOUR OWN, FLASH.
YOU'RE ABOUT TO LEARN WHY WE BUILT OUR WALLS SO THICK.

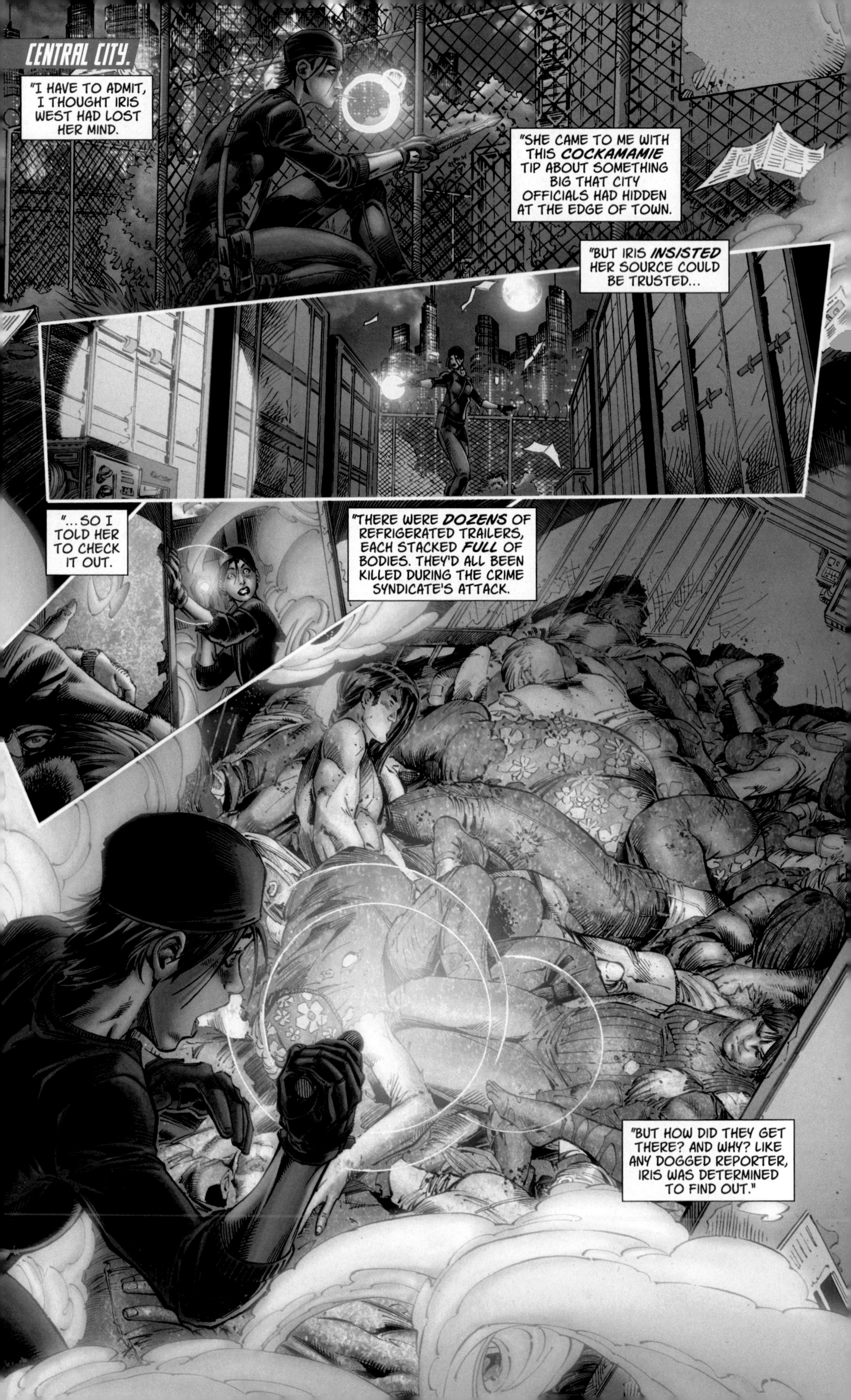
CENTRAL CITY.
"I HAVE TO ADMIT, I THOUGHT IRIS WEST HAD LOST HER MIND.
"SHE CAME TO ME WITH THIS COCKAMAMIE TIP ABOUT SOMETHING BIG THAT CITY OFFICIALS HAD HIDDEN AT THE EDGE OF TOWN.
"BUT IRIS INSISTED HER SOURCE COULD BE TRUSTED...
"...SO I TOLD HER TO CHECK IT OUT.
"THERE WERE DOZENS OF REFRIGERATED TRAILERS, EACH STACKED FULL OF BODIES. THEY'D ALL BEEN KILLED DURING THE CRIME SYNDICATE'S ATTACK.
"BUT HOW DID THEY GET THERE? AND WHY? LIKE ANY DOGGED REPORTER, IRIS WAS DETERMINED TO FIND OUT."

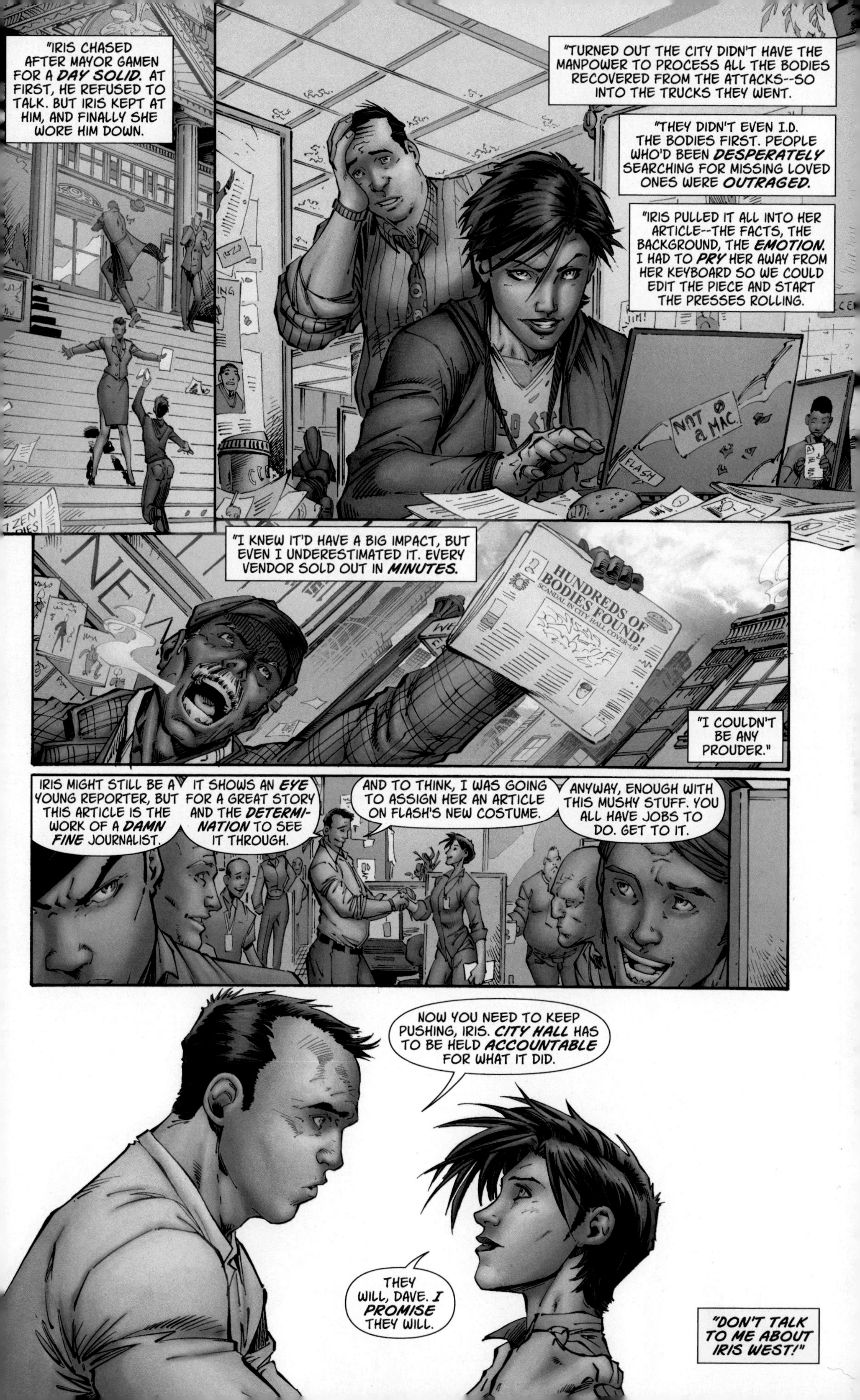
"IRIS CHASED AFTER MAYOR GAMEN FOR A DAY SOLID. AT FIRST, HE REFUSED TO TALK. BUT IRIS KEPT AT HIM, AND FINALLY SHE WORE HIM DOWN.
"TURNED OUT THE CITY DIDN'T HAVE THE MANPOWER TO PROCESS ALL THE BODIES RECOVERED FROM THE ATTACKS--SO INTO THE TRUCKS THEY WENT.
"THEY DIDN'T EVEN I.D. THE BODIES FIRST. PEOPLE WHO'D BEEN DESPERATELY SEARCHING FOR MISSING LOVED ONES WERE OUTRAGED.
"IRIS PULLED IT ALL INTO HER ARTICLE--THE FACTS, THE BACKGROUND, THE EMOTION. I HAD TO PRY HER AWAY FROM HER KEYBOARD SO WE COULD EDIT THE PIECE AND START THE PRESSES ROLLING.
NOT a MAC.
FLASH
"I KNEW IT'D HAVE A BIG IMPACT, BUT EVEN I UNDERESTIMATED IT. EVERY VENDOR SOLD OUT IN MINUTES.
HUNDREDS OF BODIES FOUND!
SCANDAL IN CITY HALL COVER-UP
"I COULDN'T BE ANY PROUDER."
IRIS MIGHT STILL BE A YOUNG REPORTER, BUT THIS ARTICLE IS THE WORK OF A DAMN FINE JOURNALIST.
IT SHOWS AN EYE FOR A GREAT STORY AND THE DETERMINATION TO SEE IT THROUGH.
AND TO THINK, I WAS GOING TO ASSIGN HER AN ARTICLE ON FLASH'S NEW COSTUME.
ANYWAY, ENOUGH WITH THIS MUSHY STUFF. YOU ALL HAVE JOBS TO DO. GET TO IT.
NOW YOU NEED TO KEEP PUSHING, IRIS. CITY HALL HAS TO BE HELD ACCOUNTABLE FOR WHAT IT DID.
THEY WILL, DAVE. I PROMISE THEY WILL.
"DON'T TALK TO ME ABOUT IRIS WEST!"

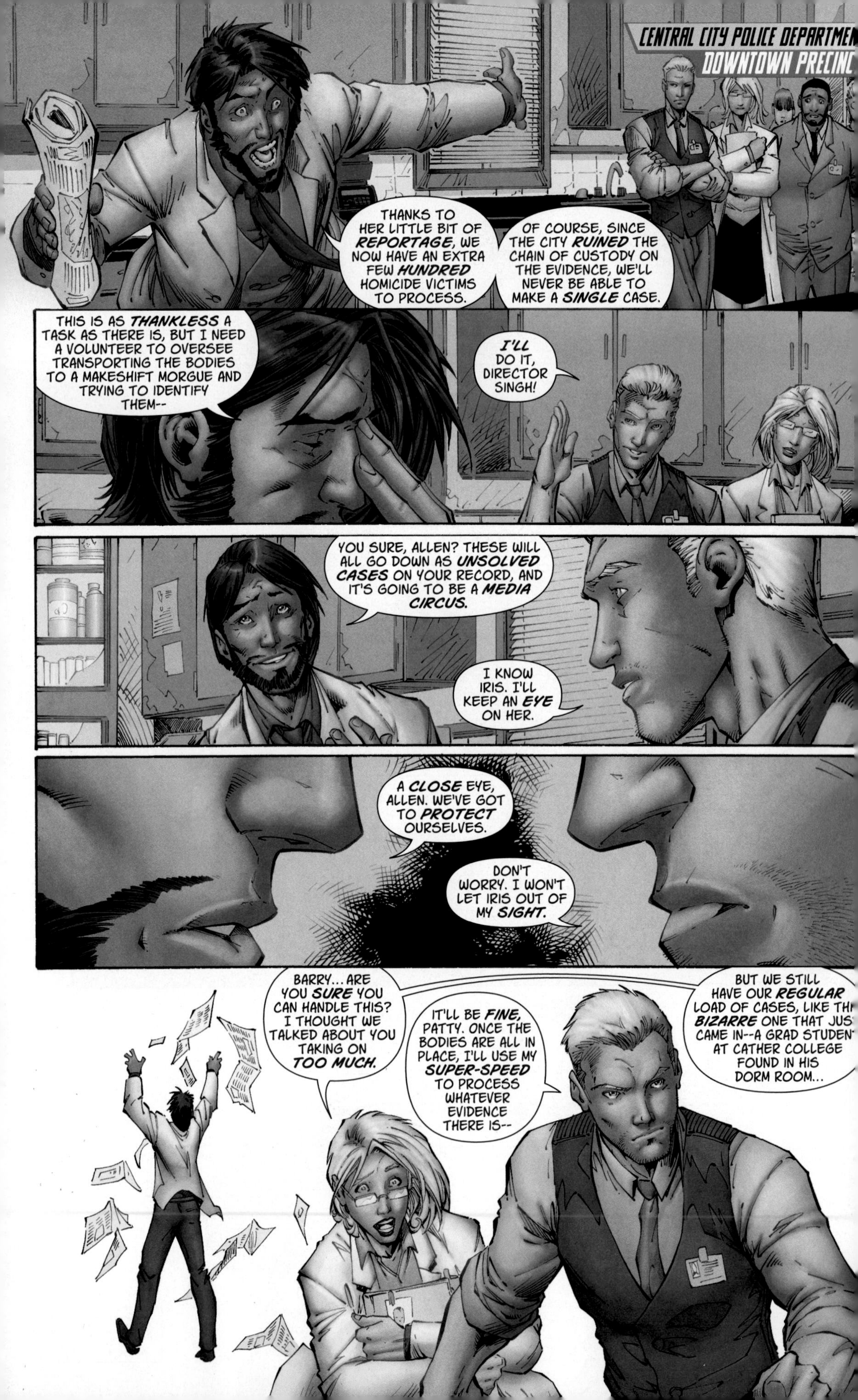
CENTRAL CITY POLICE DEPARTMEN
DOWNTOWN PRECINC
THANKS TO HER LITTLE BIT OF REPORTAGE, WE NOW HAVE AN EXTRA FEW HUNDRED HOMICIDE VICTIMS TO PROCESS.
OF COURSE, SINCE THE CITY RUINED THE CHAIN OF CUSTODY ON THE EVIDENCE, WE'LL NEVER BE ABLE TO MAKE A SINGLE CASE.
THIS IS AS THANKLESS A TASK AS THERE IS, BUT I NEED A VOLUNTEER TO OVERSEE TRANSPORTING THE BODIES TO A MAKESHIFT MORGUE AND TRYING TO IDENTIFY THEM--
I'LL DO IT, DIRECTOR SINGH!
YOU SURE, ALLEN? THESE WILL ALL GO DOWN AS UNSOLVED CASES ON YOUR RECORD, AND IT'S GOING TO BE A MEDIA CIRCUS.
I KNOW IRIS. I'LL KEEP AN EYE ON HER.
A CLOSE EYE, ALLEN. WE'VE GOT TO PROTECT OURSELVES.
DON'T WORRY. I WON'T LET IRIS OUT OF MY SIGHT.
BARRY... ARE YOU SURE YOU CAN HANDLE THIS? I THOUGHT WE TALKED ABOUT YOU TAKING ON TOO MUCH.
IT'LL BE FINE, PATTY. ONCE THE BODIES ARE ALL IN PLACE, I'LL USE MY SUPER-SPEED TO PROCESS WHATEVER EVIDENCE THERE IS--
BUT WE STILL HAVE OUR REGULAR LOAD OF CASES, LIKE THI BIZARRE ONE THAT JUS CAME IN--A GRAD STUDEN AT CATHER COLLEGE FOUND IN HIS DORM ROOM...

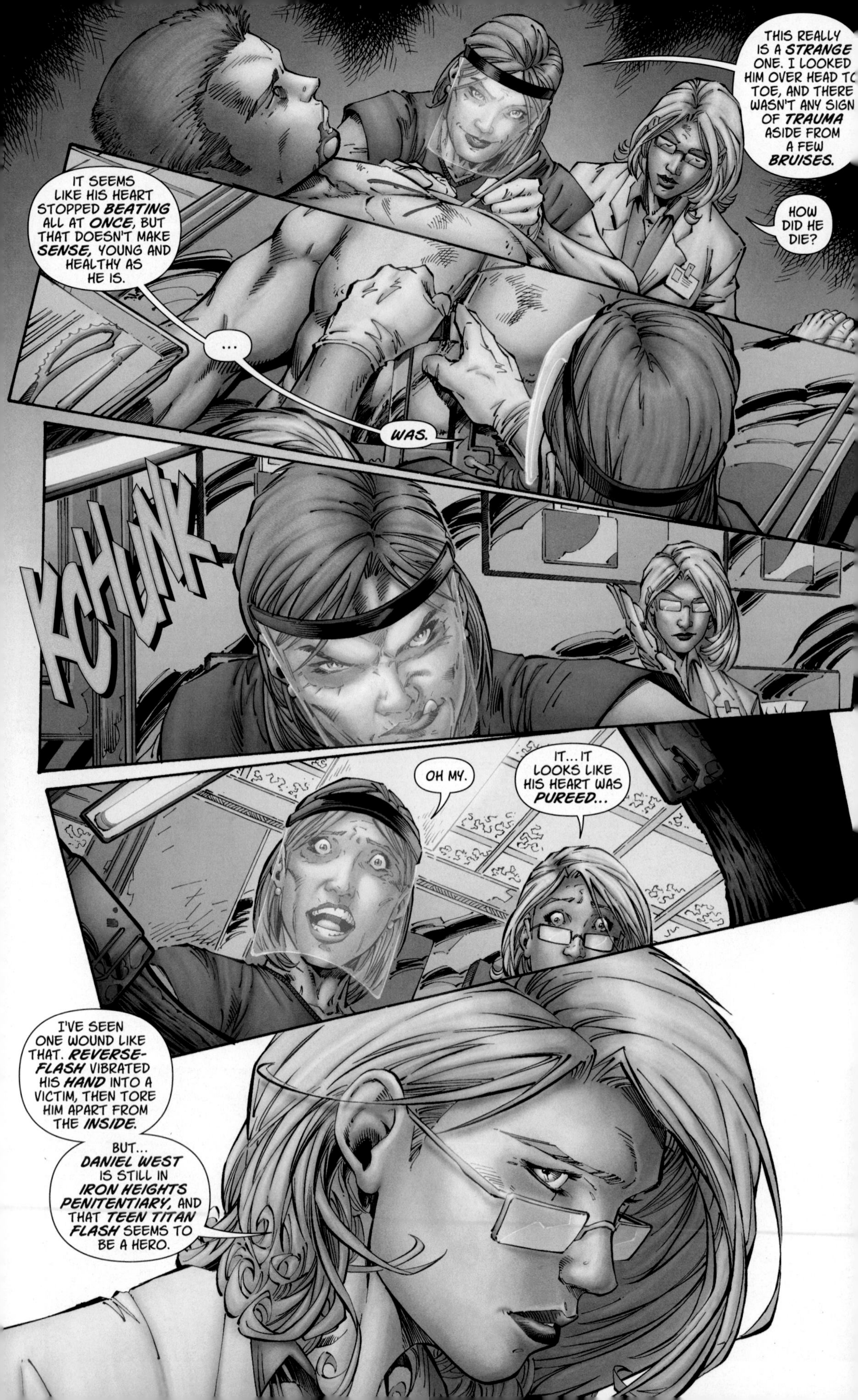
THIS REALLY IS A STRANGE ONE. I LOOKED HIM OVER HEAD TO TOE, AND THERE WASN'T ANY SIGN OF TRAUMA ASIDE FROM A FEW BRUISES.
HOW DID HE DIE?
IT SEEMS LIKE HIS HEART STOPPED BEATING ALL AT ONCE, BUT THAT DOESN'T MAKE SENSE, YOUNG AND HEALTHY AS HE IS.
...
WAS.
KCHUNK
OH MY.
IT... IT LOOKS LIKE HIS HEART WAS PUREED...
I'VE SEEN ONE WOUND LIKE THAT. REVERSE-FLASH VIBRATED HIS HAND INTO A VICTIM, THEN TORE HIM APART FROM THE INSIDE.
BUT... DANIEL WEST IS STILL IN IRON HEIGHTS PENITENTIARY, AND THAT TEEN TITAN FLASH SEEMS TO BE A HERO.

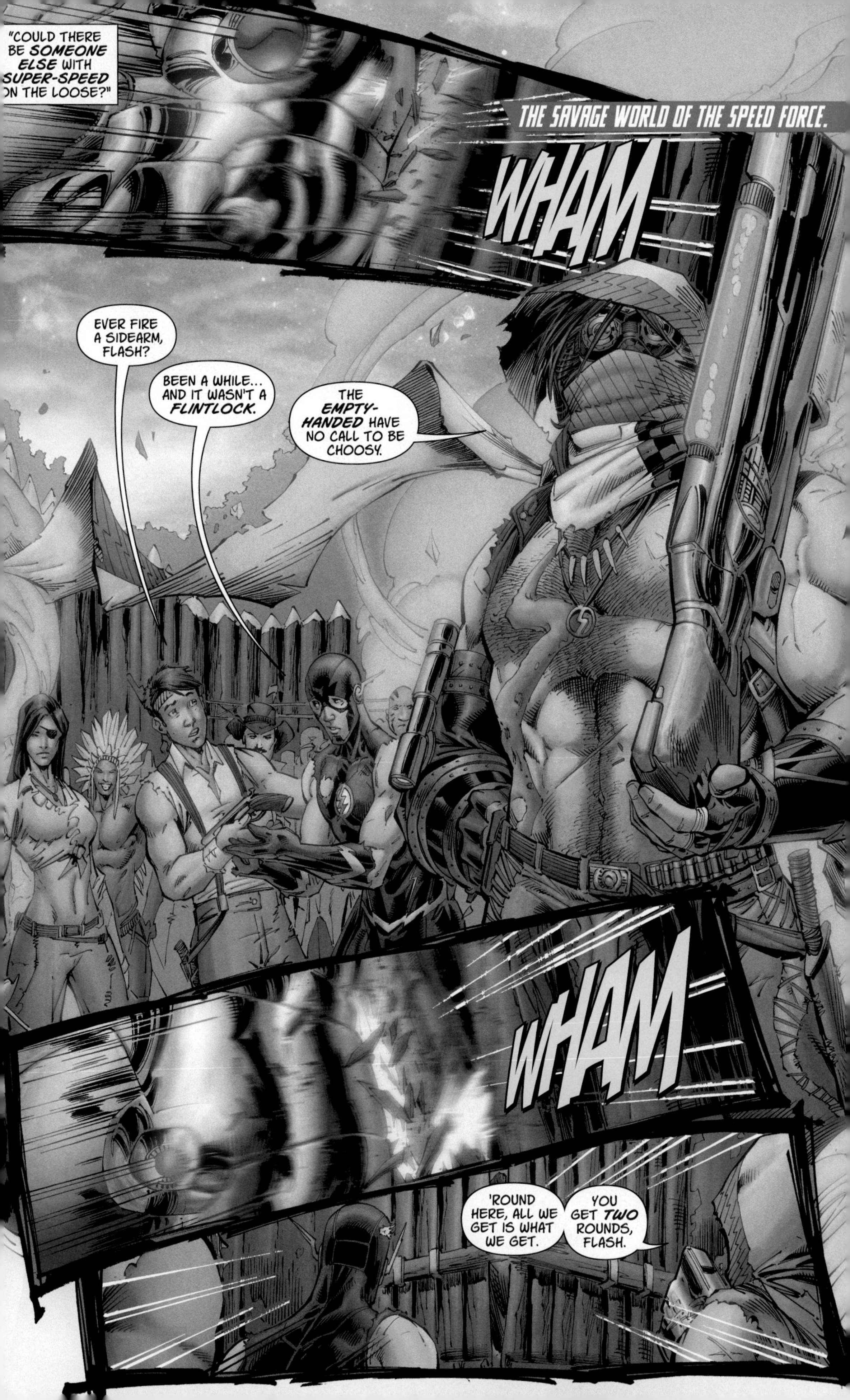
"COULD THERE BE SOMEONE ELSE WITH SUPER-SPEED ON THE LOOSE?"
THE SAVAGE WORLD OF THE SPEED FORCE.
WHAM
EVER FIRE A SIDEARM, FLASH?
BEEN A WHILE... AND IT WASN'T A FLINTLOCK.
THE EMPTY-HANDED HAVE NO CALL TO BE CHOOSY.
WHAM
'ROUND HERE, ALL WE GET IS WHAT WE GET.
YOU GET TWO ROUNDS, FLASH.

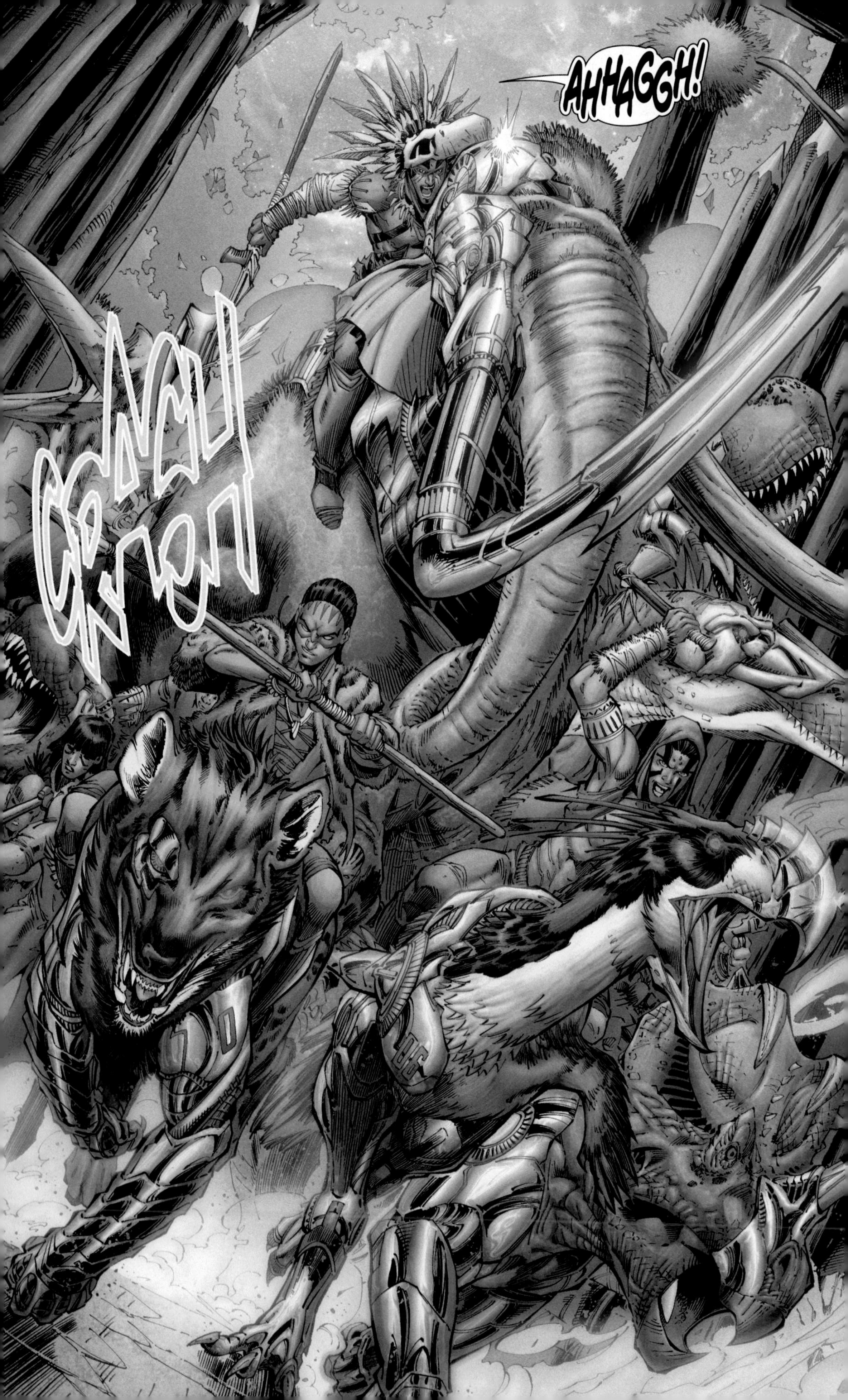
AHHAGGH!

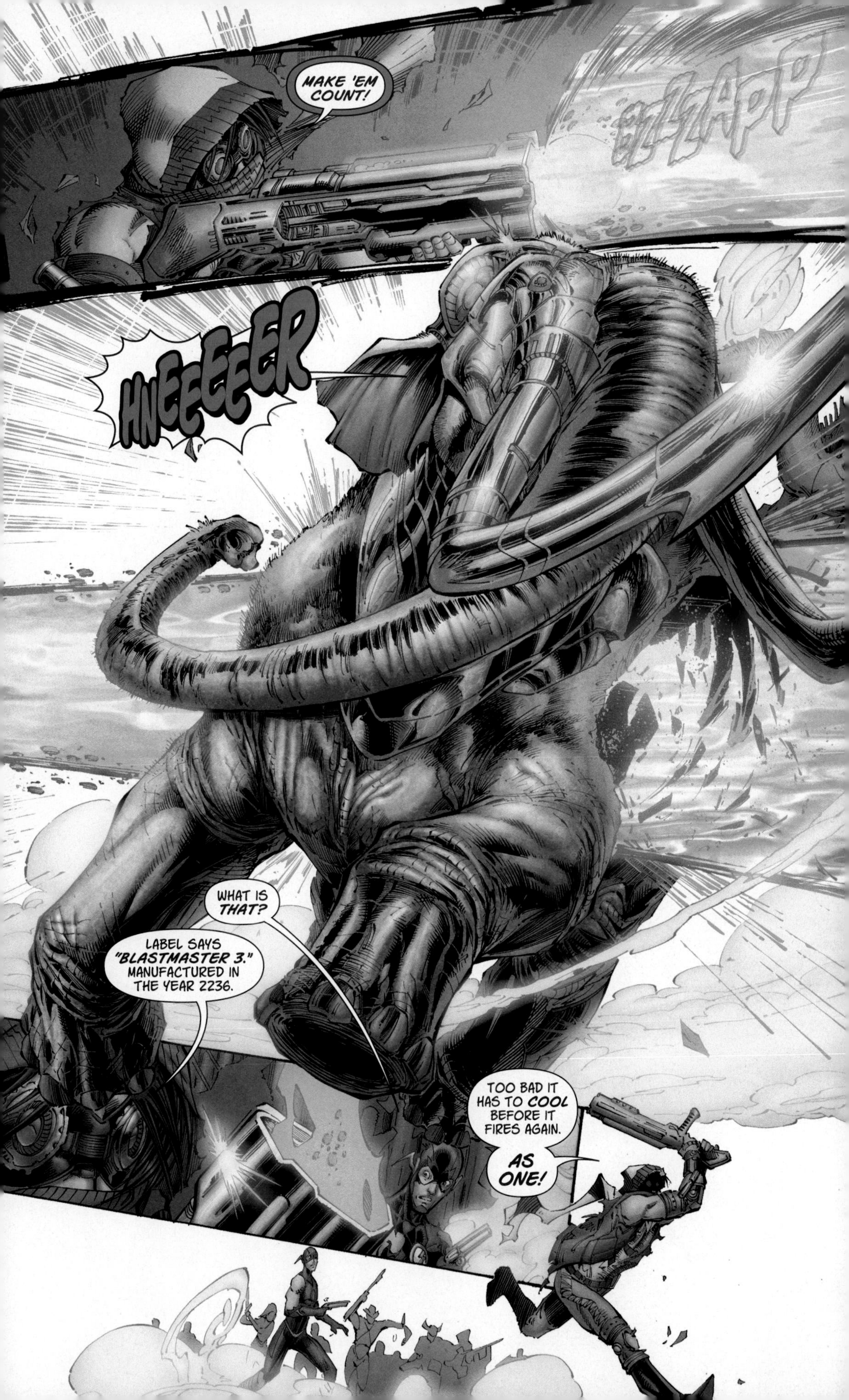
MAKE 'EM COUNT!
HNEEEEEER
WHAT IS THAT?
LABEL SAYS "BLASTMASTER 3." MANUFACTURED IN THE YEAR 2236.
TOO BAD IT HAS TO COOL BEFORE IT FIRES AGAIN.
AS ONE!

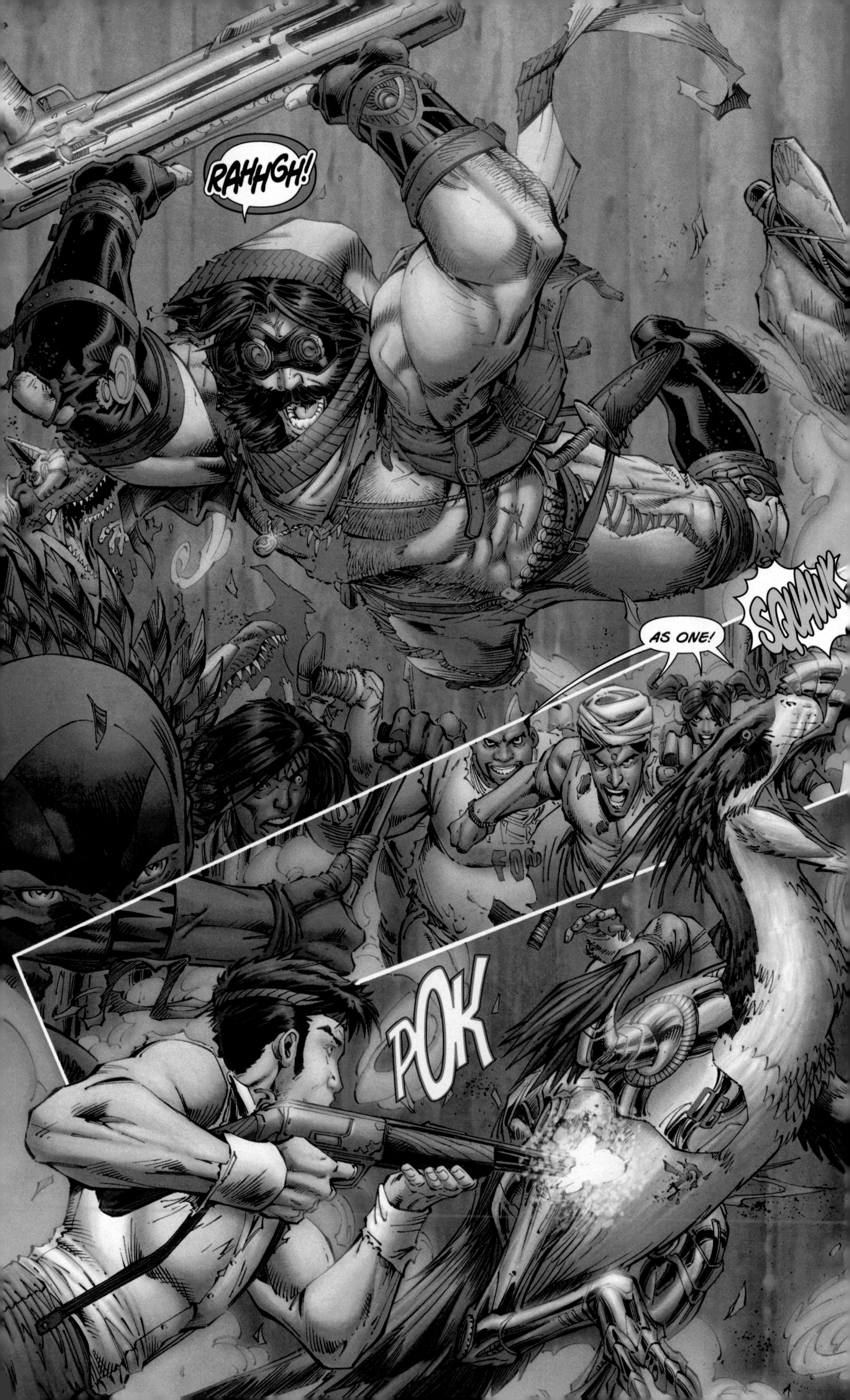
RAHHGH!
AS ONE!
SQUAWK
POK

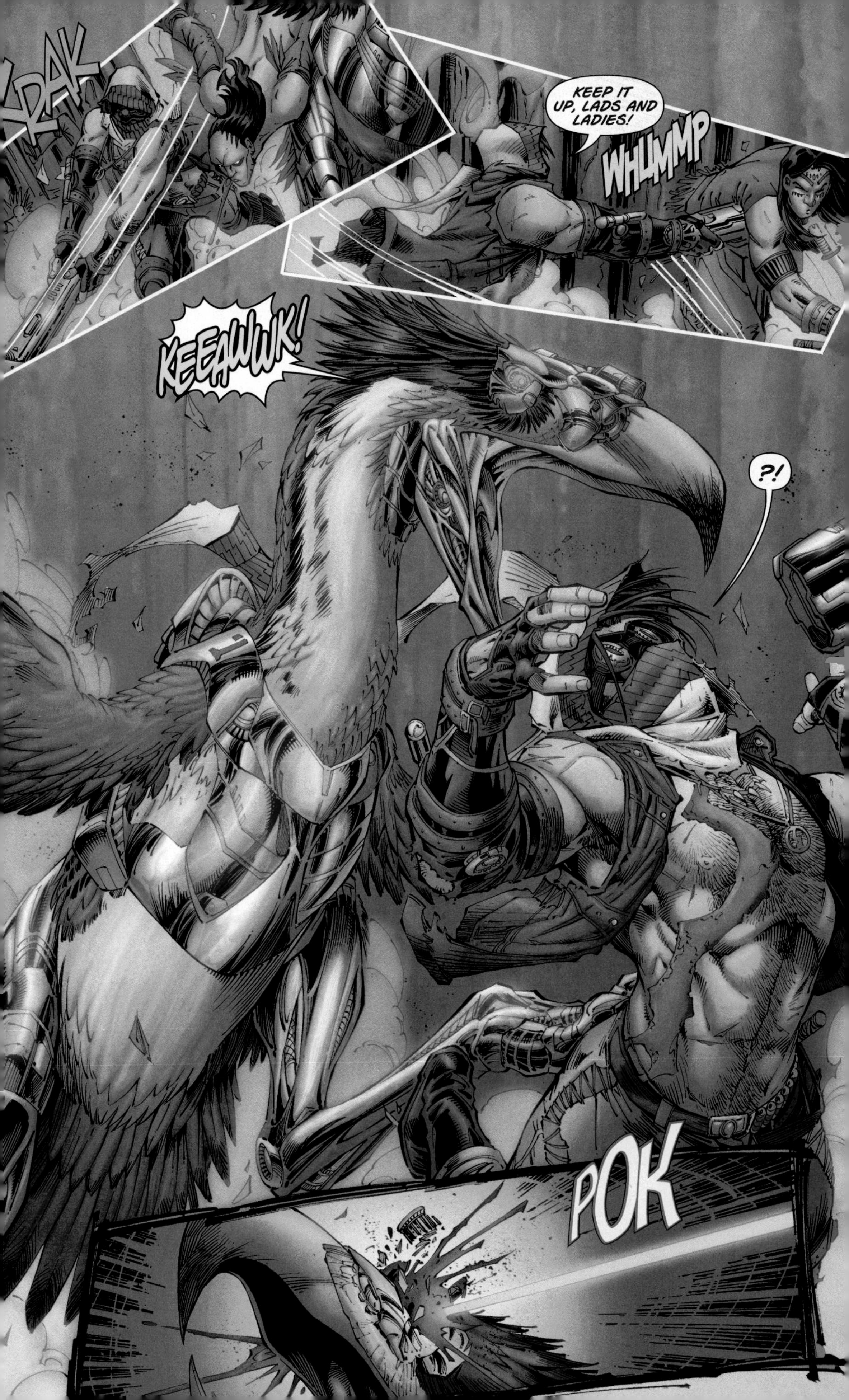

KRAK
KEEP IT UP, LADS AND LADIES!
WHUMMP
KEEAWWK!
?!
POK

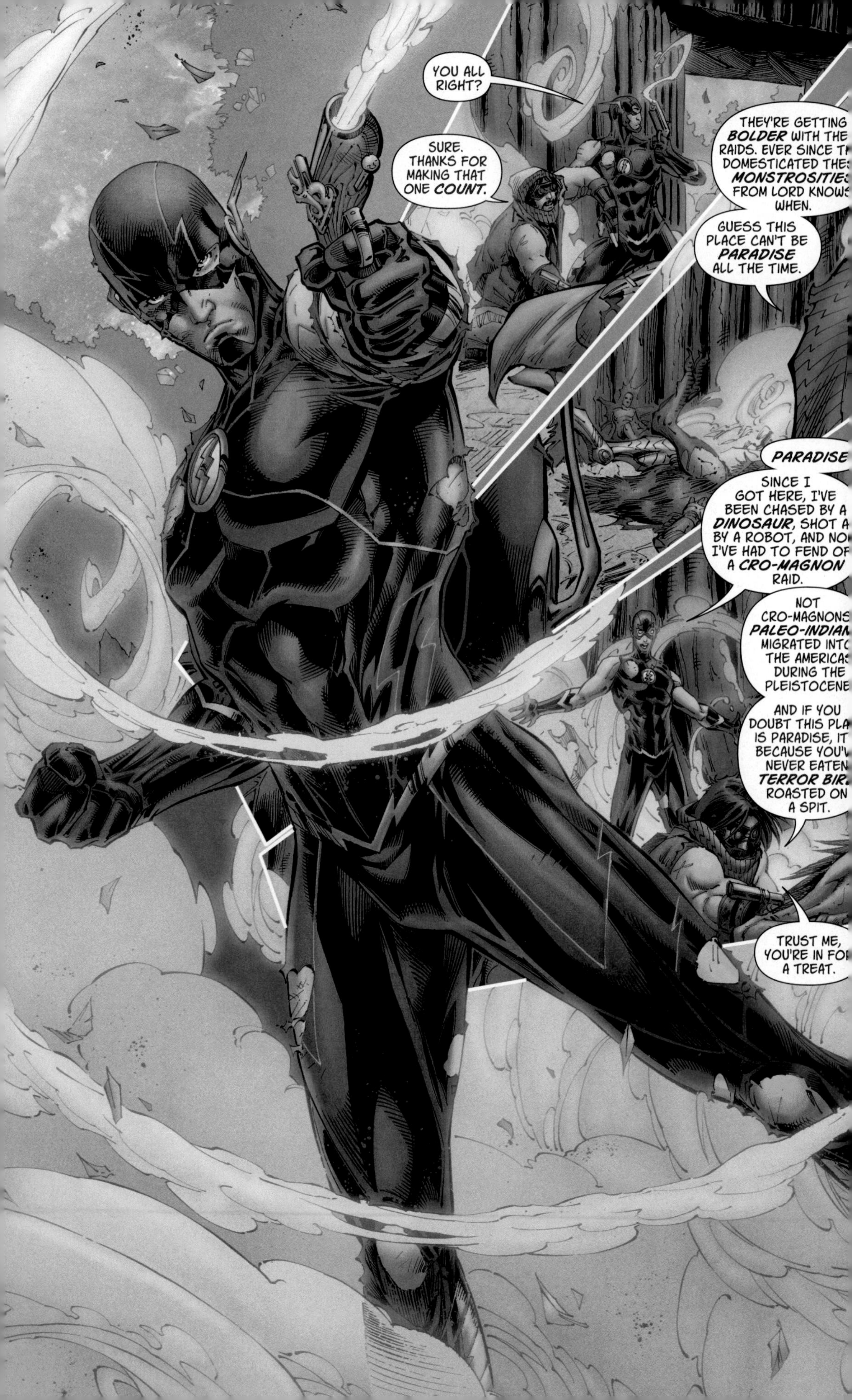
YOU ALL RIGHT?
SURE. THANKS FOR MAKING THAT ONE COUNT.
THEY'RE GETTING BOLDER WITH THE RAIDS. EVER SINCE T DOMESTICATED THES MONSTROSITIE FROM LORD KNOWS WHEN.
GUESS THIS PLACE CAN'T BE PARADISE ALL THE TIME.
PARADISE
SINCE I GOT HERE, I'VE BEEN CHASED BY A DINOSAUR, SHOT A BY A ROBOT, AND NO I'VE HAD TO FEND OF A CRO-MAGNON RAID.
NOT CRO-MAGNONS PALEO-INDIAN MIGRATED INTO THE AMERICAS DURING THE PLEISTOCENE
AND IF YOU DOUBT THIS PLA IS PARADISE, IT BECAUSE YOU' NEVER EATEN TERROR BIR ROASTED ON A SPIT.
TRUST ME, YOU'RE IN FO A TREAT.

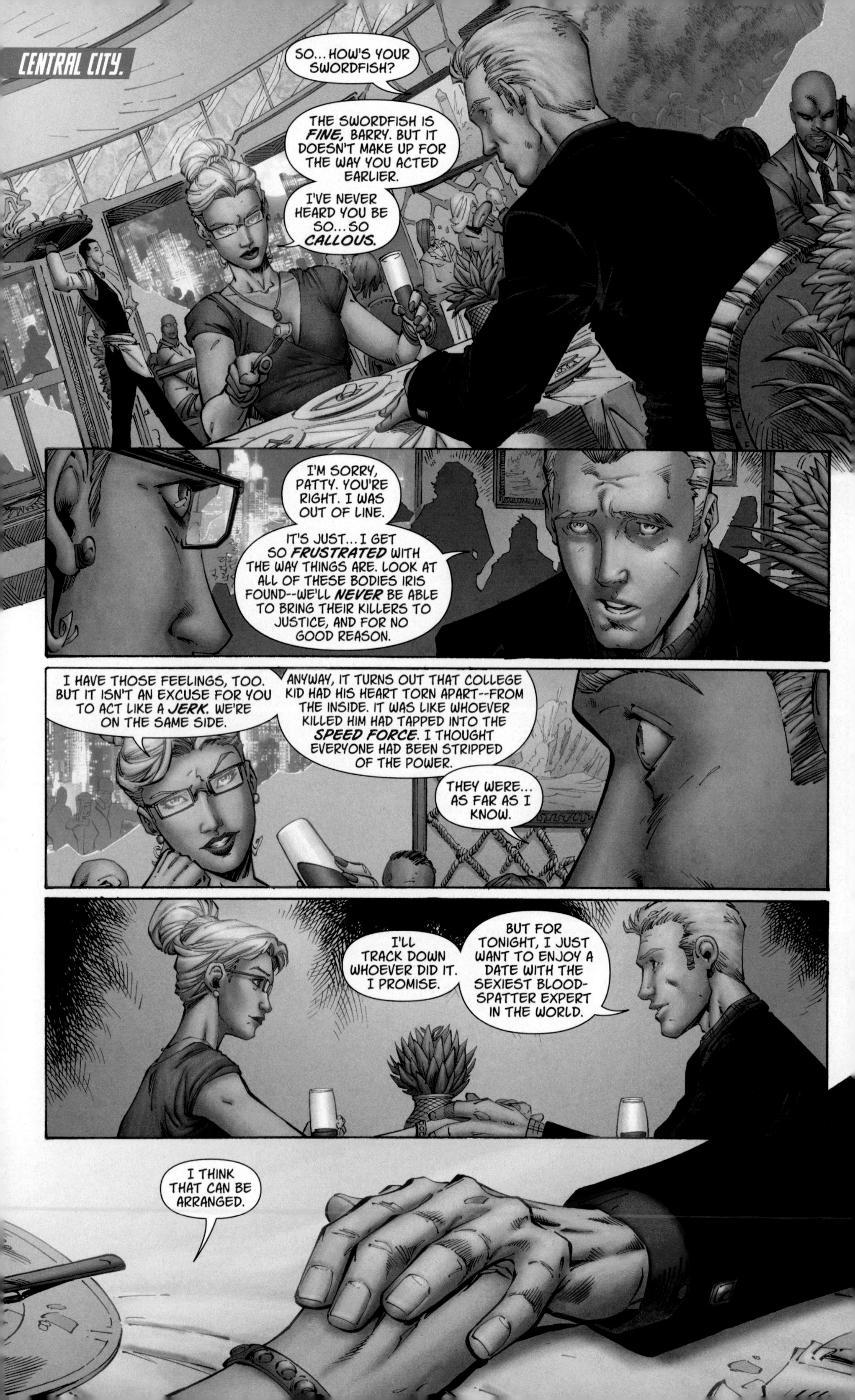
CENTRAL CITY.
SO... HOW'S YOUR SWORDFISH?
THE SWORDFISH IS FINE, BARRY. BUT IT DOESN'T MAKE UP FOR THE WAY YOU ACTED EARLIER.
I'VE NEVER HEARD YOU BE SO... SO CALLOUS.
I'M SORRY, PATTY. YOU'RE RIGHT. I WAS OUT OF LINE.
IT'S JUST... I GET SO FRUSTRATED WITH THE WAY THINGS ARE. LOOK AT ALL OF THESE BODIES IRIS FOUND--WE'LL NEVER BE ABLE TO BRING THEIR KILLERS TO JUSTICE, AND FOR NO GOOD REASON.
I HAVE THOSE FEELINGS, TOO. BUT IT ISN'T AN EXCUSE FOR YOU TO ACT LIKE A JERK. WE'RE ON THE SAME SIDE.
ANYWAY, IT TURNS OUT THAT COLLEGE KID HAD HIS HEART TORN APART--FROM THE INSIDE. IT WAS LIKE WHOEVER KILLED HIM HAD TAPPED INTO THE SPEED FORCE. I THOUGHT EVERYONE HAD BEEN STRIPPED OF THE POWER.
THEY WERE... AS FAR AS I KNOW.
I'LL TRACK DOWN WHOEVER DID IT. I PROMISE.
BUT FOR TONIGHT, I JUST WANT TO ENJOY A DATE WITH THE SEXIEST BLOOD-SPATTER EXPERT IN THE WORLD.
I THINK THAT CAN BE ARRANGED.

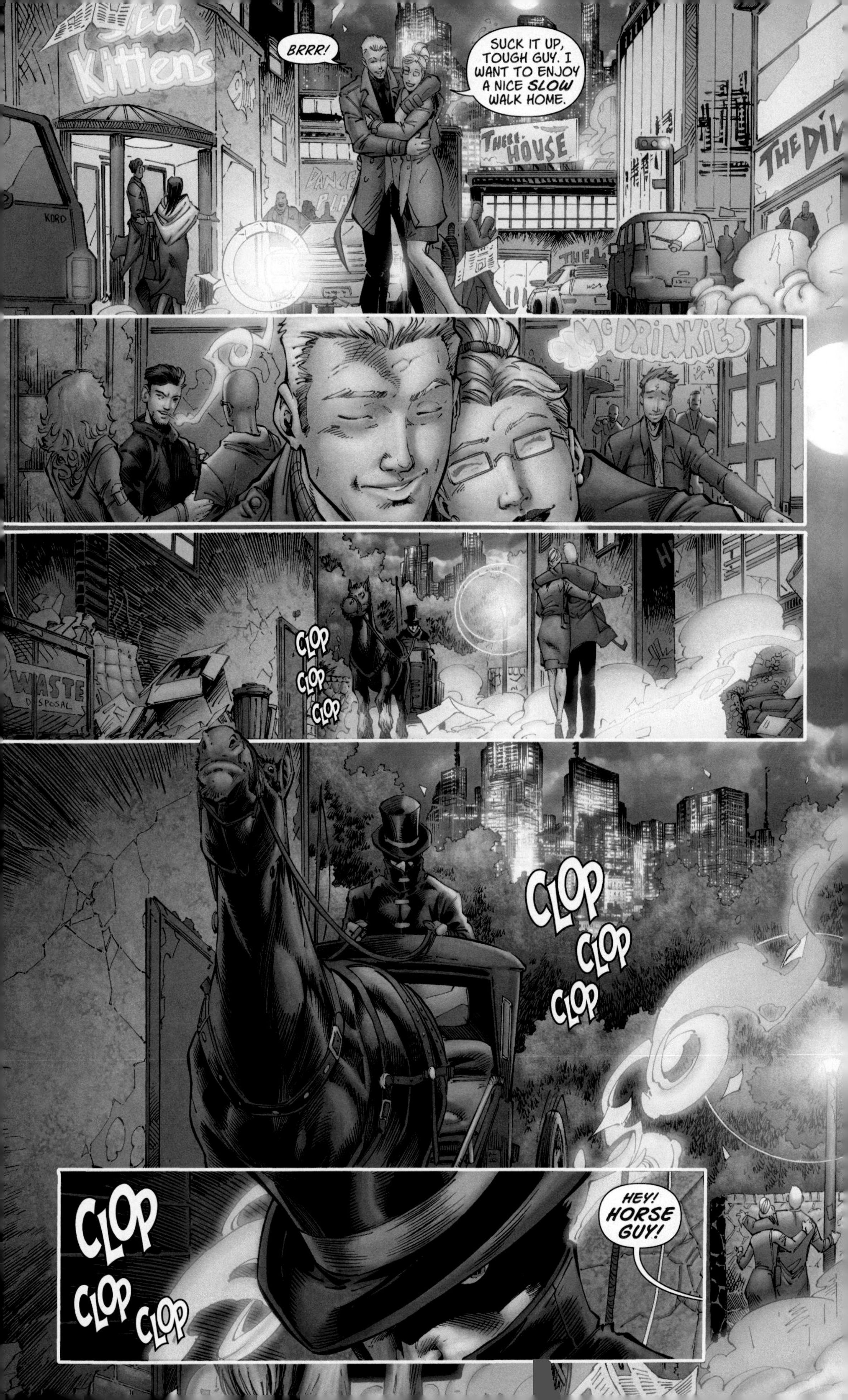
BRRR!
SUCK IT UP, TOUGH GUY. I WANT TO ENJOY A NICE SLOW WALK HOME.
CLOP CLOP CLOP
CLOP CLOP CLOP
CLOP CLOP CLOP
HEY! HORSE GUY!

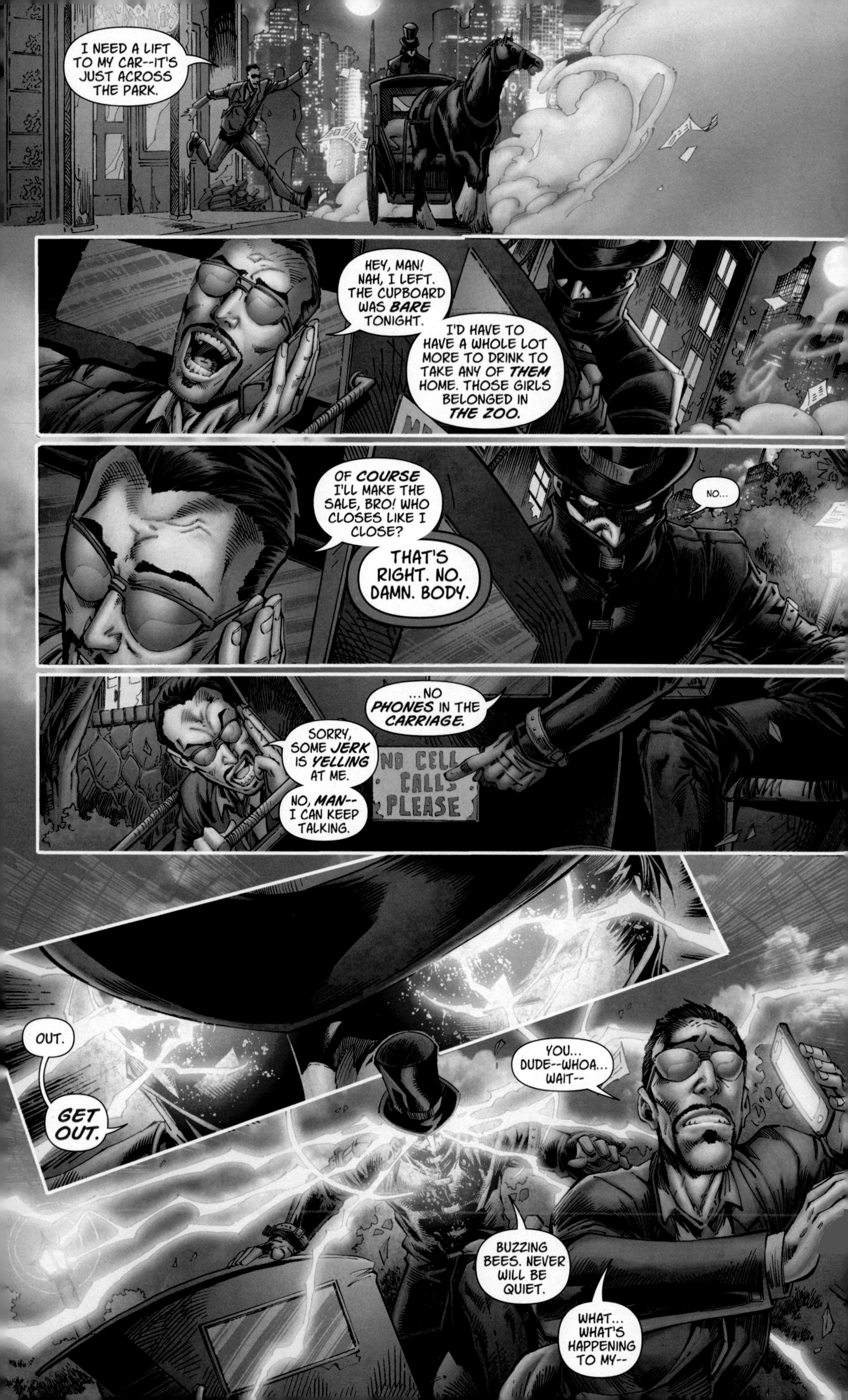
I NEED A LIFT TO MY CAR--IT'S JUST ACROSS THE PARK.
HEY, MAN! NAH, I LEFT. THE CUPBOARD WAS BARE TONIGHT.
I'D HAVE TO HAVE A WHOLE LOT MORE TO DRINK TO TAKE ANY OF THEM HOME. THOSE GIRLS BELONGED IN THE ZOO.
OF COURSE I'LL MAKE THE SALE, BRO! WHO CLOSES LIKE I CLOSE?
THAT'S RIGHT. NO. DAMN. BODY.
NO...
...NO PHONES IN THE CARRIAGE.
SORRY, SOME JERK IS YELLING AT ME.
NO CELL CALLS PLEASE
NO, MAN-- I CAN KEEP TALKING.
OUT.
GET OUT.
YOU... DUDE--WHOA... WAIT--
BUZZING BEES. NEVER WILL BE QUIET.
WHAT... WHAT'S HAPPENING TO MY--

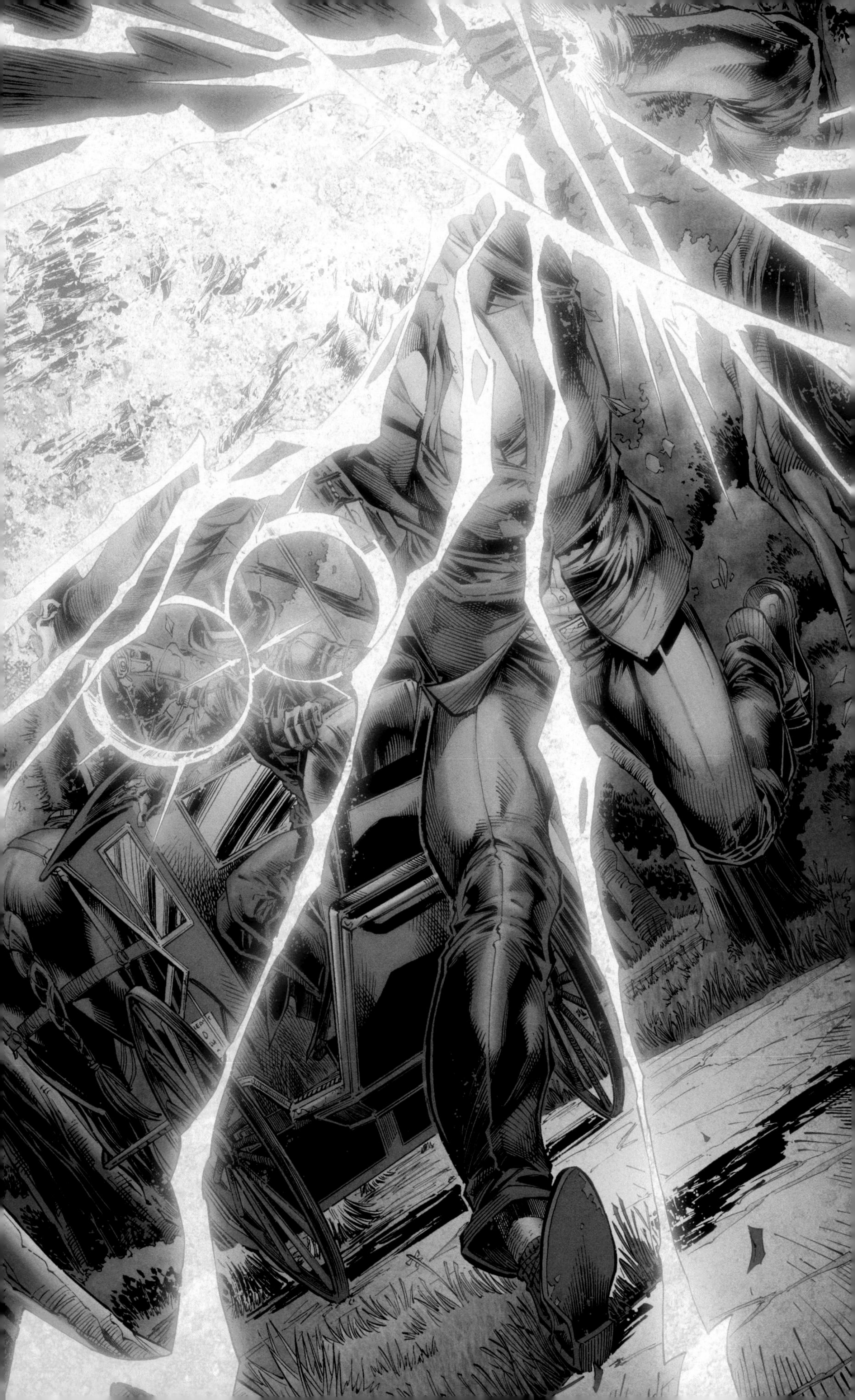

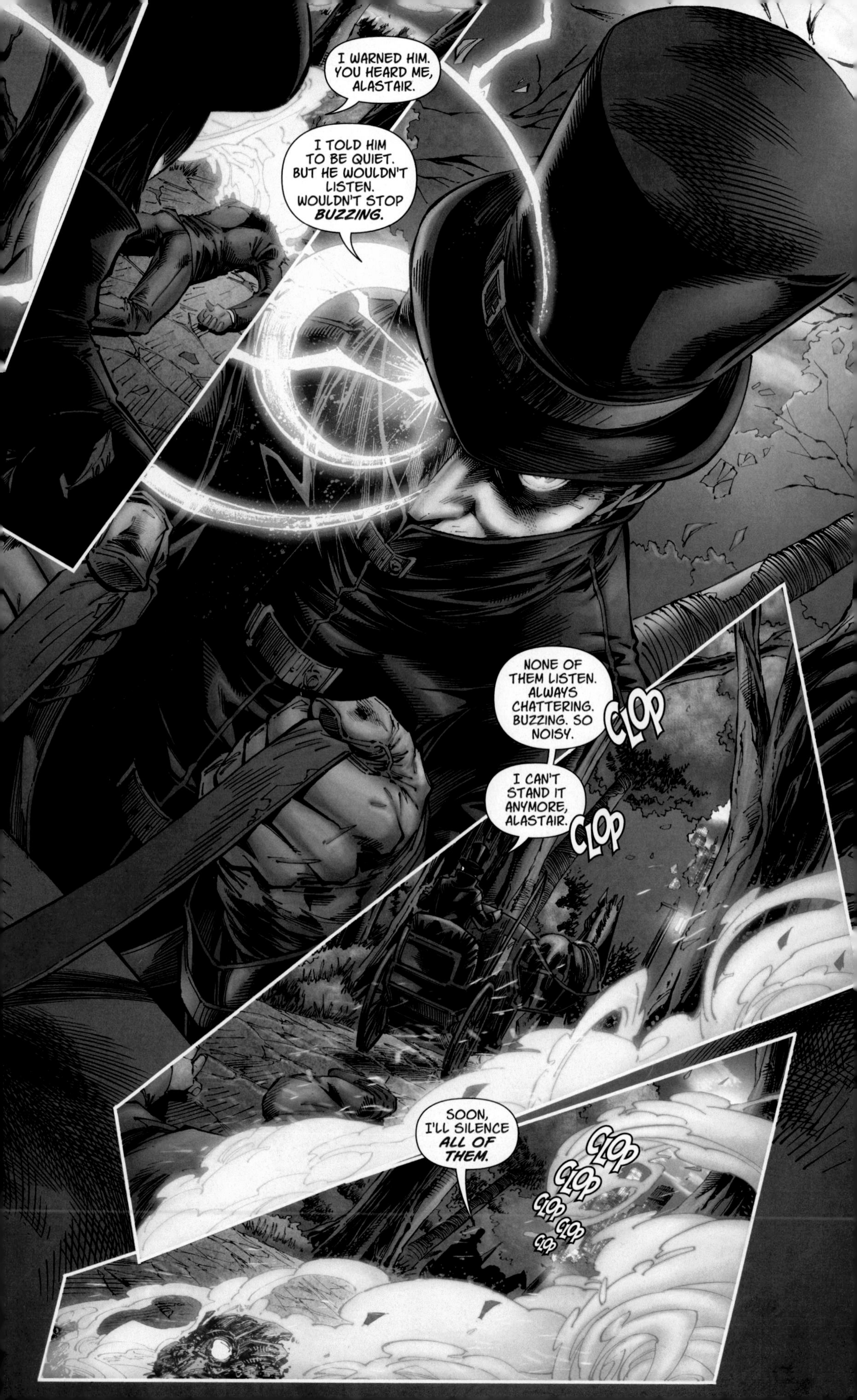
I WARNED HIM. YOU HEARD ME, ALASTAIR.
I TOLD HIM TO BE QUIET. BUT HE WOULDN'T LISTEN. WOULDN'T STOP *BUZZING*.
NONE OF THEM LISTEN. ALWAYS CHATTERING. BUZZING. SO NOISY.
CLOP
I CAN'T STAND IT ANYMORE, ALASTAIR.
CLOP
SOON, I'LL SILENCE *ALL OF THEM*.
CLOP
CLOP
CLOP CLOP
CLOP

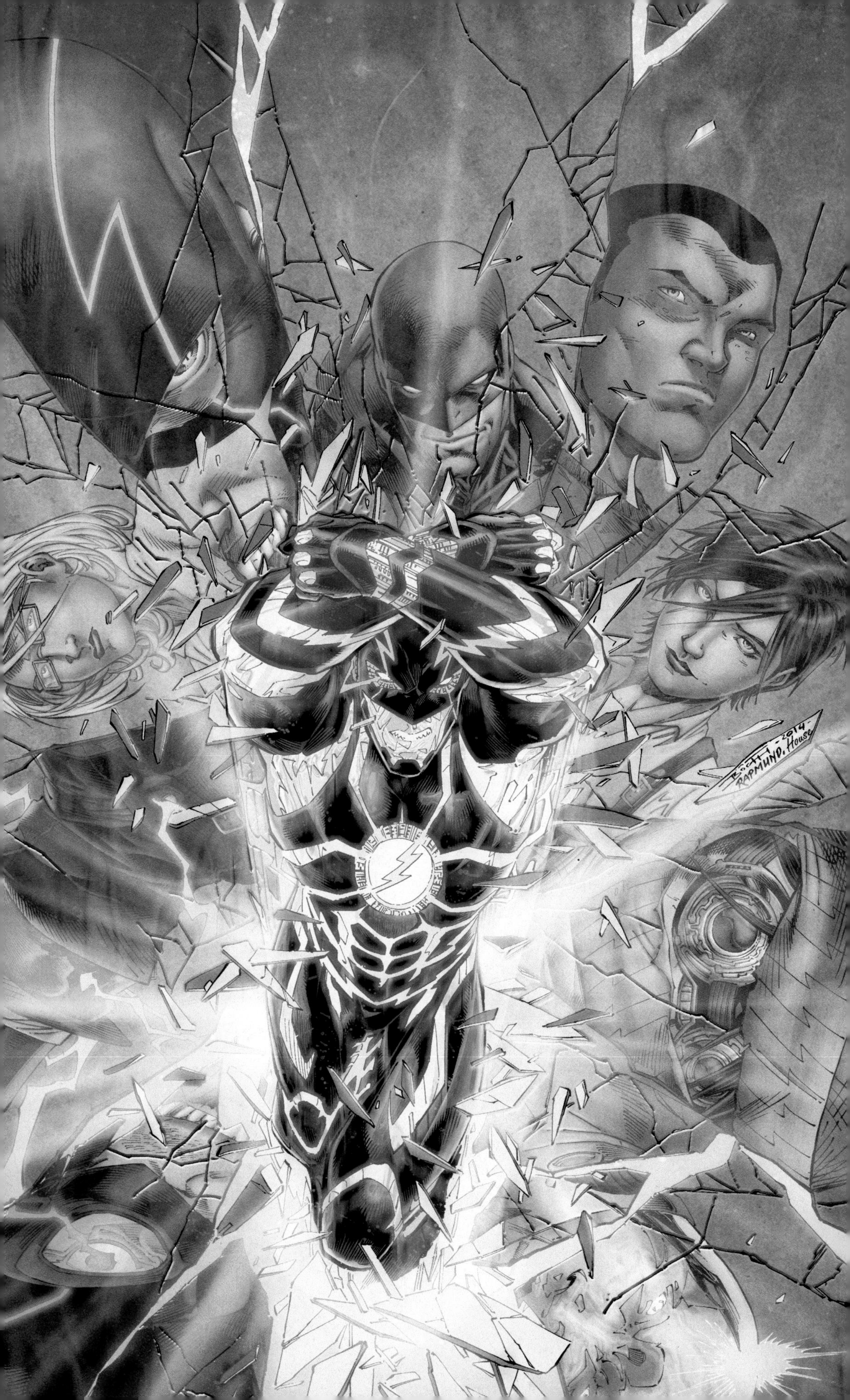
-2014-
RAPMUND. House

SKELETONS IN THE CLOSET

ROBERT VENDITTI & VAN JENSEN writers BRETT BOOTH penciller NORM RAPMUND inker ANDREW DALHOUSE colorist PAT BROSSEAU letterer
cover by BRETT BOOTH, NORM RAPMUND & ANDREW DALHOUSE

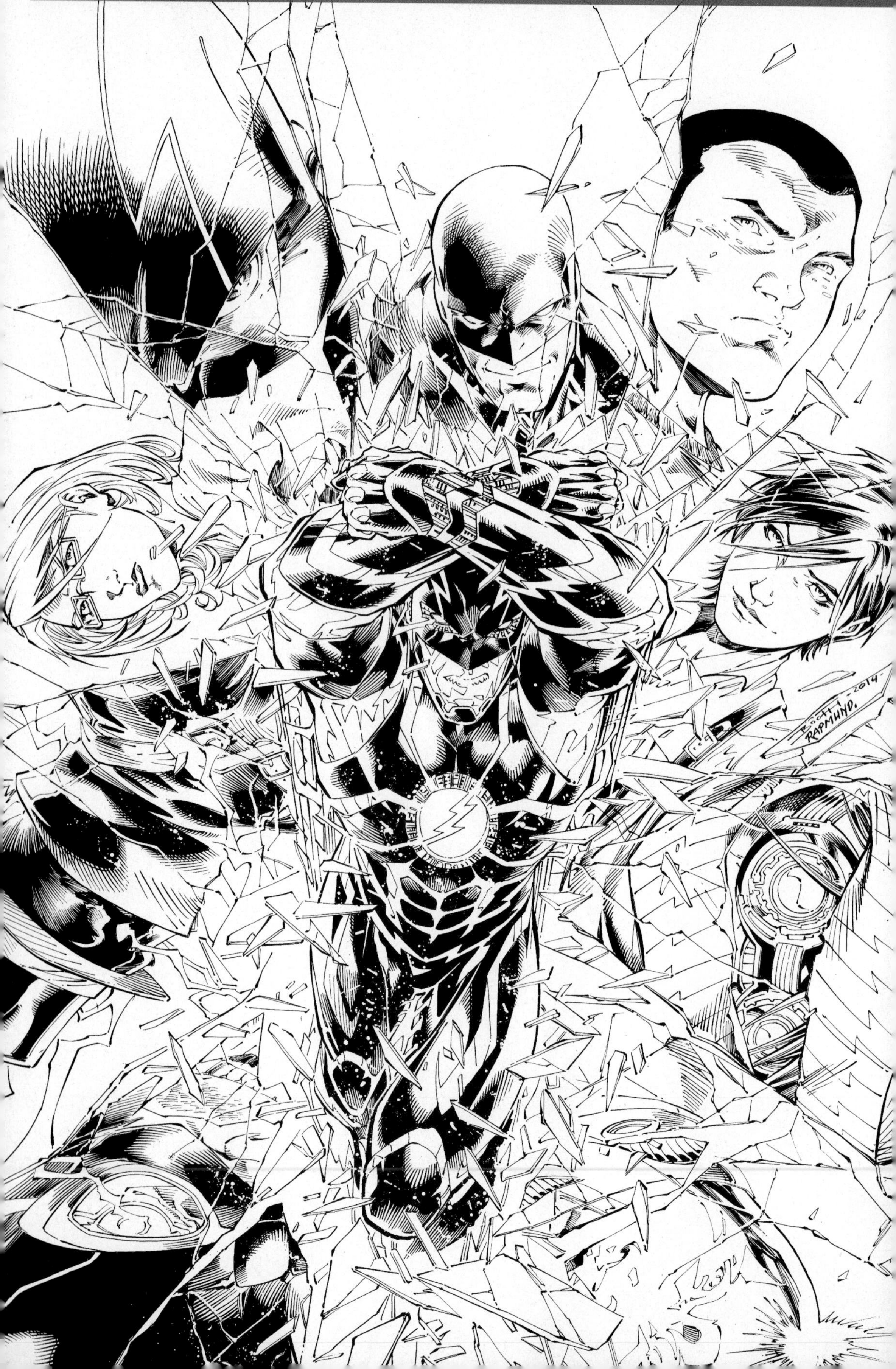

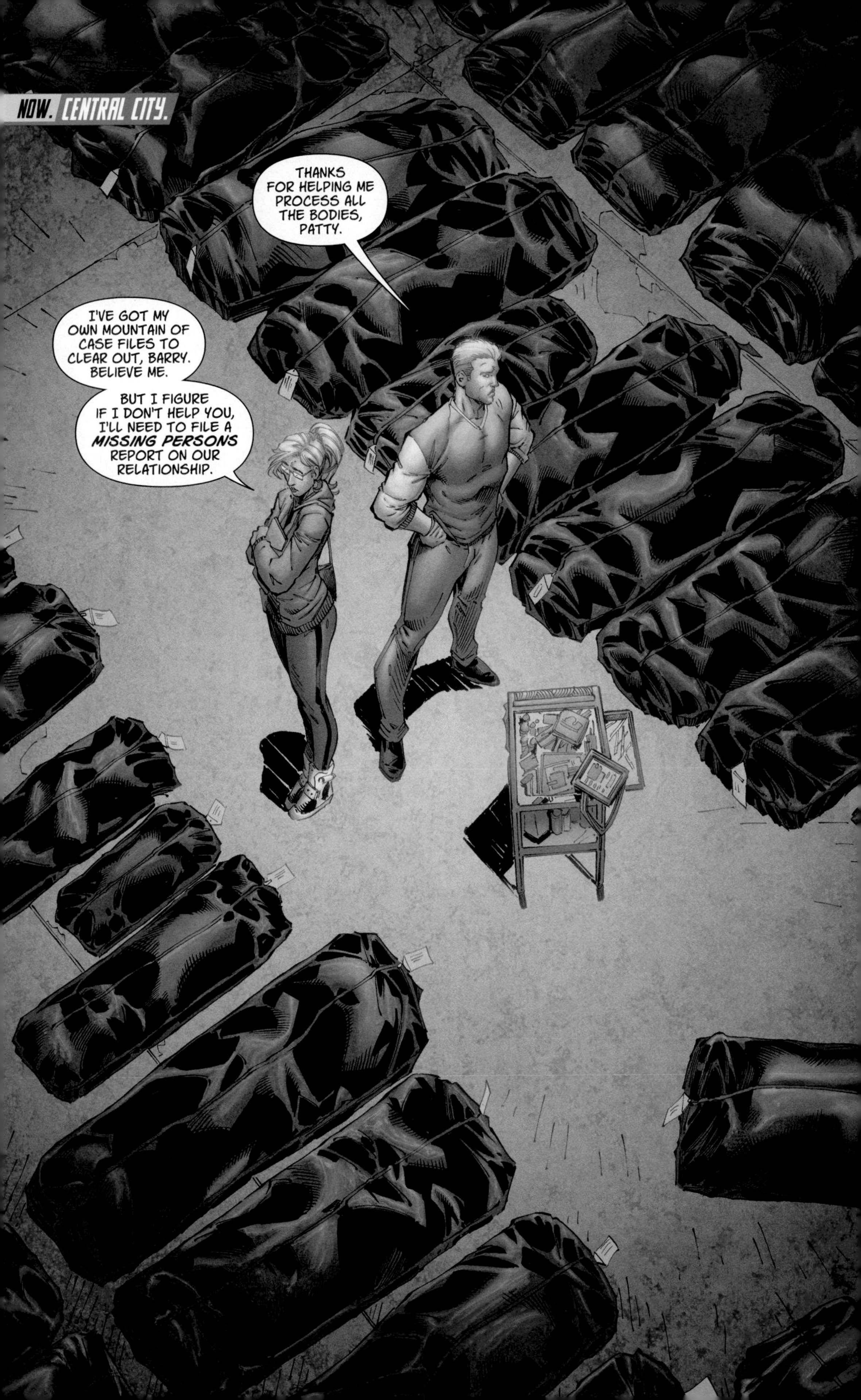
NOW. CENTRAL CITY.
THANKS FOR HELPING ME PROCESS ALL THE BODIES, PATTY.
I'VE GOT MY OWN MOUNTAIN OF CASE FILES TO CLEAR OUT, BARRY. BELIEVE ME.
BUT I FIGURE IF I DON'T HELP YOU, I'LL NEED TO FILE A MISSING PERSONS REPORT ON OUR RELATIONSHIP.

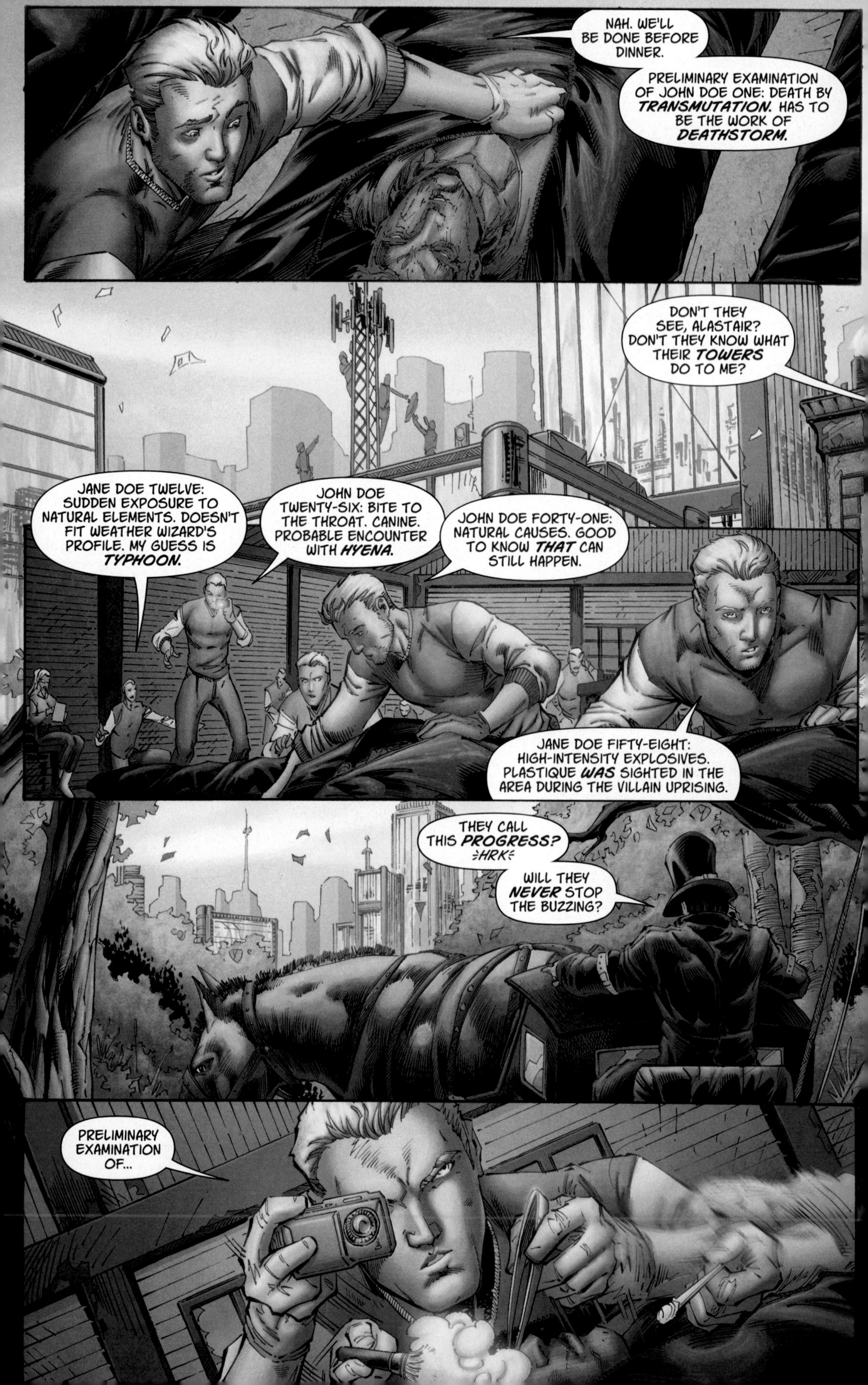
NAH. WE'LL BE DONE BEFORE DINNER.
PRELIMINARY EXAMINATION OF JOHN DOE ONE: DEATH BY TRANSMUTATION. HAS TO BE THE WORK OF DEATHSTORM.
DON'T THEY SEE, ALASTAIR? DON'T THEY KNOW WHAT THEIR TOWERS DO TO ME?
JANE DOE TWELVE: SUDDEN EXPOSURE TO NATURAL ELEMENTS. DOESN'T FIT WEATHER WIZARD'S PROFILE. MY GUESS IS TYPHOON.
JOHN DOE TWENTY-SIX: BITE TO THE THROAT. CANINE. PROBABLE ENCOUNTER WITH HYENA.
JOHN DOE FORTY-ONE: NATURAL CAUSES. GOOD TO KNOW THAT CAN STILL HAPPEN.
JANE DOE FIFTY-EIGHT: HIGH-INTENSITY EXPLOSIVES. PLASTIQUE WAS SIGHTED IN THE AREA DURING THE VILLAIN UPRISING.
THEY CALL THIS PROGRESS? HRK
WILL THEY NEVER STOP THE BUZZING?
PRELIMINARY EXAMINATION OF...

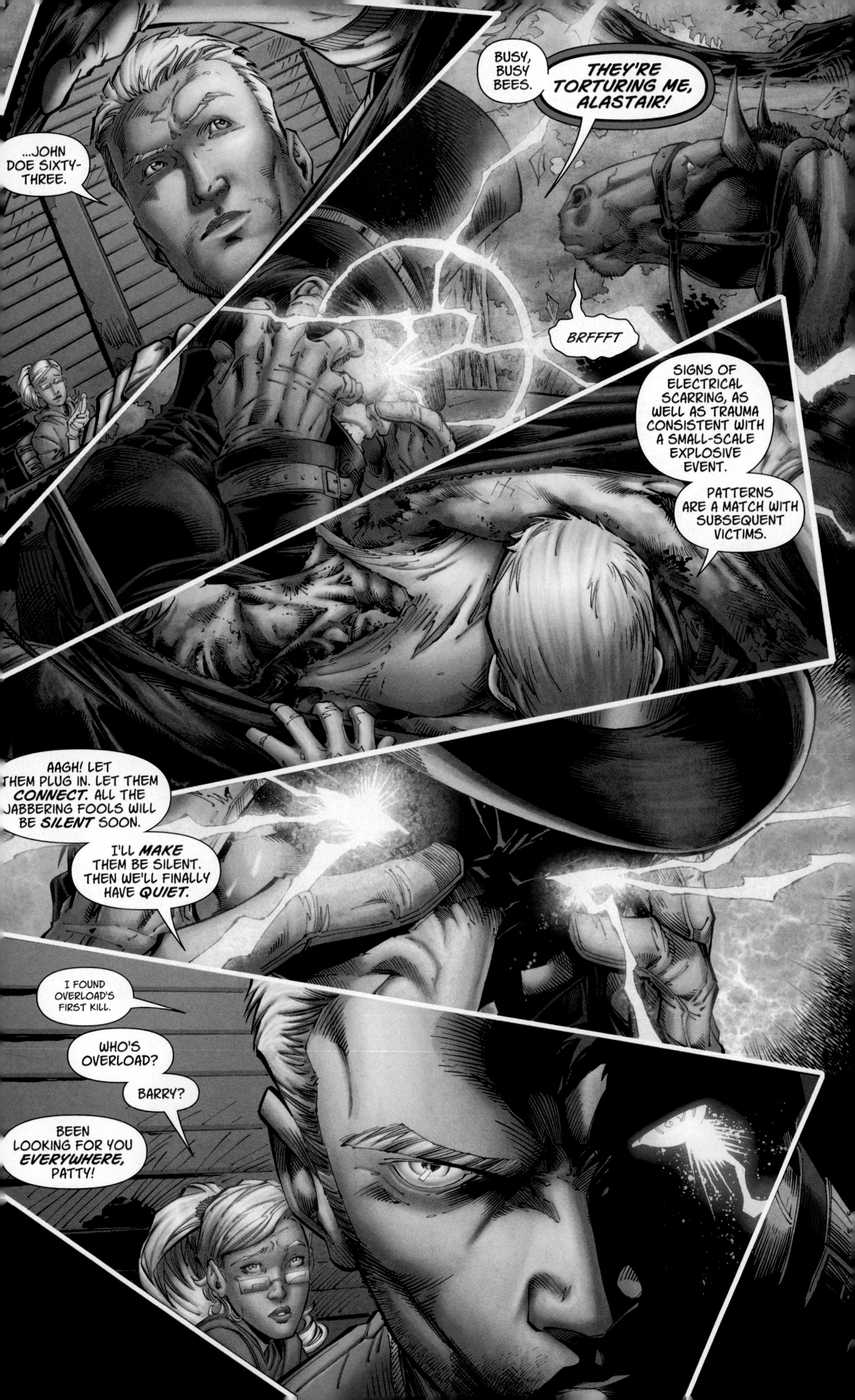
...JOHN DOE SIXTY-THREE.
BUSY, BUSY BEES.
THEY'RE TORTURING ME, ALASTAIR!
BRFFFT
SIGNS OF ELECTRICAL SCARRING, AS WELL AS TRAUMA CONSISTENT WITH A SMALL-SCALE EXPLOSIVE EVENT.
PATTERNS ARE A MATCH WITH SUBSEQUENT VICTIMS.
AAGH! LET THEM PLUG IN. LET THEM CONNECT. ALL THE JABBERING FOOLS WILL BE SILENT SOON.
I'LL MAKE THEM BE SILENT. THEN WE'LL FINALLY HAVE QUIET.
I FOUND OVERLOAD'S FIRST KILL.
WHO'S OVERLOAD?
BARRY?
BEEN LOOKING FOR YOU EVERYWHERE, PATTY!

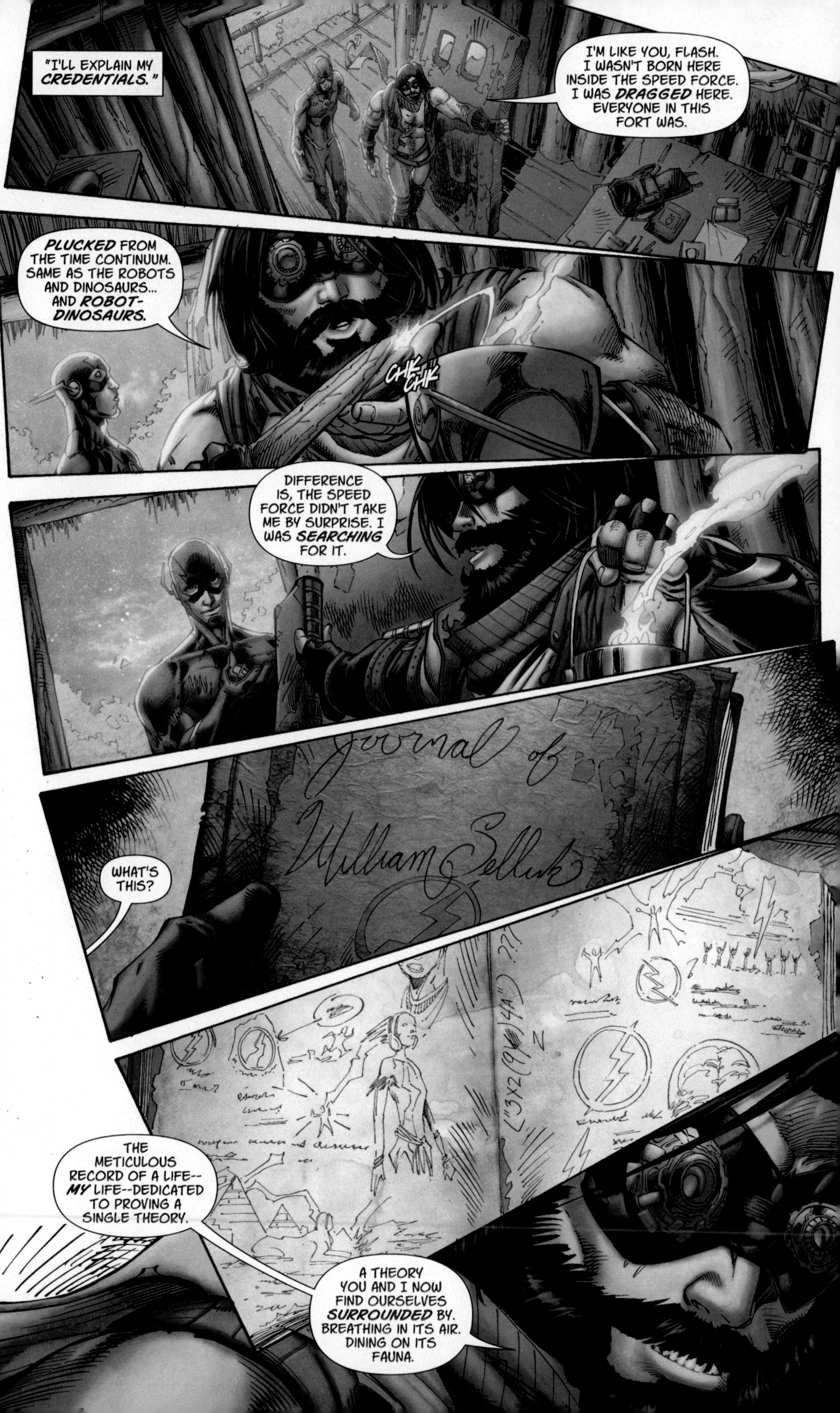
"I'LL EXPLAIN MY CREDENTIALS."
I'M LIKE YOU, FLASH. I WASN'T BORN HERE INSIDE THE SPEED FORCE. I WAS DRAGGED HERE. EVERYONE IN THIS FORT WAS.
PLUCKED FROM THE TIME CONTINUUM. SAME AS THE ROBOTS AND DINOSAURS... AND ROBOT-DINOSAURS.
CHK CHK
DIFFERENCE IS, THE SPEED FORCE DIDN'T TAKE ME BY SURPRISE. I WAS SEARCHING FOR IT.
Journal of William Sellick
WHAT'S THIS?
THE METICULOUS RECORD OF A LIFE-- MY LIFE--DEDICATED TO PROVING A SINGLE THEORY.
A THEORY YOU AND I NOW FIND OURSELVES SURROUNDED BY. BREATHING IN ITS AIR. DINING ON ITS FAUNA.

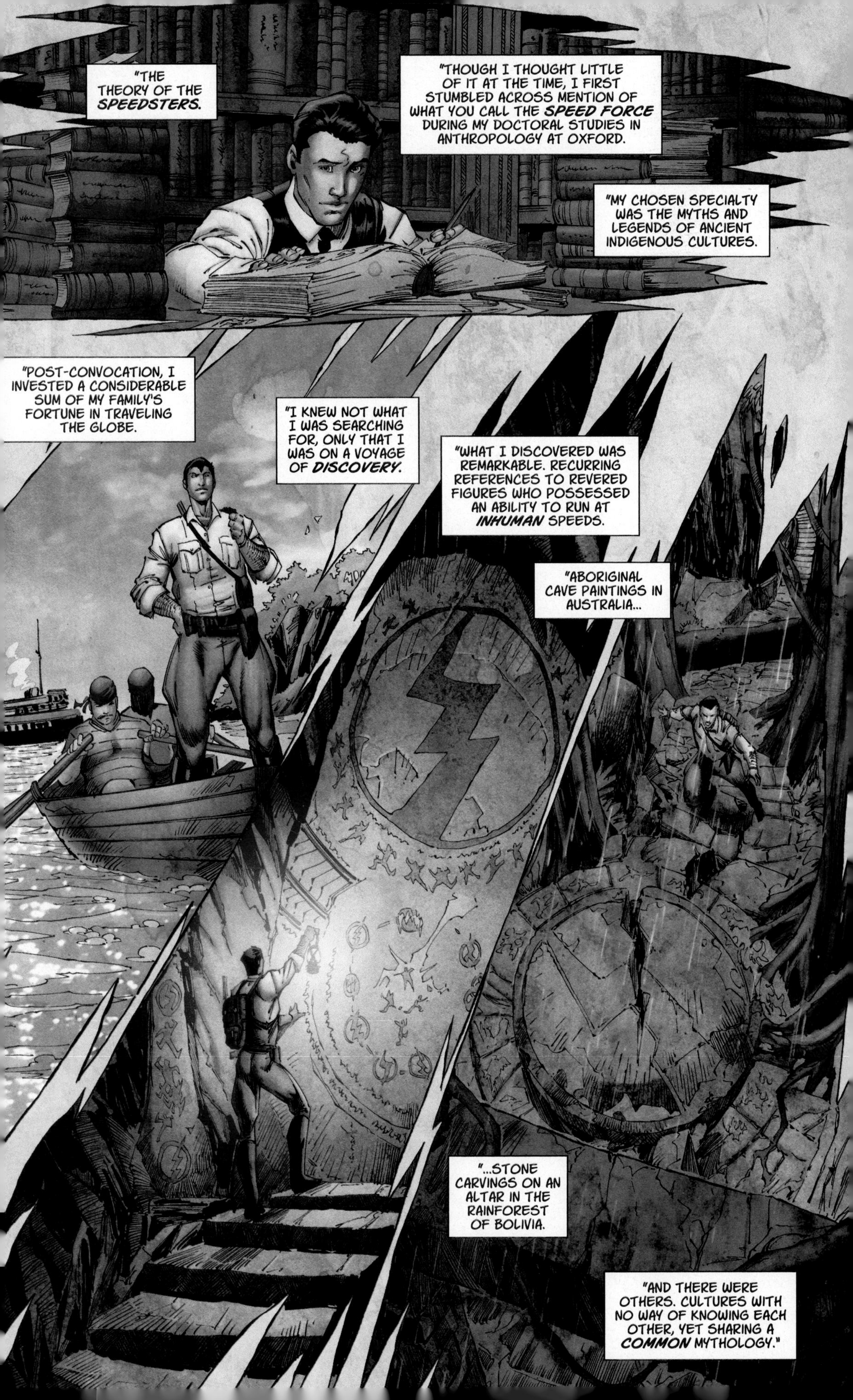
"THE THEORY OF THE SPEEDSTERS.
"THOUGH I THOUGHT LITTLE OF IT AT THE TIME, I FIRST STUMBLED ACROSS MENTION OF WHAT YOU CALL THE SPEED FORCE DURING MY DOCTORAL STUDIES IN ANTHROPOLOGY AT OXFORD.
"MY CHOSEN SPECIALTY WAS THE MYTHS AND LEGENDS OF ANCIENT INDIGENOUS CULTURES.
"POST-CONVOCATION, I INVESTED A CONSIDERABLE SUM OF MY FAMILY'S FORTUNE IN TRAVELING THE GLOBE.
"I KNEW NOT WHAT I WAS SEARCHING FOR, ONLY THAT I WAS ON A VOYAGE OF DISCOVERY.
"WHAT I DISCOVERED WAS REMARKABLE. RECURRING REFERENCES TO REVERED FIGURES WHO POSSESSED AN ABILITY TO RUN AT INHUMAN SPEEDS.
"ABORIGINAL CAVE PAINTINGS IN AUSTRALIA...
"...STONE CARVINGS ON AN ALTAR IN THE RAINFOREST OF BOLIVIA.
"AND THERE WERE OTHERS. CULTURES WITH NO WAY OF KNOWING EACH OTHER, YET SHARING A COMMON MYTHOLOGY."

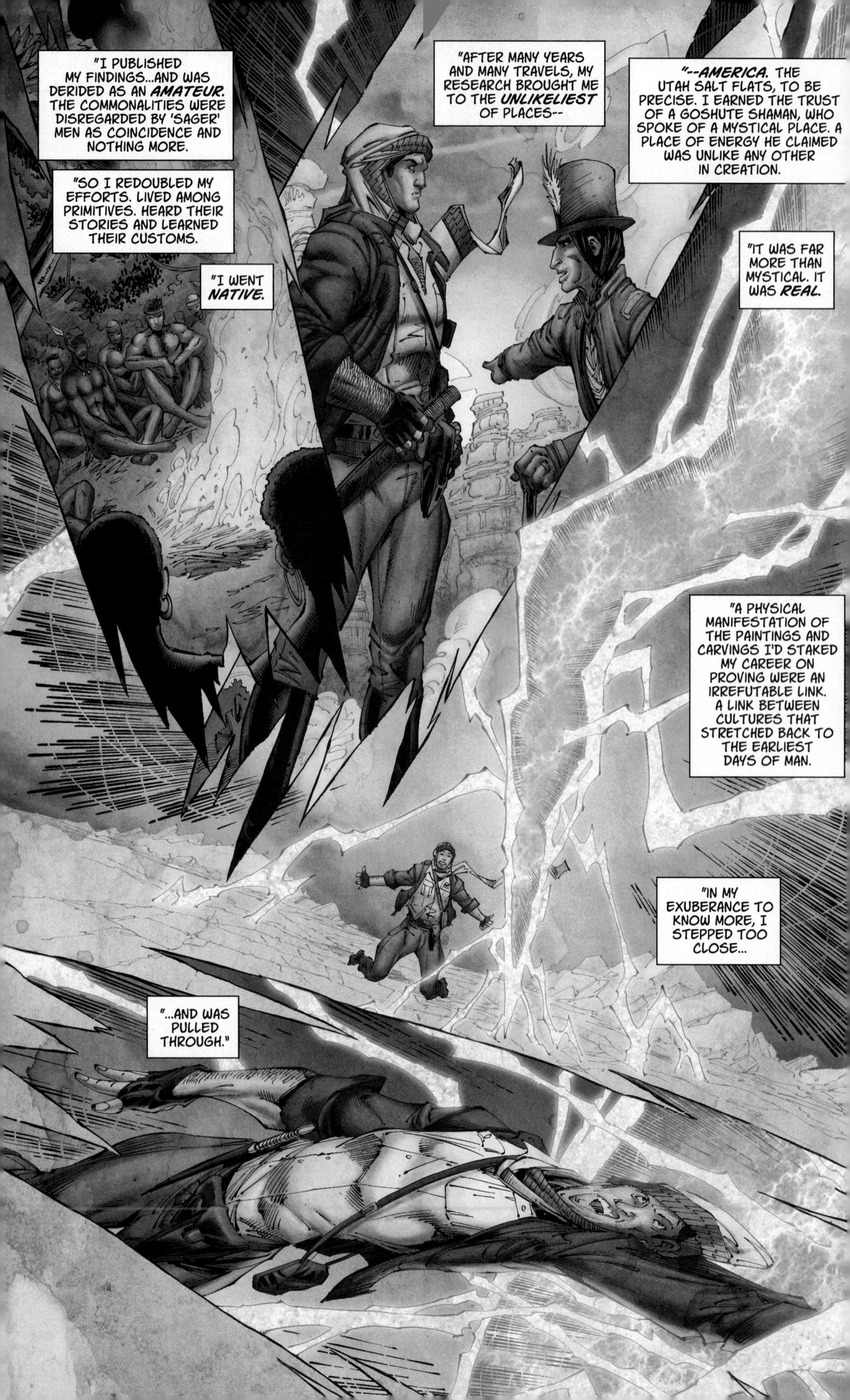
"I PUBLISHED MY FINDINGS...AND WAS DERIDED AS AN AMATEUR. THE COMMONALITIES WERE DISREGARDED BY 'SAGER' MEN AS COINCIDENCE AND NOTHING MORE.
"SO I REDOUBLED MY EFFORTS. LIVED AMONG PRIMITIVES. HEARD THEIR STORIES AND LEARNED THEIR CUSTOMS.
"I WENT NATIVE.
"AFTER MANY YEARS AND MANY TRAVELS, MY RESEARCH BROUGHT ME TO THE UNLIKELIEST OF PLACES--
"--AMERICA. THE UTAH SALT FLATS, TO BE PRECISE. I EARNED THE TRUST OF A GOSHUTE SHAMAN, WHO SPOKE OF A MYSTICAL PLACE. A PLACE OF ENERGY HE CLAIMED WAS UNLIKE ANY OTHER IN CREATION.
"IT WAS FAR MORE THAN MYSTICAL. IT WAS REAL.
"A PHYSICAL MANIFESTATION OF THE PAINTINGS AND CARVINGS I'D STAKED MY CAREER ON PROVING WERE AN IRREFUTABLE LINK. A LINK BETWEEN CULTURES THAT STRETCHED BACK TO THE EARLIEST DAYS OF MAN.
"IN MY EXUBERANCE TO KNOW MORE, I STEPPED TOO CLOSE...
"...AND WAS PULLED THROUGH."

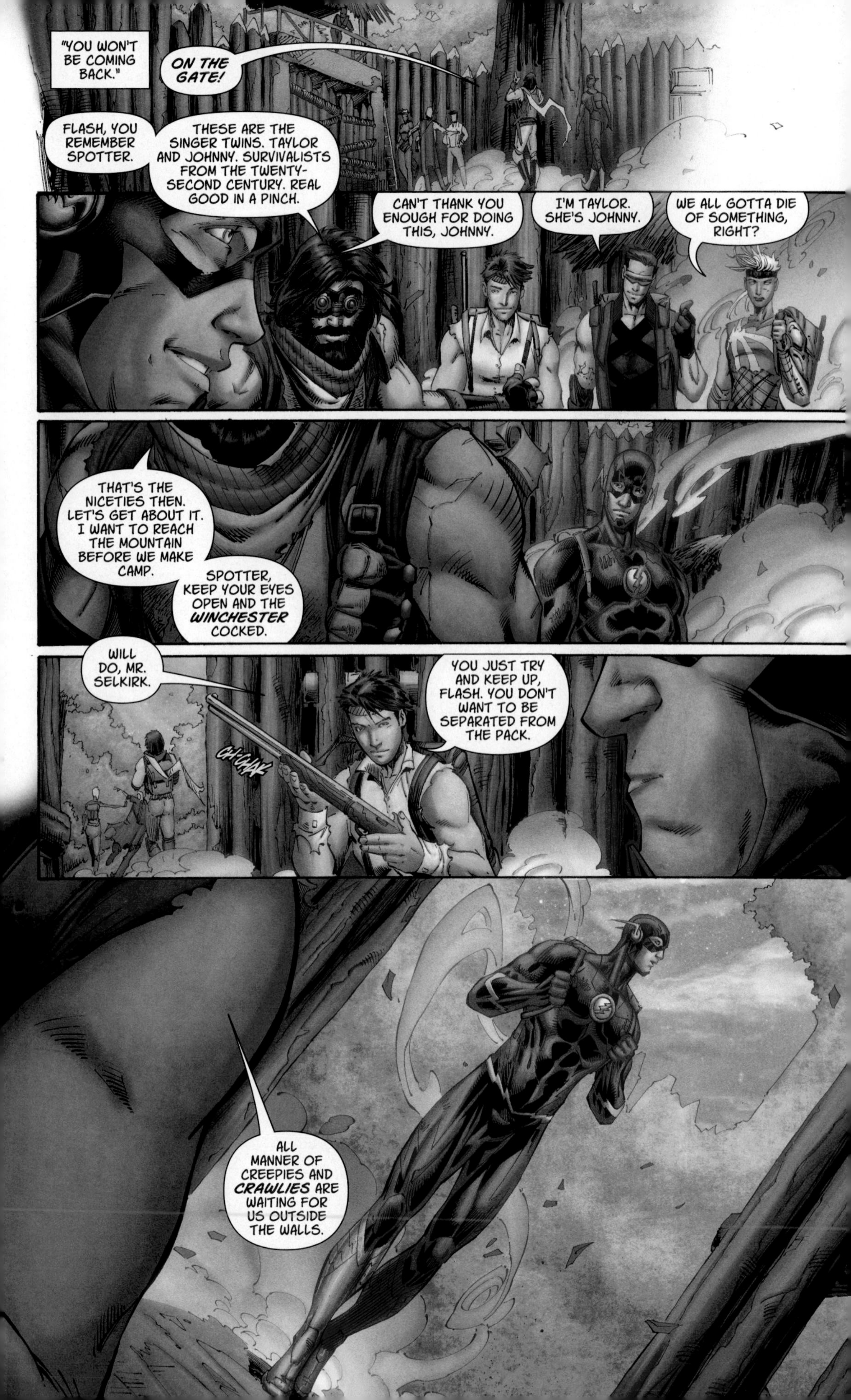
"YOU WON'T BE COMING BACK."
ON THE GATE!
FLASH, YOU REMEMBER SPOTTER.
THESE ARE THE SINGER TWINS. TAYLOR AND JOHNNY. SURVIVALISTS FROM THE TWENTY-SECOND CENTURY. REAL GOOD IN A PINCH.
CAN'T THANK YOU ENOUGH FOR DOING THIS, JOHNNY.
I'M TAYLOR. SHE'S JOHNNY.
WE ALL GOTTA DIE OF SOMETHING, RIGHT?
THAT'S THE NICETIES THEN. LET'S GET ABOUT IT. I WANT TO REACH THE MOUNTAIN BEFORE WE MAKE CAMP.
SPOTTER, KEEP YOUR EYES OPEN AND THE WINCHESTER COCKED.
WILL DO, MR. SELKIRK.
CH-CHAK
YOU JUST TRY AND KEEP UP, FLASH. YOU DON'T WANT TO BE SEPARATED FROM THE PACK.
ALL MANNER OF CREEPIES AND CRAWLIES ARE WAITING FOR US OUTSIDE THE WALLS.

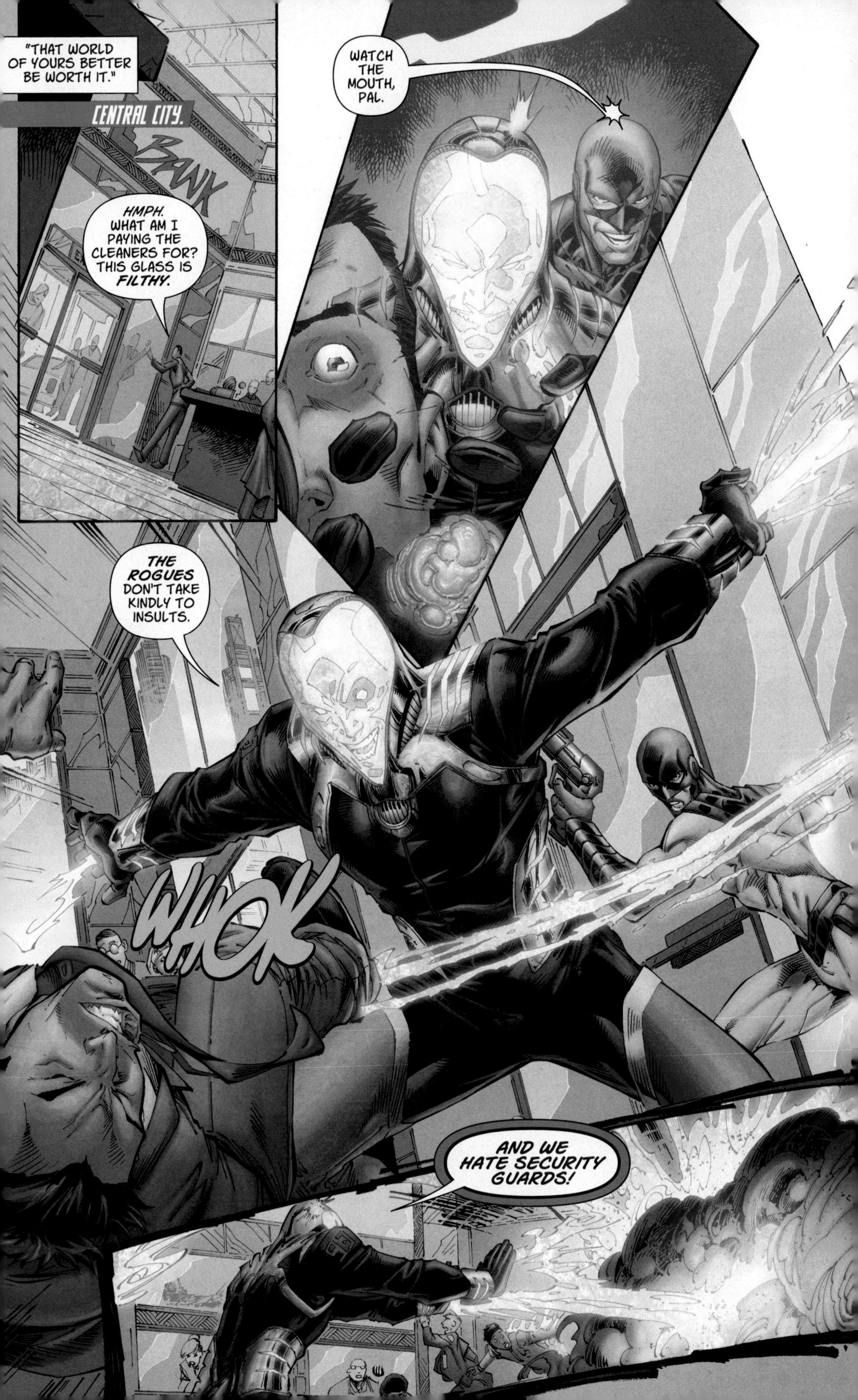
"THAT WORLD OF YOURS BETTER BE WORTH IT."
CENTRAL CITY.
BANK
HMPH. WHAT AM I PAYING THE CLEANERS FOR? THIS GLASS IS FILTHY.
WATCH THE MOUTH, PAL.
THE ROGUES DON'T TAKE KINDLY TO INSULTS.
WHOK
AND WE HATE SECURITY GUARDS!

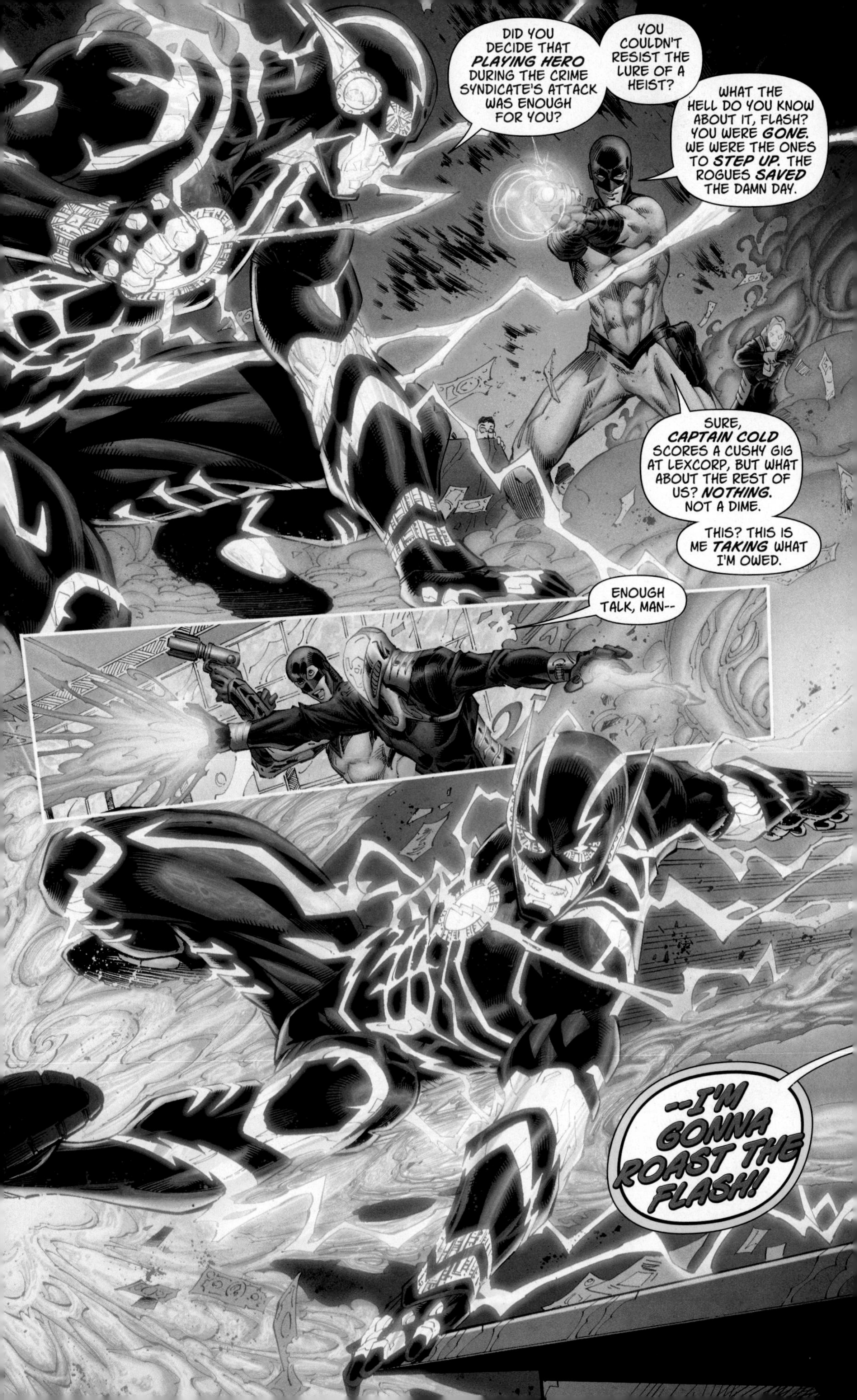
DID YOU DECIDE THAT PLAYING HERO DURING THE CRIME SYNDICATE'S ATTACK WAS ENOUGH FOR YOU?
YOU COULDN'T RESIST THE LURE OF A HEIST?
WHAT THE HELL DO YOU KNOW ABOUT IT, FLASH? YOU WERE GONE. WE WERE THE ONES TO STEP UP. THE ROGUES SAVED THE DAMN DAY.
SURE, CAPTAIN COLD SCORES A CUSHY GIG AT LEXCORP, BUT WHAT ABOUT THE REST OF US? NOTHING. NOT A DIME.
THIS? THIS IS ME TAKING WHAT I'M OWED.
ENOUGH TALK, MAN--
--I'M GONNA ROAST THE FLASH!

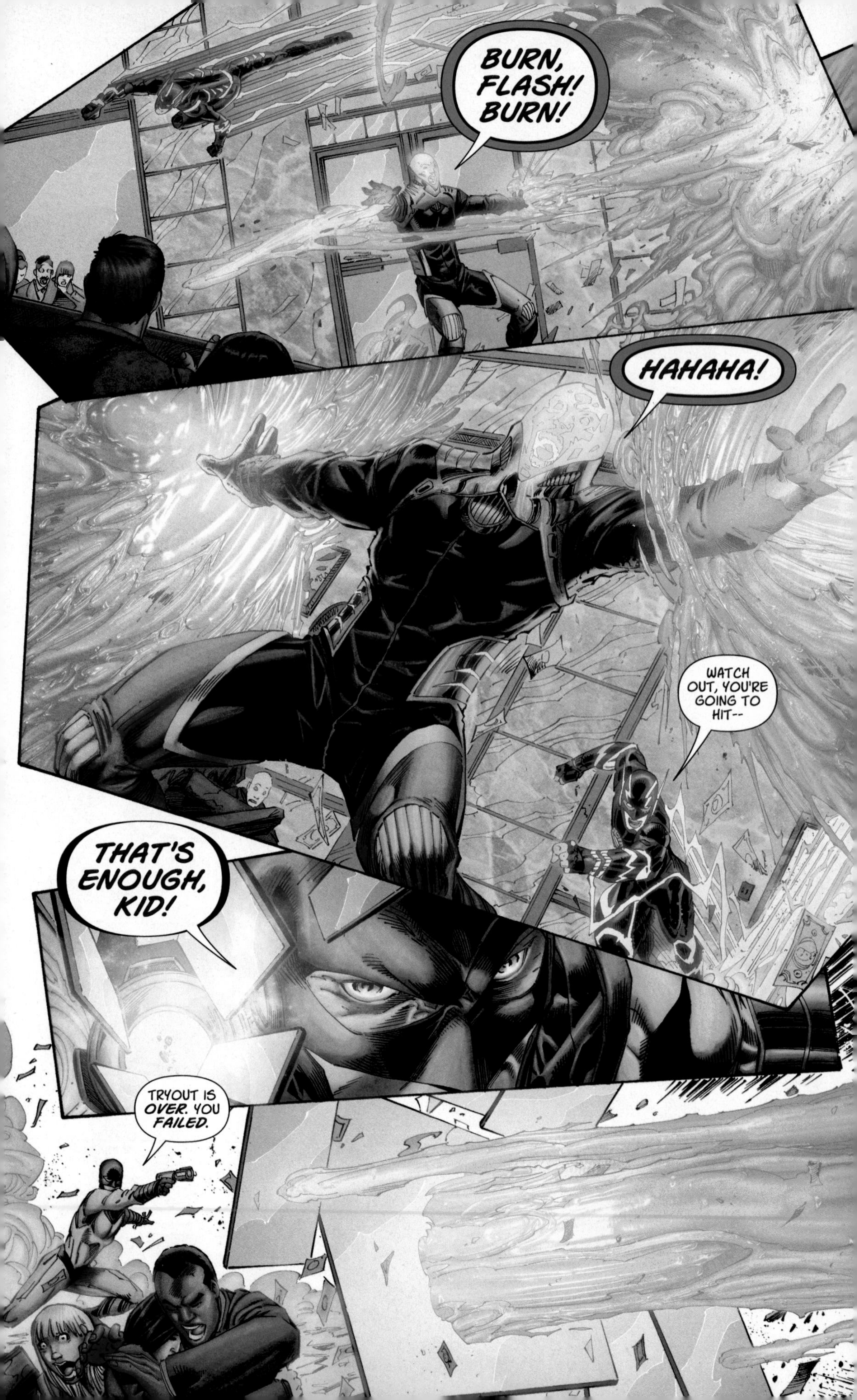
BURN, FLASH! BURN!
HAHAHA!
WATCH OUT, YOU'RE GOING TO HIT--
THAT'S ENOUGH, KID!
TRYOUT IS *OVER*. YOU *FAILED*.

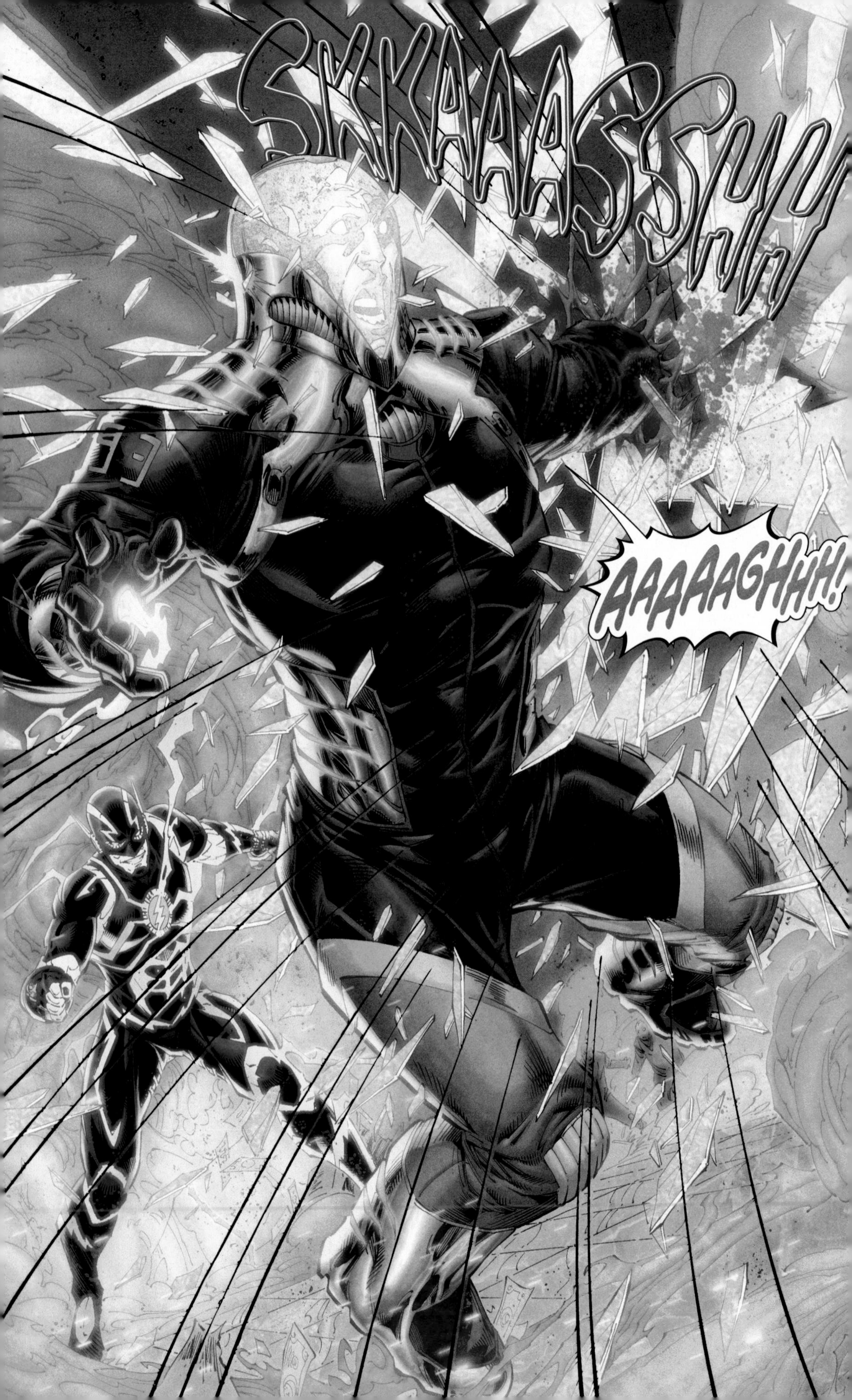
SKKAAAASSHH
AAAAAGHHH!

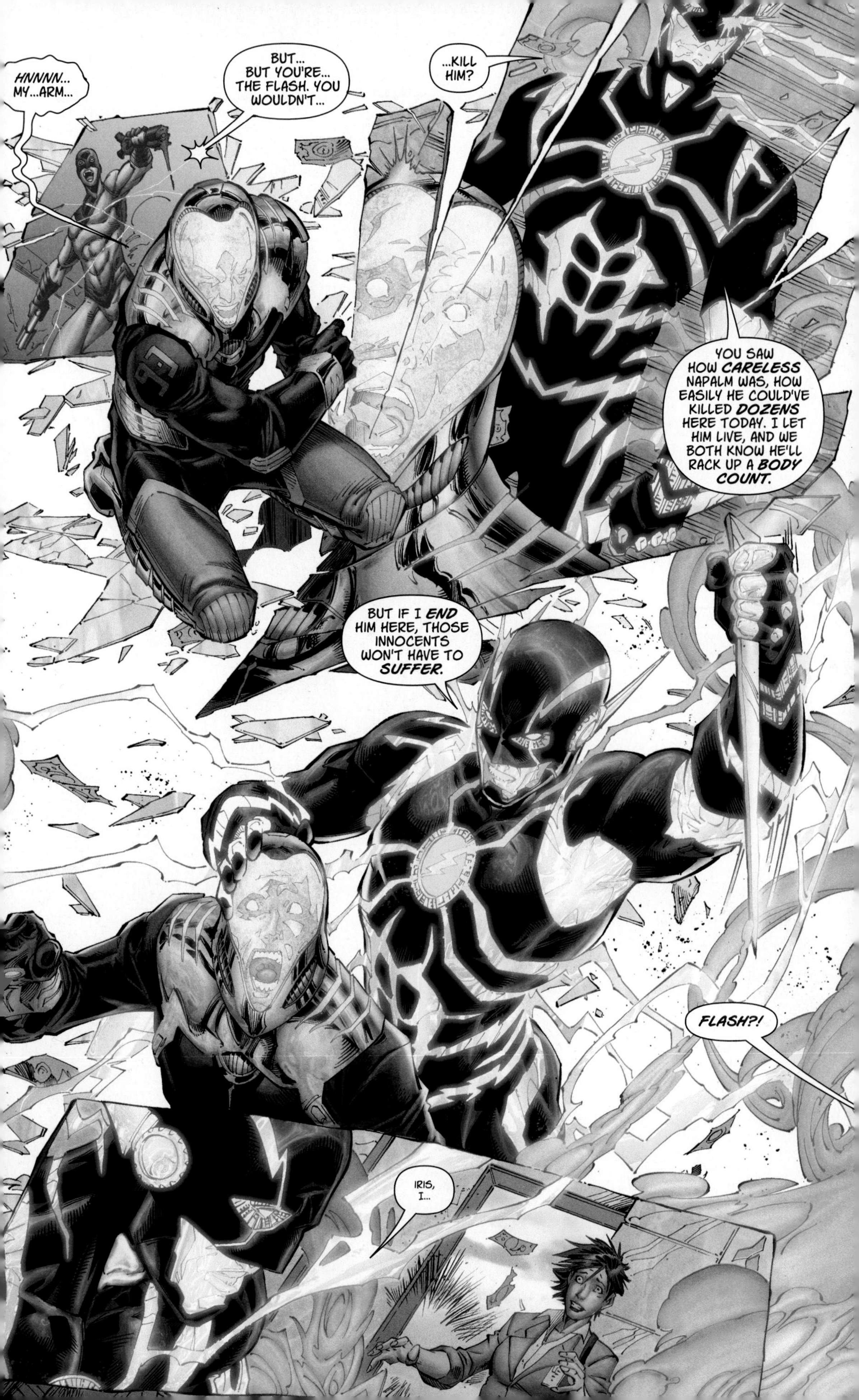
HNNNN... MY...ARM...
BUT... BUT YOU'RE... THE FLASH. YOU WOULDN'T...
...KILL HIM?
YOU SAW HOW CARELESS NAPALM WAS, HOW EASILY HE COULD'VE KILLED DOZENS HERE TODAY. I LET HIM LIVE, AND WE BOTH KNOW HE'LL RACK UP A BODY COUNT.
BUT IF I END HIM HERE, THOSE INNOCENTS WON'T HAVE TO SUFFER.
FLASH?!
IRIS, I...

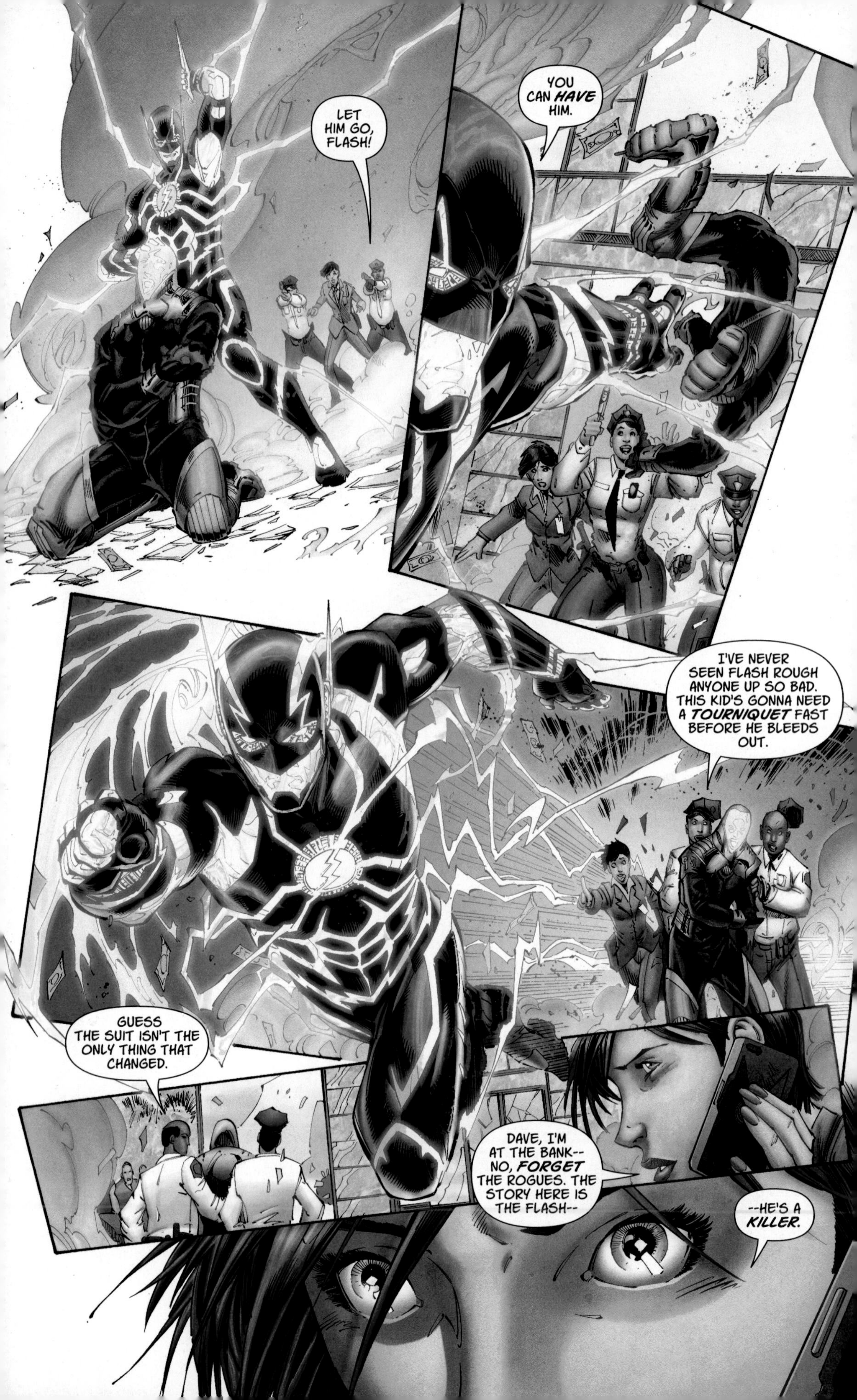
LET HIM GO, FLASH!
YOU CAN *HAVE* HIM.
I'VE NEVER SEEN FLASH ROUGH ANYONE UP SO BAD. THIS KID'S GONNA NEED A *TOURNIQUET* FAST BEFORE HE BLEEDS OUT.
GUESS THE SUIT ISN'T THE ONLY THING THAT CHANGED.
DAVE, I'M AT THE BANK-- NO, *FORGET* THE ROGUES. THE STORY HERE IS THE FLASH--
--HE'S A *KILLER.*

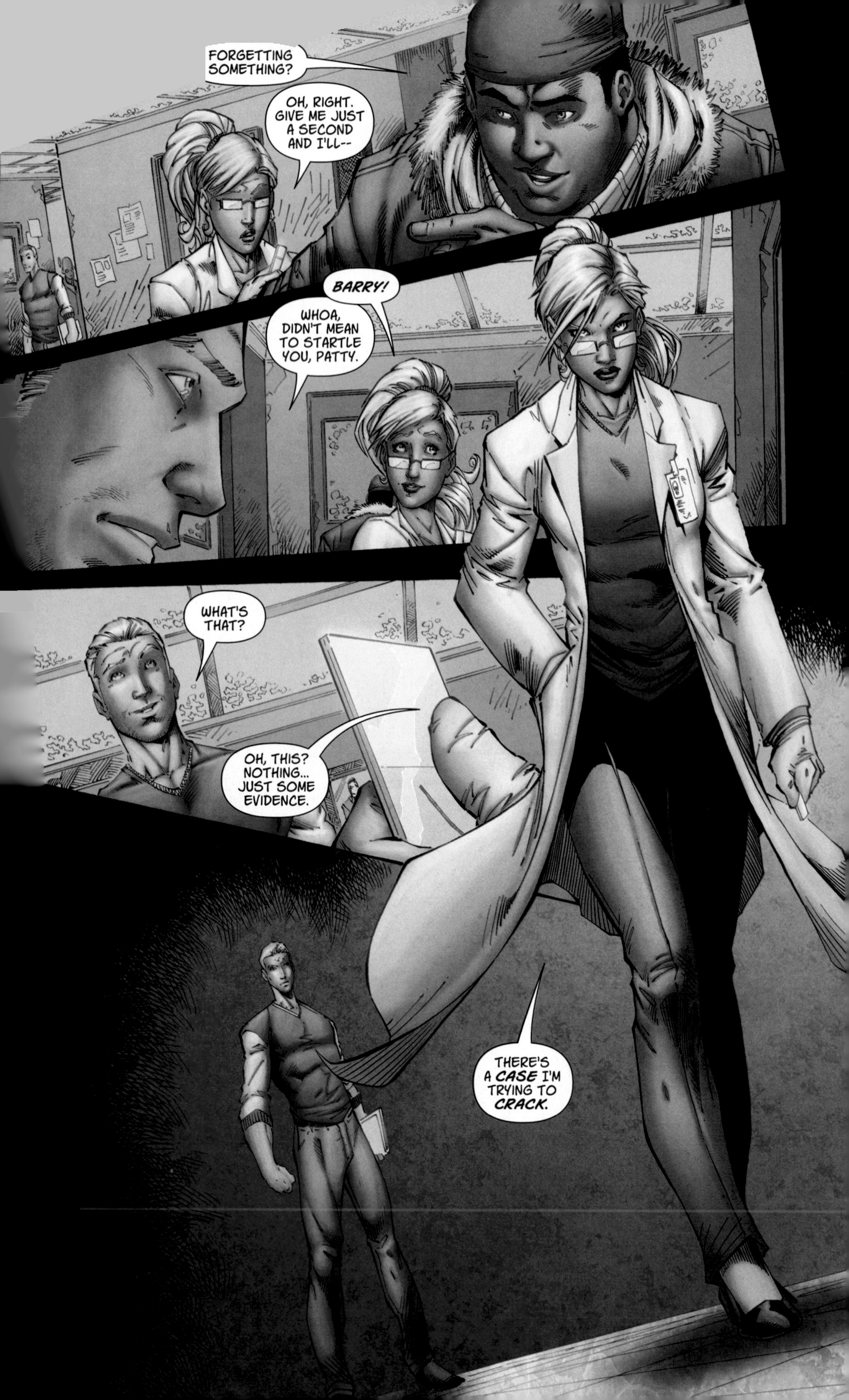
FORGETTING SOMETHING?
OH, RIGHT. GIVE ME JUST A SECOND AND I'LL--
BARRY!
WHOA, DIDN'T MEAN TO STARTLE YOU, PATTY.
WHAT'S THAT?
OH, THIS? NOTHING... JUST SOME EVIDENCE.
THERE'S A CASE I'M TRYING TO CRACK.

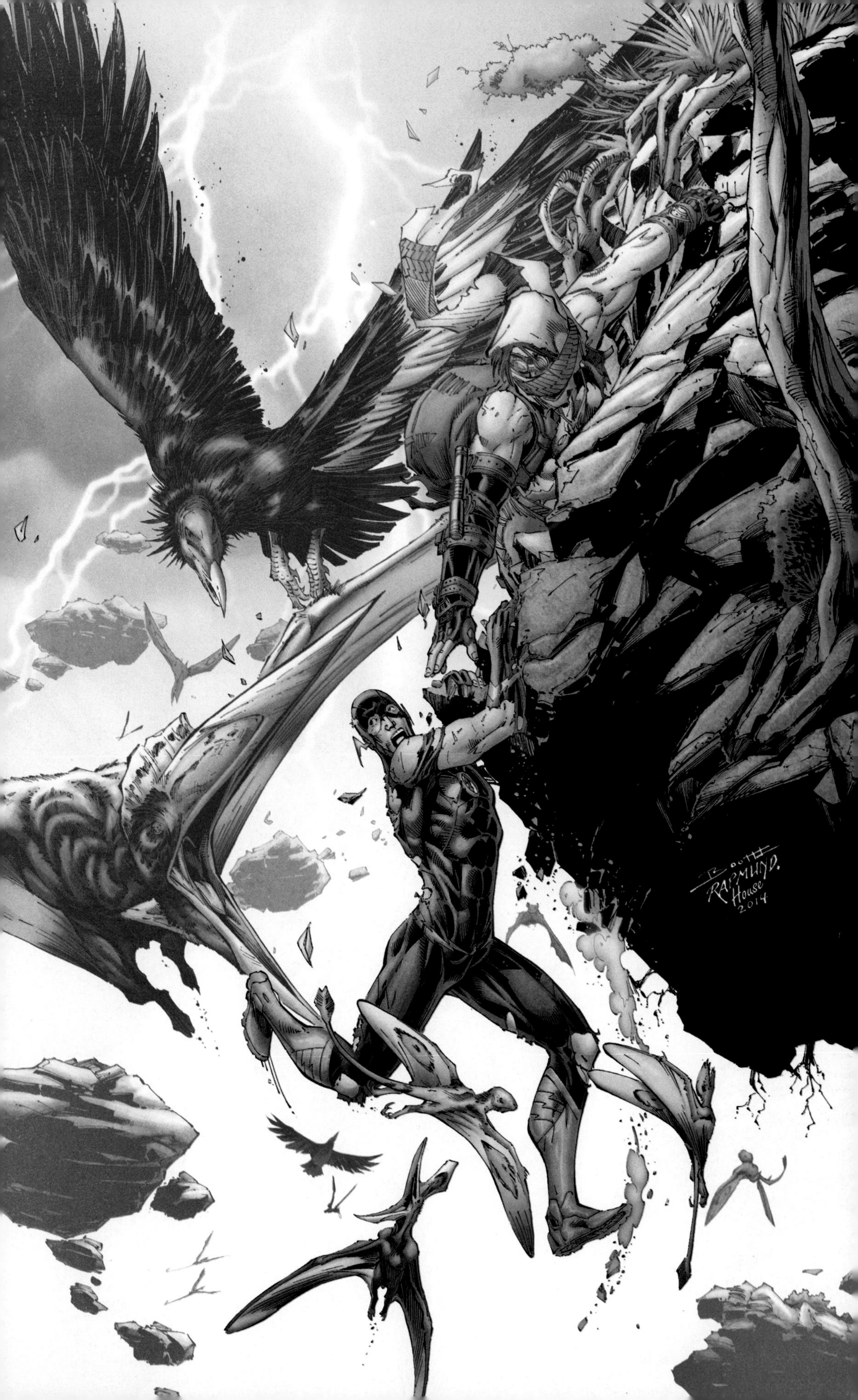

Booth
Rapmund.
House
2014

POWER LOSS

ROBERT VENDITTI & VAN JENSEN writers BRETT BOOTH penciller NORM RAPMUND inker ANDREW DALHOUSE colorist PAT BROSSEAU letterer
cover by BRETT BOOTH, NORM RAPMUND & ANDREW DALHOUSE

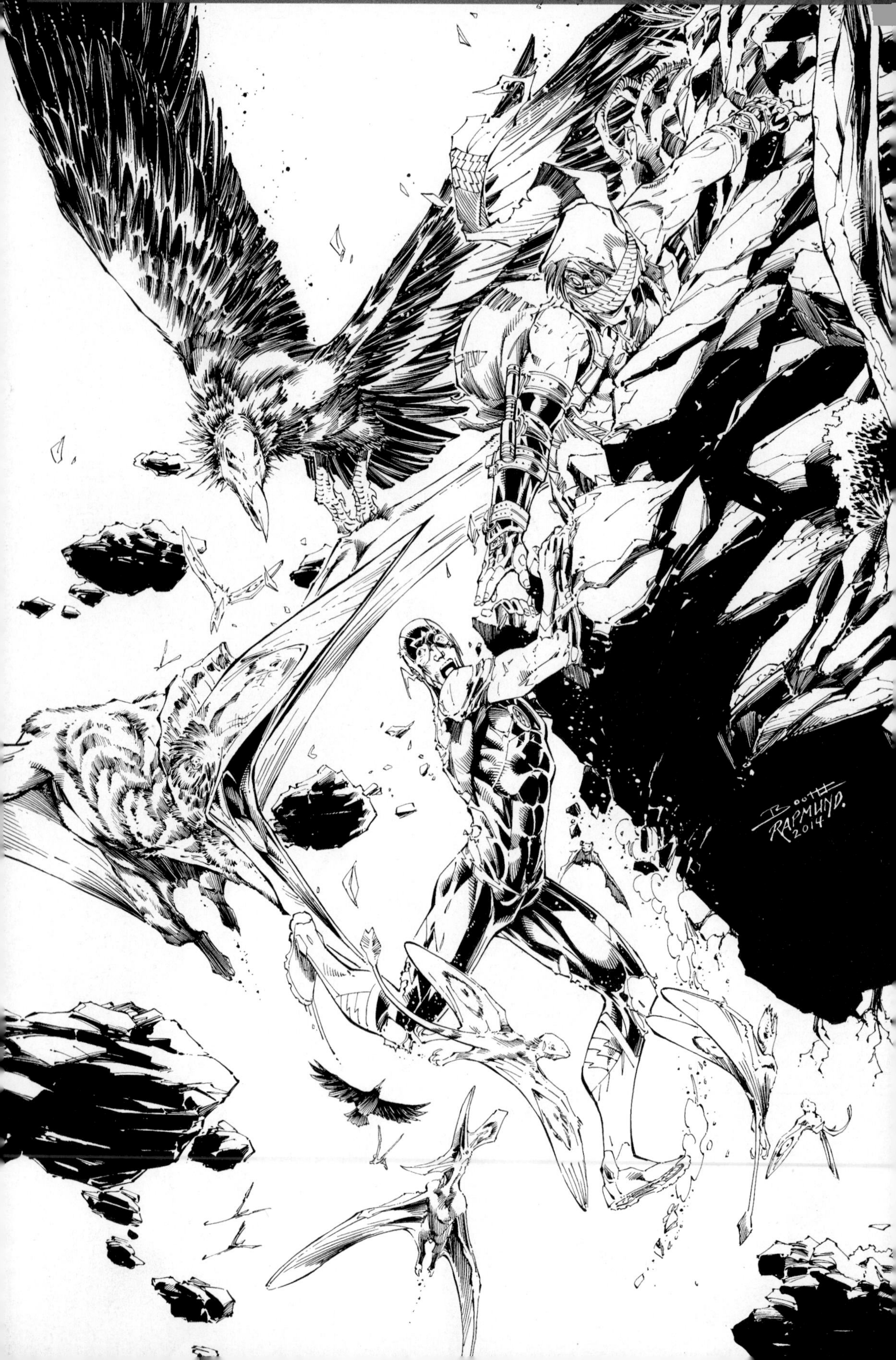
BOOTH
RAPMUND
2014

"DO YOU REMEMBER, ALASTAIR? THE WHOLE TOWN WAS *DARK* EXCEPT FOR THE FIRES.

"THE HEROES WERE *DISAPPEARED,* THEY SAID.

"THE POLICEMEN AND FIREMEN COULDN'T KEEP UP.

"A *MASSACRE.* BUT WHAT I REMEMBER *MOST* WAS THE *BLACKOUT.*

"NO TVS OR COMPUTERS. NO RADIOS. NO PHONES.

"NO *BUZZING.*

"FINALLY, I FELT *GOOD.* "

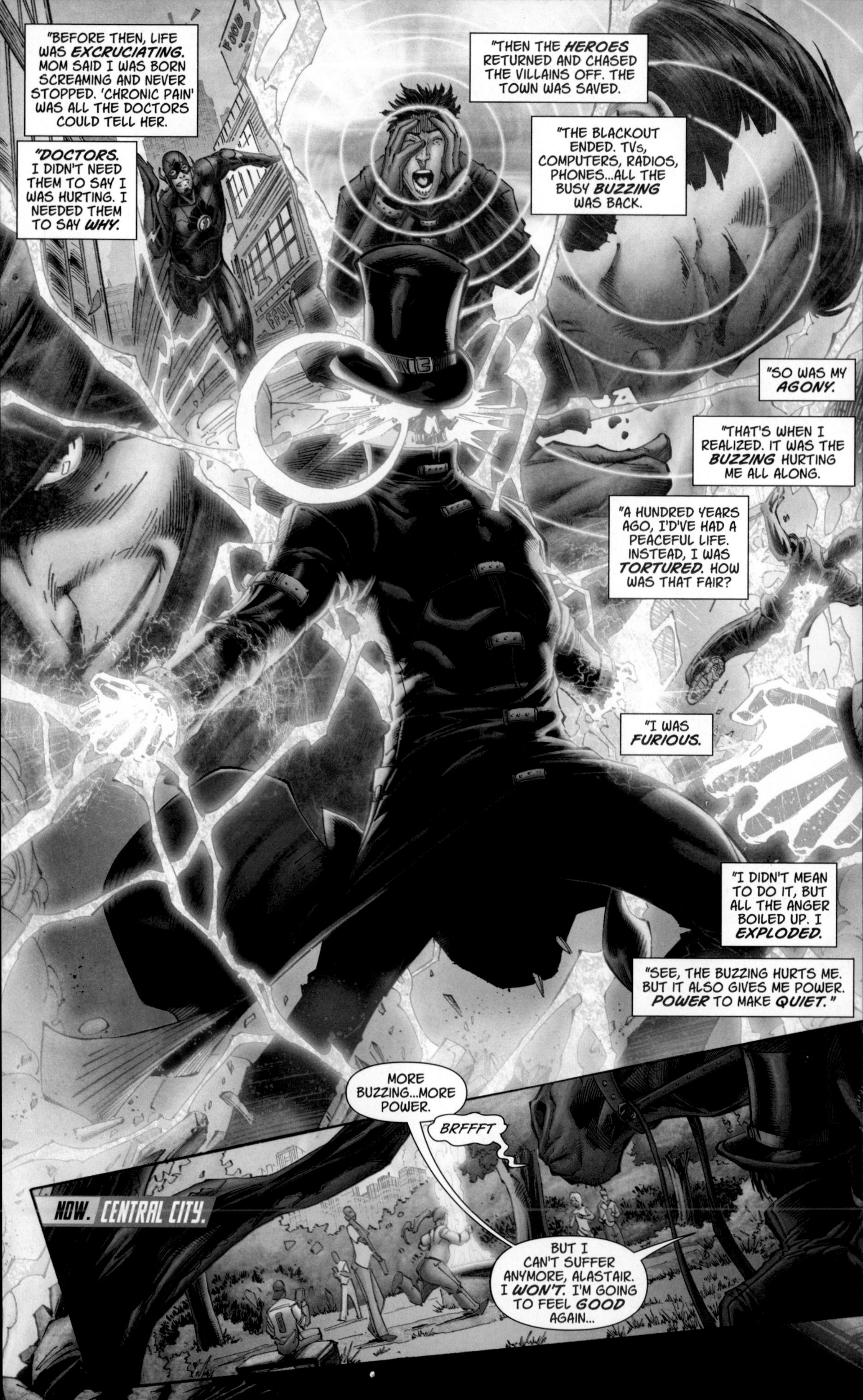
"BEFORE THEN, LIFE WAS **EXCRUCIATING**. MOM SAID I WAS BORN SCREAMING AND NEVER STOPPED. 'CHRONIC PAIN' WAS ALL THE DOCTORS COULD TELL HER.
"**DOCTORS**. I DIDN'T NEED THEM TO SAY I WAS HURTING. I NEEDED THEM TO SAY **WHY**.
"THEN THE **HEROES** RETURNED AND CHASED THE VILLAINS OFF. THE TOWN WAS SAVED.
"THE BLACKOUT ENDED. TVs, COMPUTERS, RADIOS, PHONES...ALL THE BUSY **BUZZING** WAS BACK.
"SO WAS MY **AGONY**.
"THAT'S WHEN I REALIZED. IT WAS THE **BUZZING** HURTING ME ALL ALONG.
"A HUNDRED YEARS AGO, I'D'VE HAD A PEACEFUL LIFE. INSTEAD, I WAS **TORTURED**. HOW WAS THAT FAIR?
"I WAS **FURIOUS**.
"I DIDN'T MEAN TO DO IT, BUT ALL THE ANGER BOILED UP. I **EXPLODED**.
"SEE, THE BUZZING HURTS ME. BUT IT ALSO GIVES ME POWER. **POWER** TO MAKE **QUIET**."
NOW. CENTRAL CITY.
MORE BUZZING...MORE POWER.
BRFFFT
BUT I CAN'T SUFFER ANYMORE, ALASTAIR. I **WON'T**. I'M GOING TO FEEL **GOOD** AGAIN...

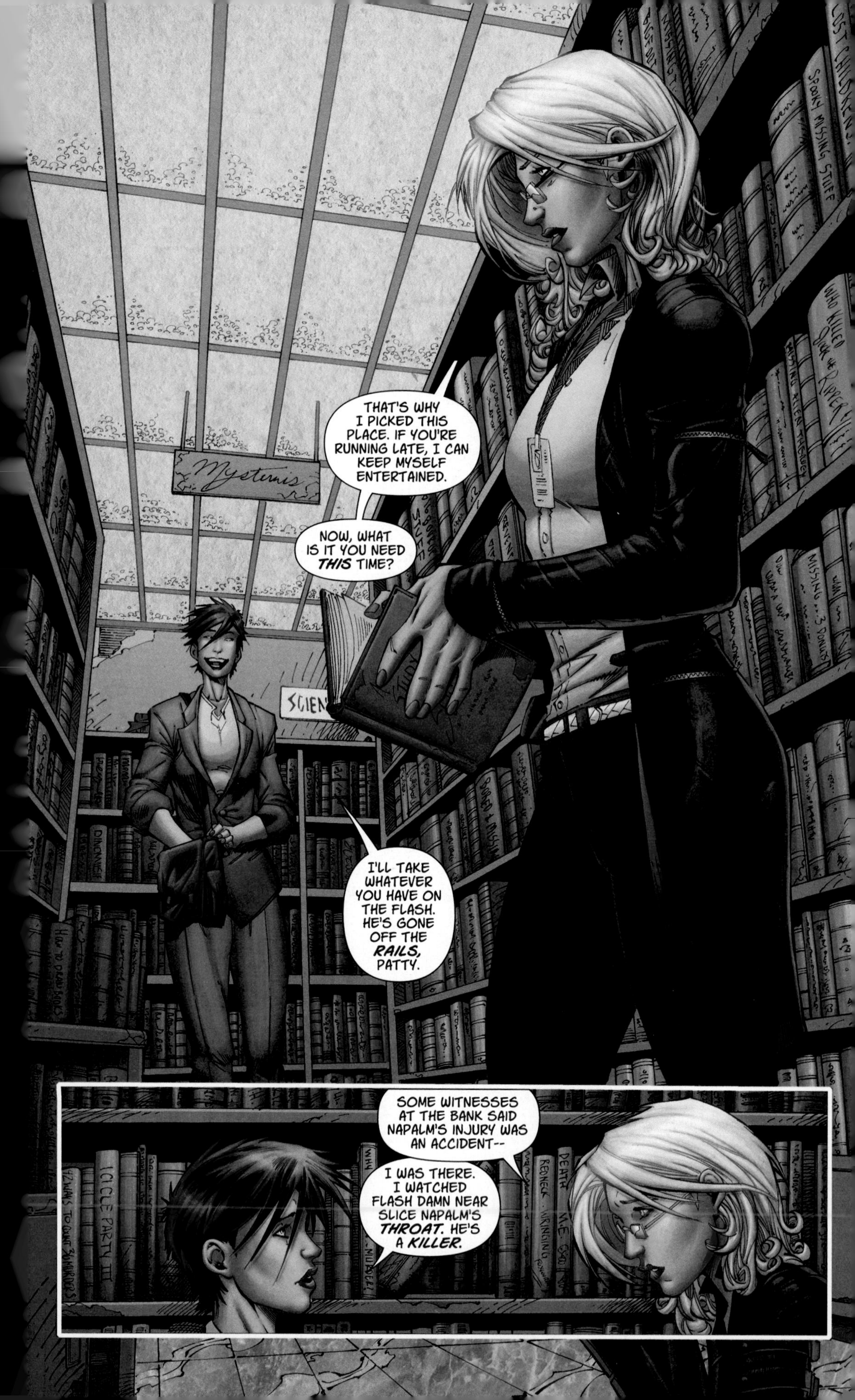
THAT'S WHY I PICKED THIS PLACE. IF YOU'RE RUNNING LATE, I CAN KEEP MYSELF ENTERTAINED.
NOW, WHAT IS IT YOU NEED *THIS* TIME?
I'LL TAKE WHATEVER YOU HAVE ON THE FLASH. HE'S GONE OFF THE *RAILS,* PATTY.
SOME WITNESSES AT THE BANK SAID NAPALM'S INJURY WAS AN ACCIDENT--
I WAS THERE. I WATCHED FLASH DAMN NEAR SLICE NAPALM'S *THROAT.* HE'S A *KILLER.*

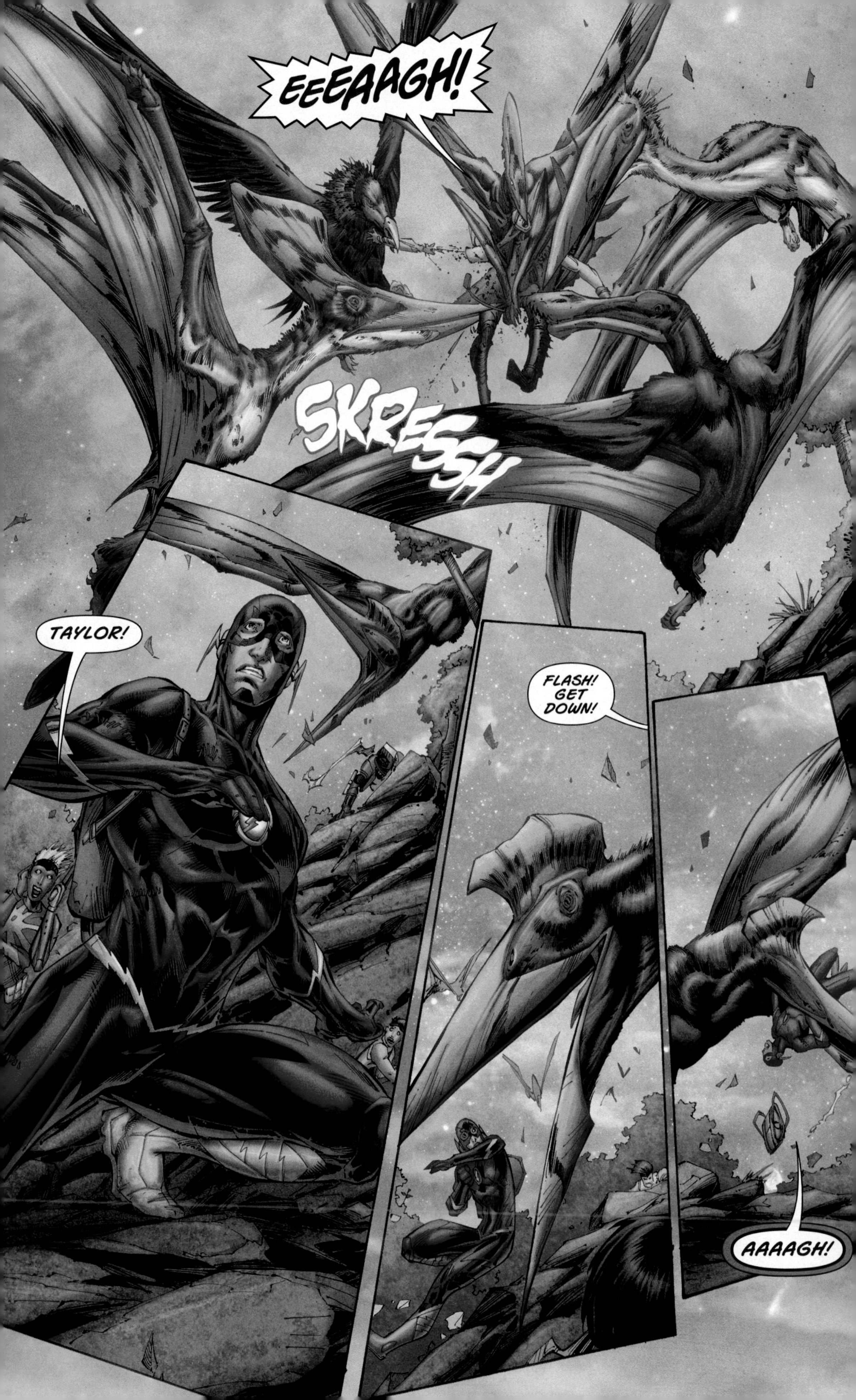
EEEAAGH!
SKRESSH
TAYLOR!
FLASH! GET DOWN!
AAAAGH!

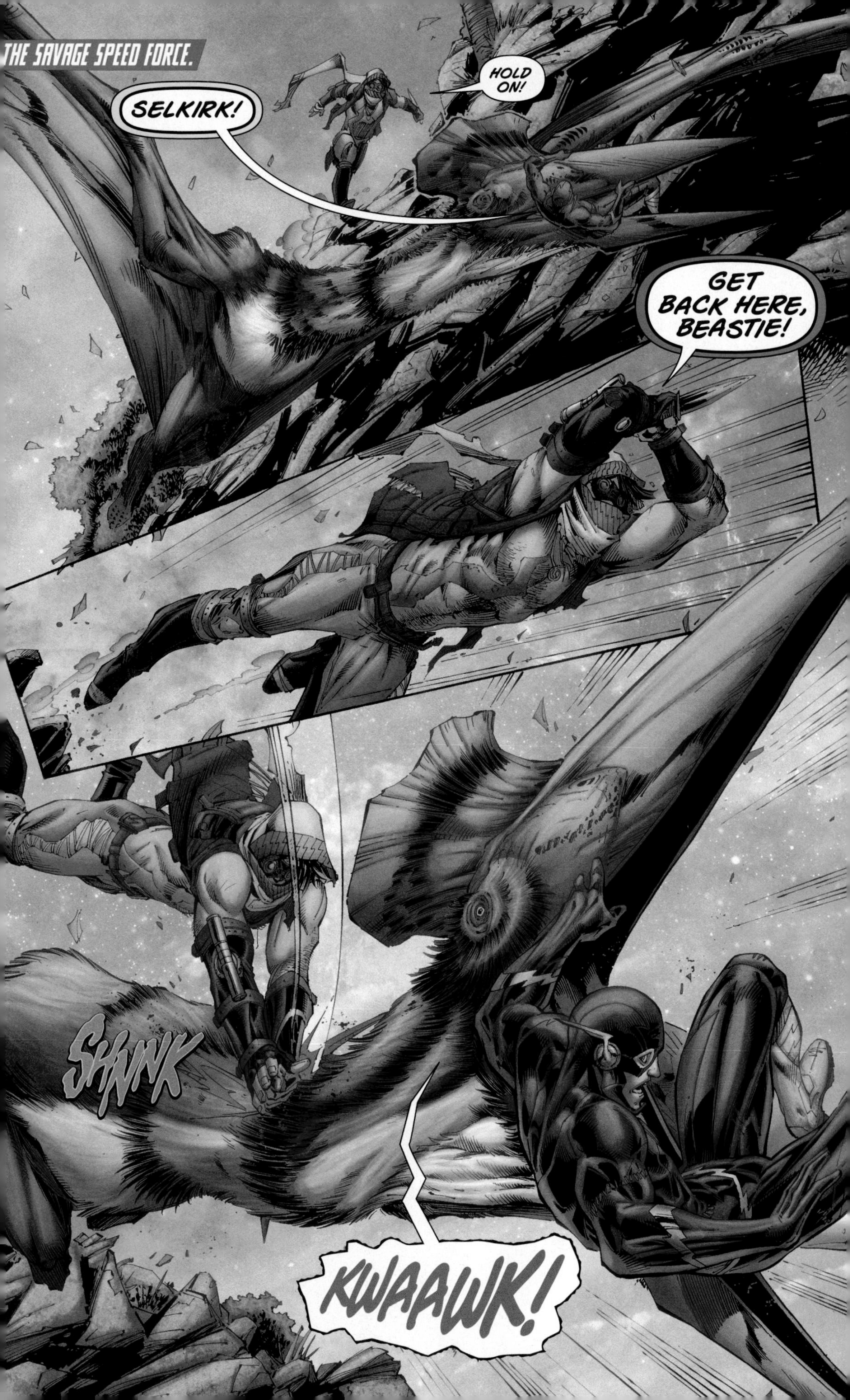
THE SAVAGE SPEED FORCE.
SELKIRK!
HOLD ON!
GET BACK HERE, BEASTIE!
SHNK
KWAAAWK!

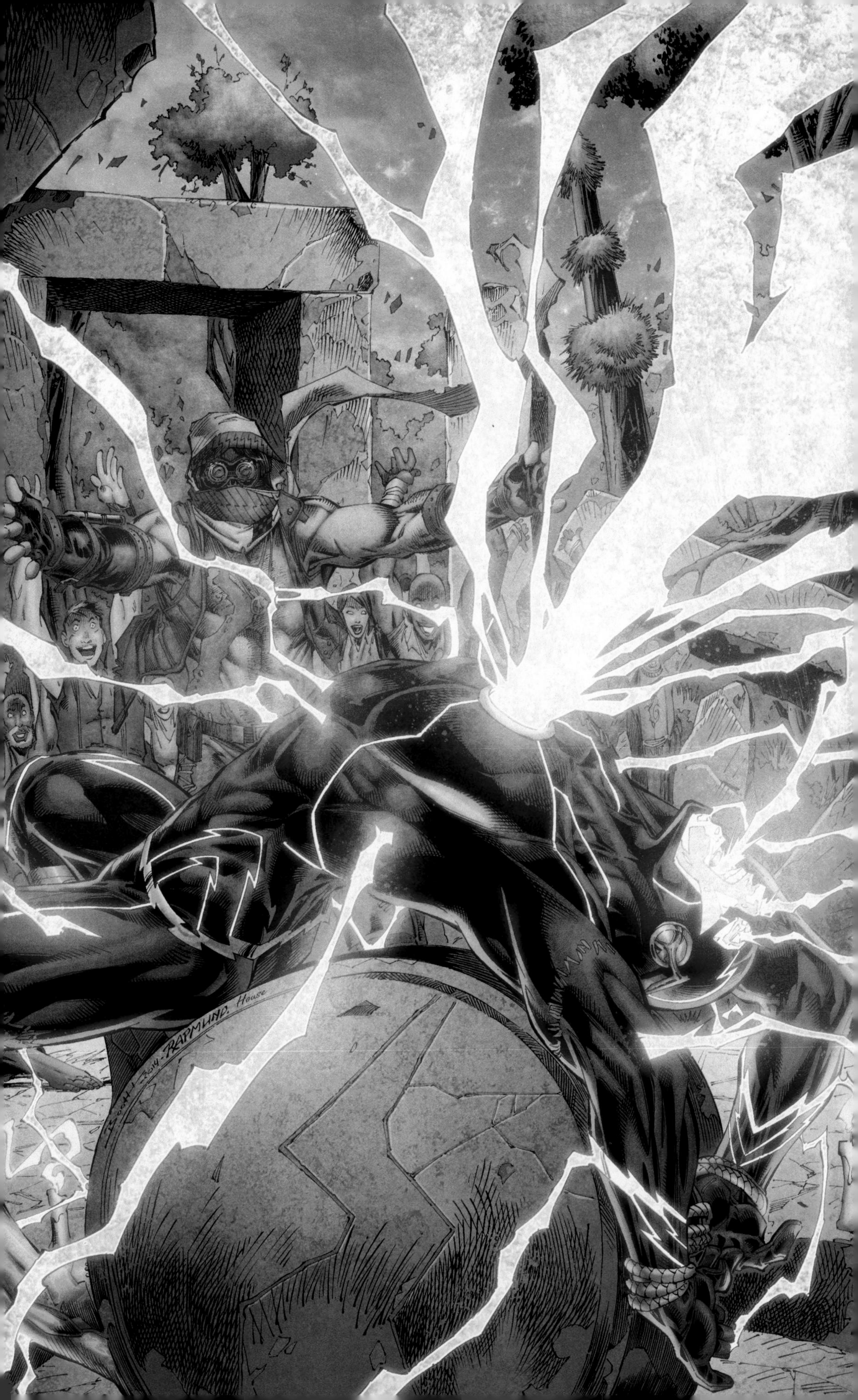

END OF THE ROAD

ROBERT VENDITTI & VAN JENSEN writers BRETT BOOTH penciller NORM RAPMUND inker ANDREW DALHOUSE colorist PAT BROSSEAU letterer
cover by BRETT BOOTH, NORM RAPMUND & ANDREW DALHOUSE

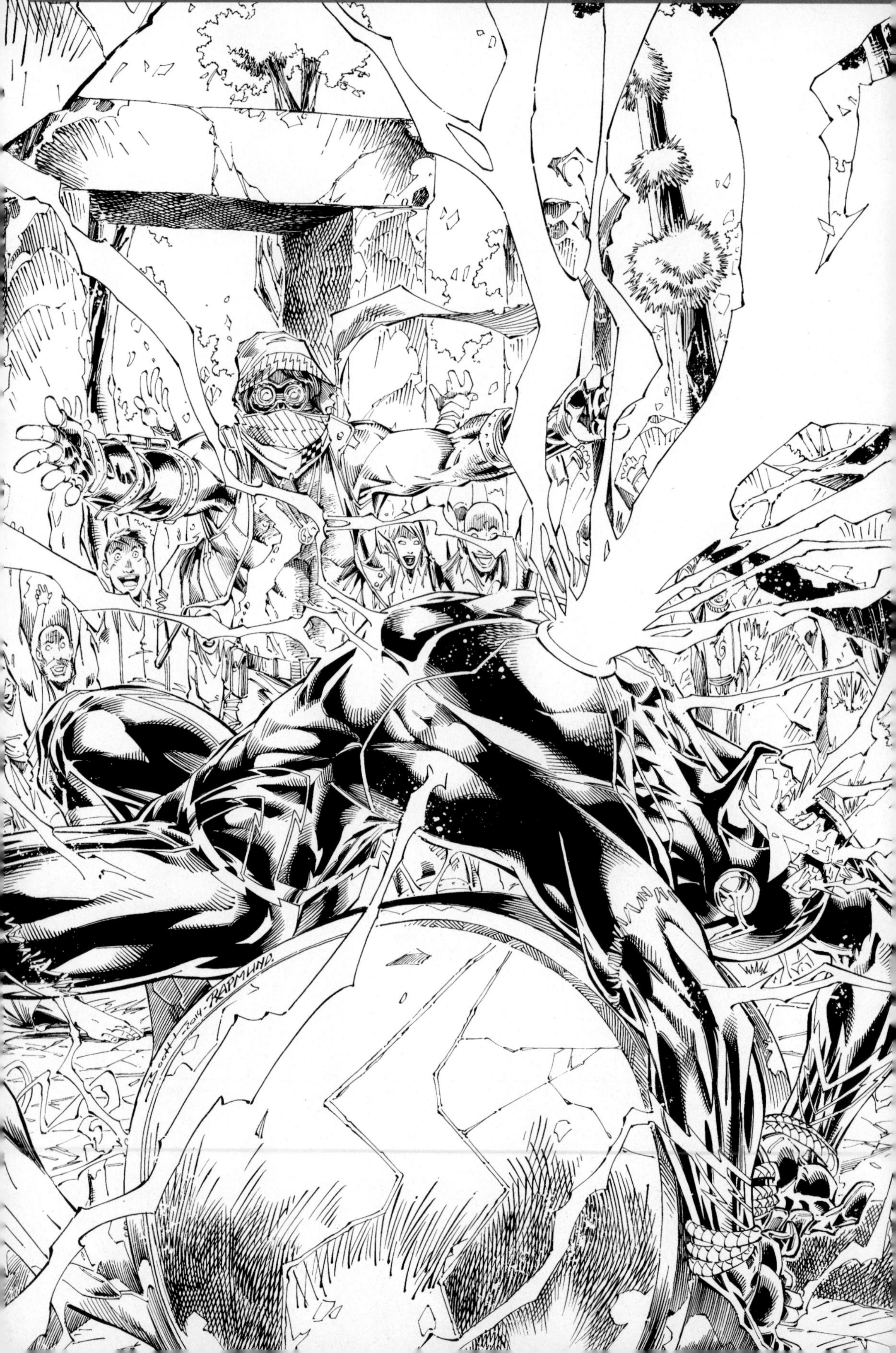

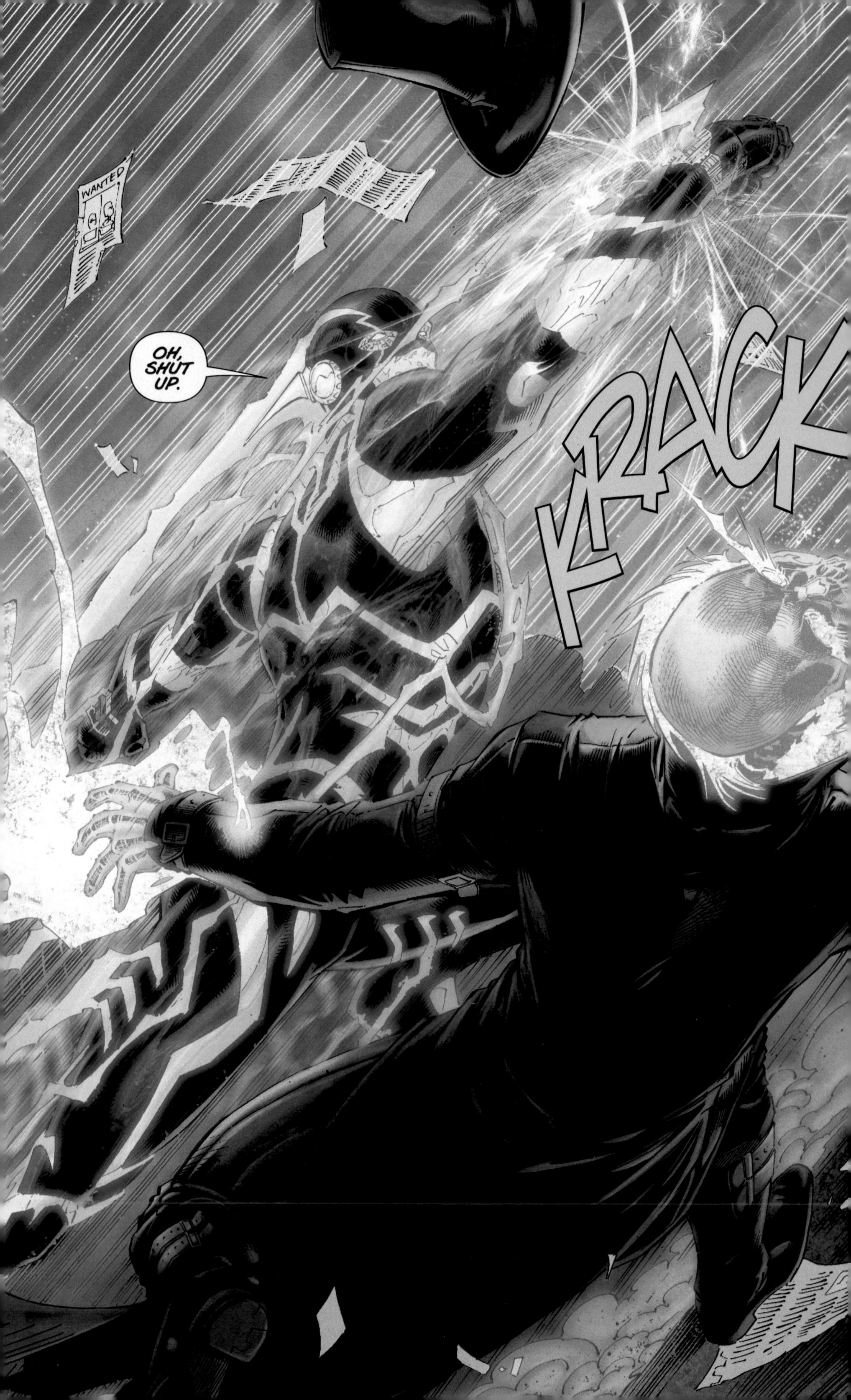
WANTED
OH, SHUT UP.
KRACK

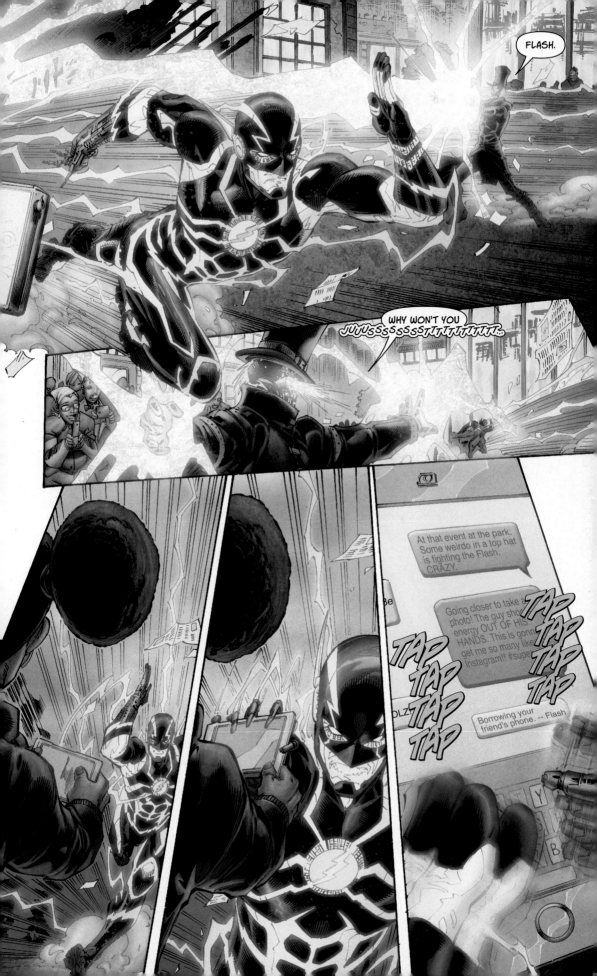

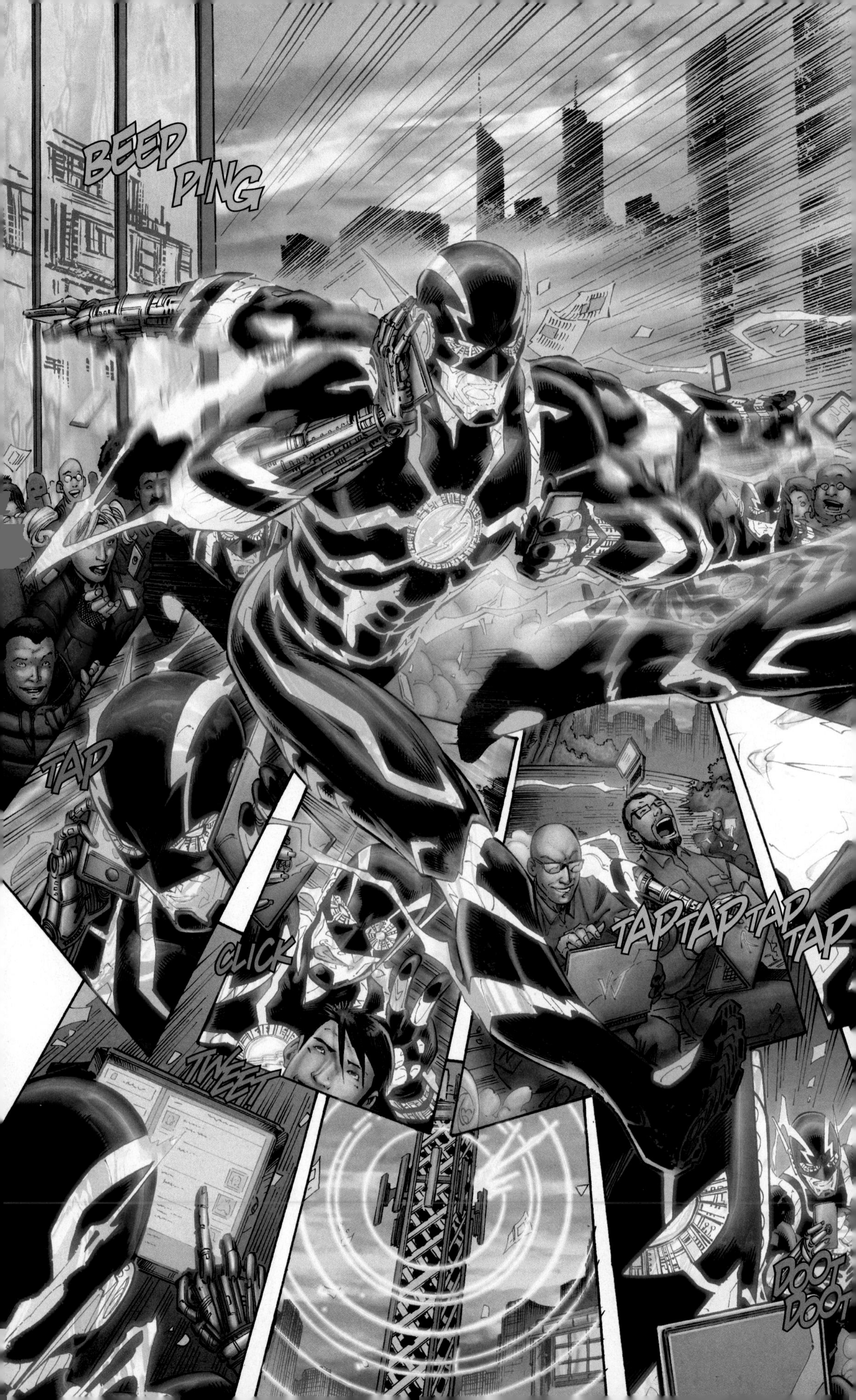
BEEP
PING
TAP
CLICK
TAPTAPTAPTAP
TWEET
DOOT
DOOT

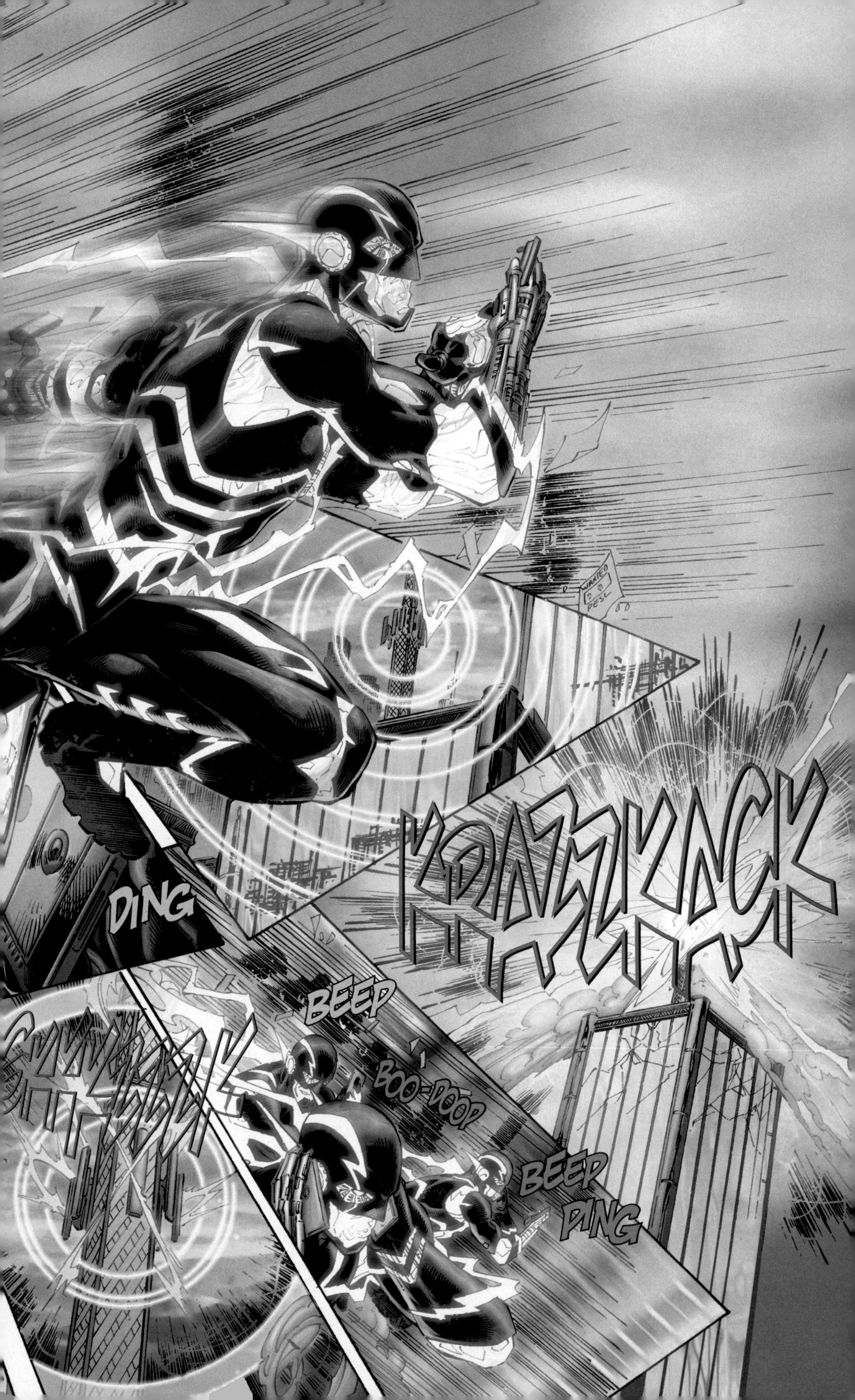
DING
KRAZZKACK
BEEP
BOO-DOOP
BEEP
DING

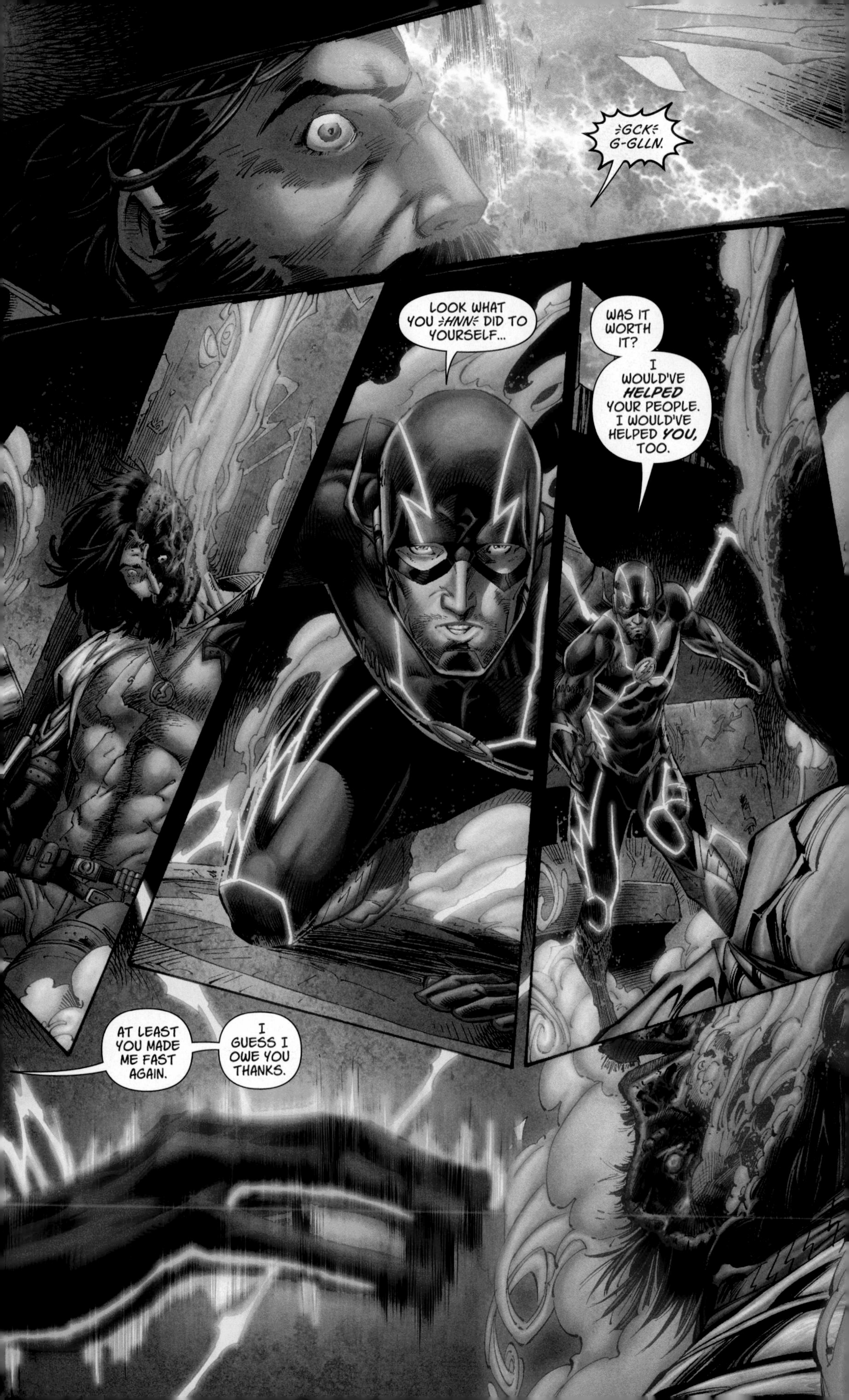
GCK G-GLLN.
LOOK WHAT YOU HNN DID TO YOURSELF...
WAS IT WORTH IT?
I WOULD'VE HELPED YOUR PEOPLE. I WOULD'VE HELPED YOU, TOO.
I GUESS I OWE YOU THANKS.
AT LEAST YOU MADE ME FAST AGAIN.

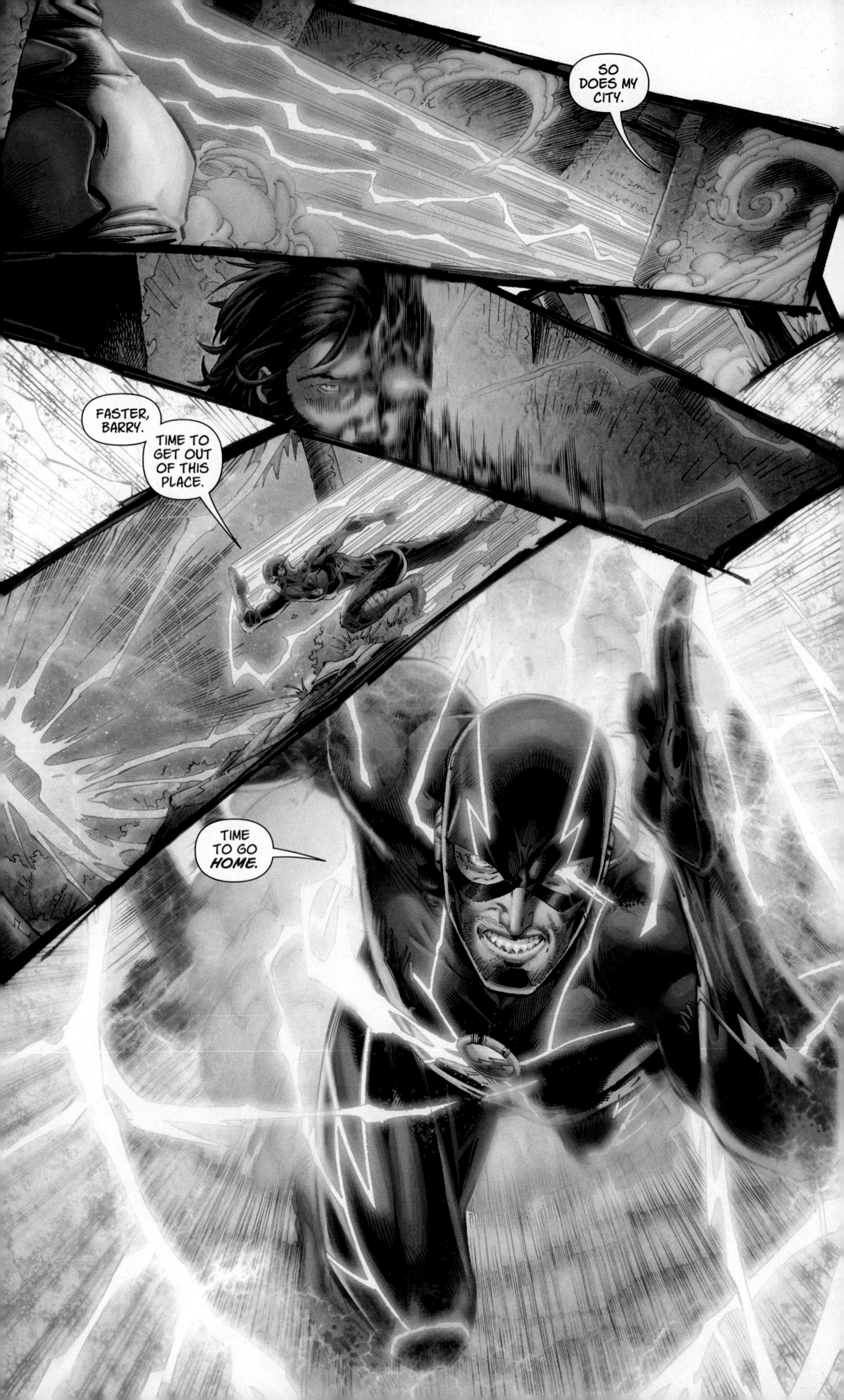
SO DOES MY CITY.
FASTER, BARRY.
TIME TO GET OUT OF THIS PLACE.
TIME TO GO *HOME*.

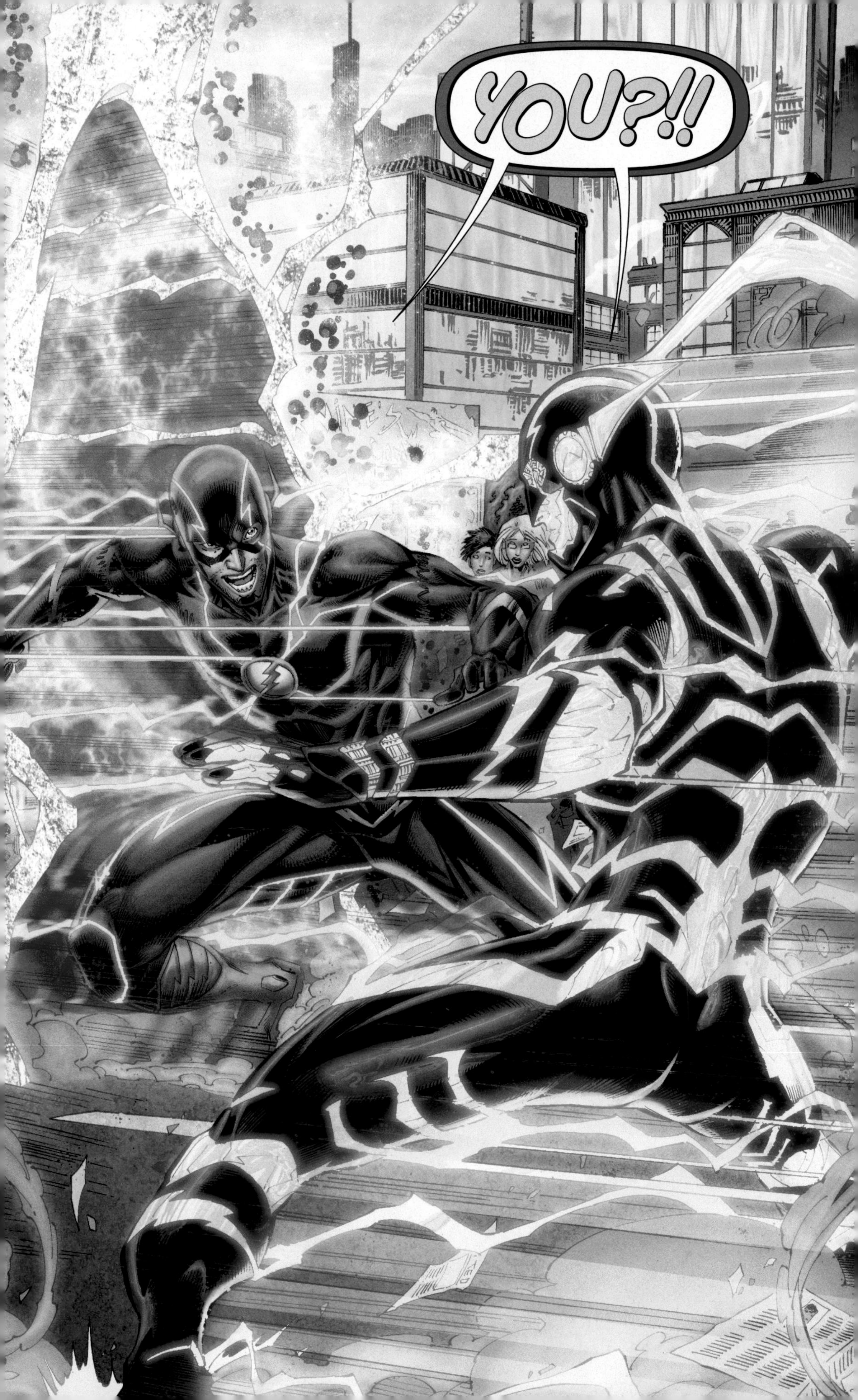
YOU?!!

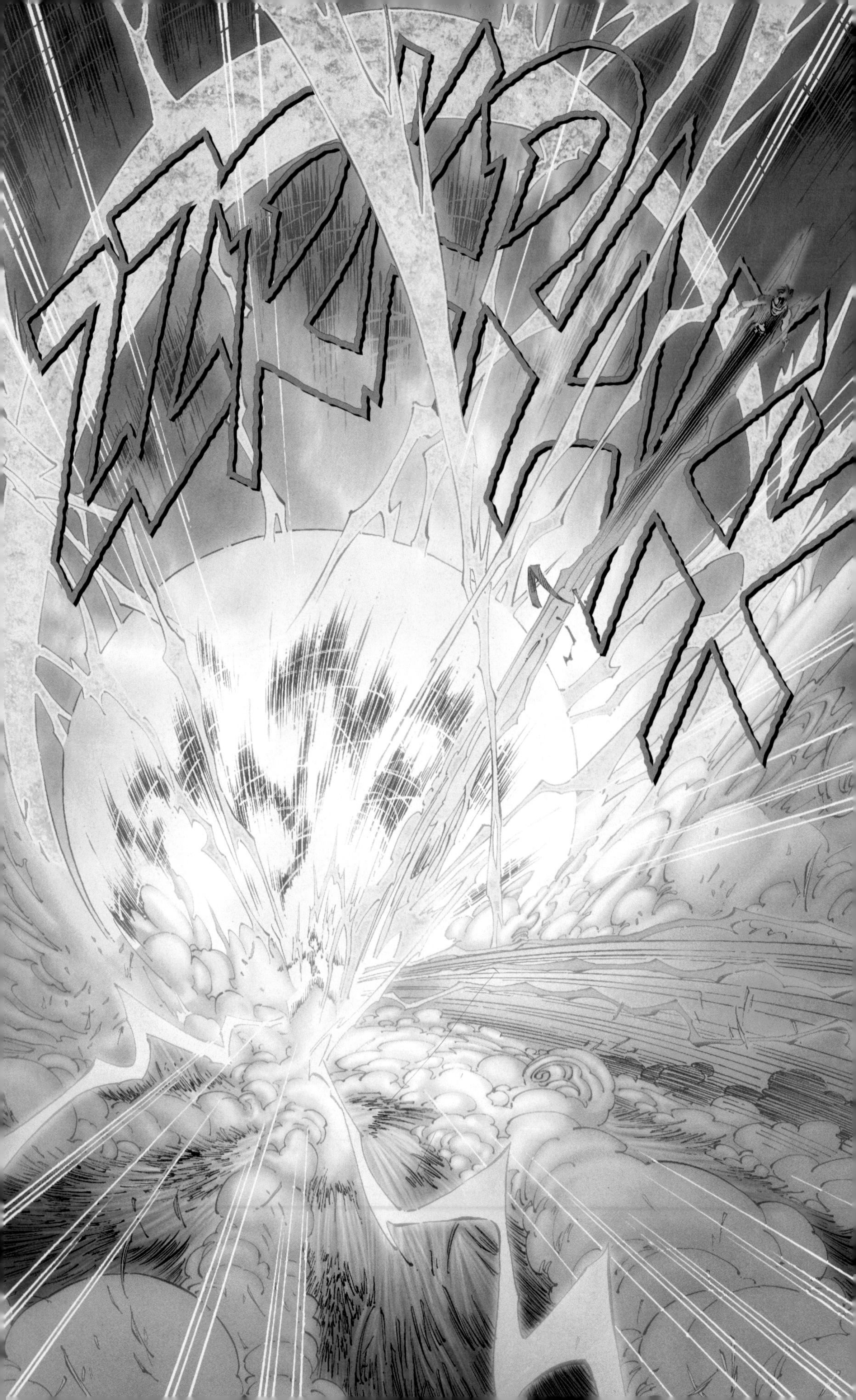

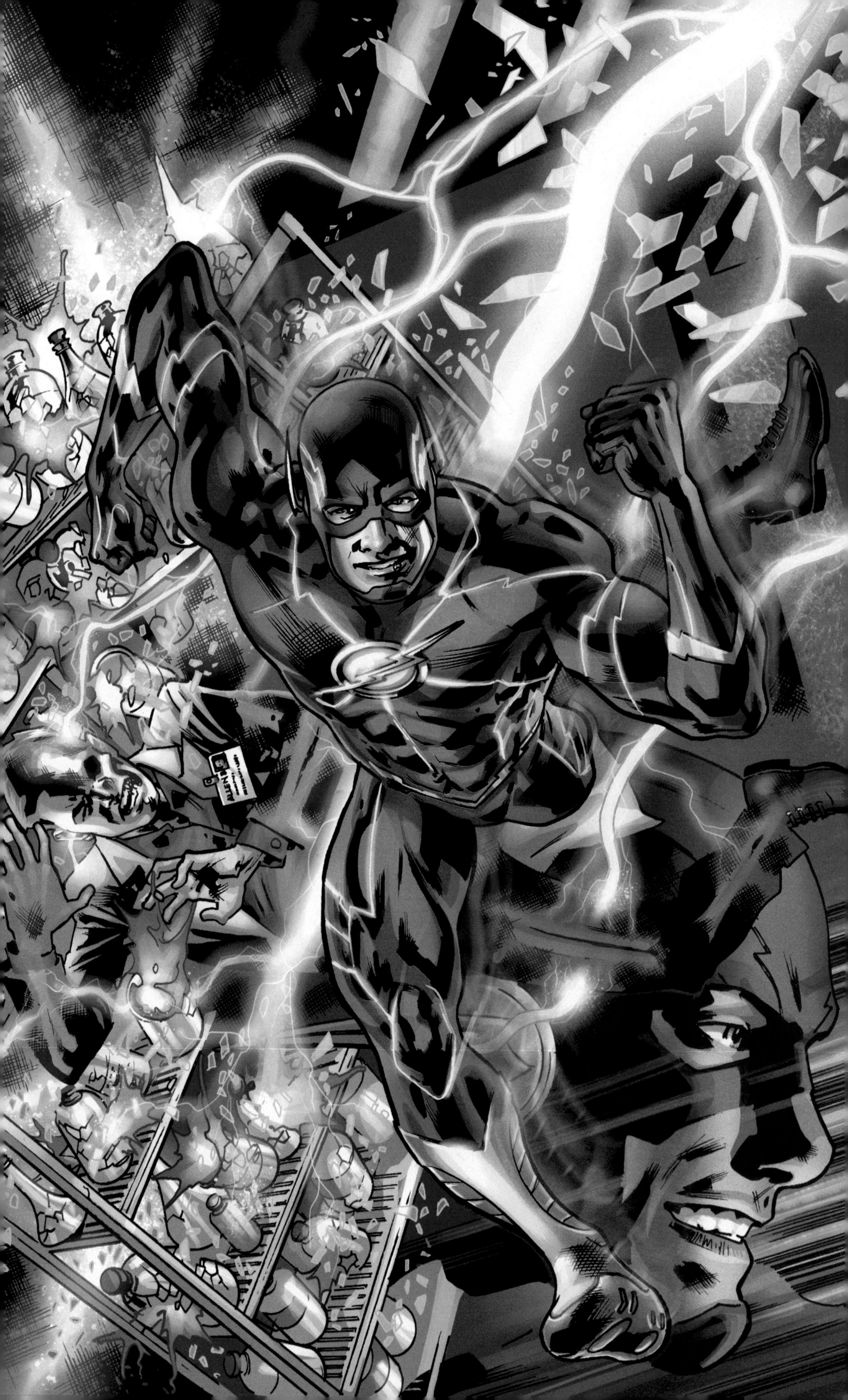

THE CHASE

ROBERT VENDITTI & VAN JENSEN writers **MIGUEL SEPULVEDA** penciller **SCOTT HANNA** inker **ANDREW DALHOUSE** colorist **TAYLOR ESPOSITO** letterer
cover by **BRYAN HITCH & ALEX SINCLAIR**

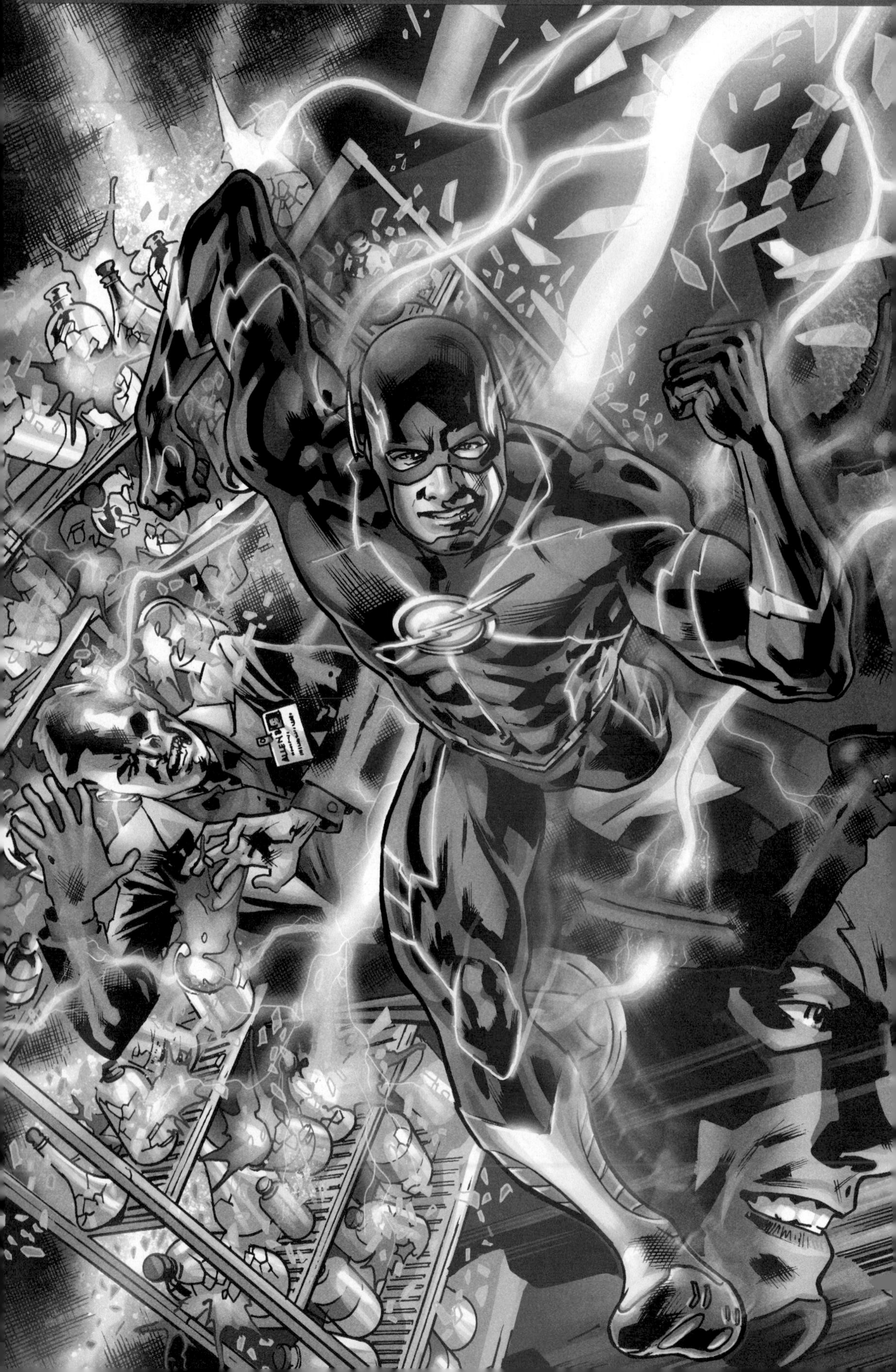
ALLEN

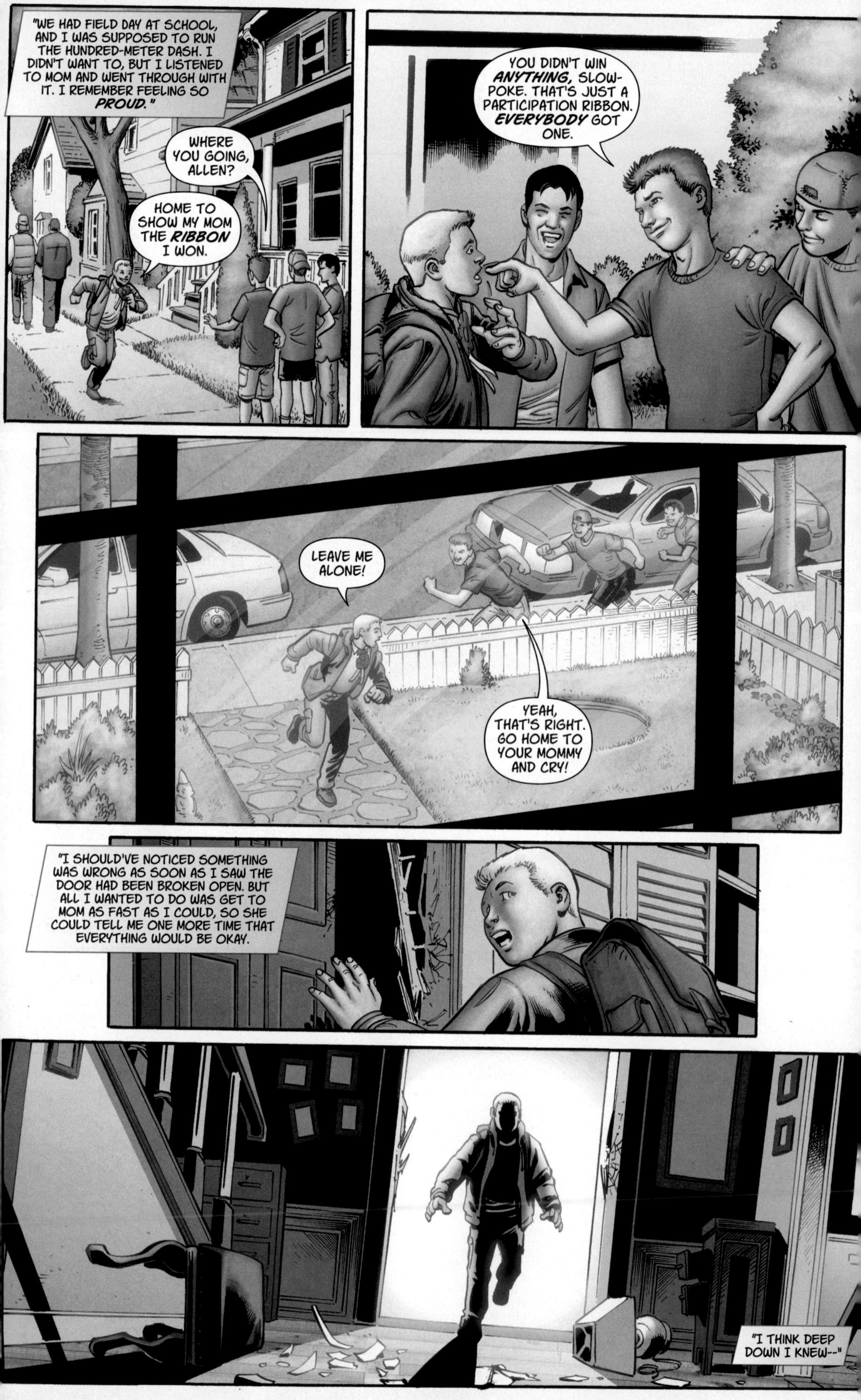
"WE HAD FIELD DAY AT SCHOOL, AND I WAS SUPPOSED TO RUN THE HUNDRED-METER DASH. I DIDN'T WANT TO, BUT I LISTENED TO MOM AND WENT THROUGH WITH IT. I REMEMBER FEELING SO PROUD."
WHERE YOU GOING, ALLEN?
HOME TO SHOW MY MOM THE RIBBON I WON.
YOU DIDN'T WIN ANYTHING, SLOW-POKE. THAT'S JUST A PARTICIPATION RIBBON. EVERYBODY GOT ONE.
LEAVE ME ALONE!
YEAH, THAT'S RIGHT. GO HOME TO YOUR MOMMY AND CRY!
"I SHOULD'VE NOTICED SOMETHING WAS WRONG AS SOON AS I SAW THE DOOR HAD BEEN BROKEN OPEN. BUT ALL I WANTED TO DO WAS GET TO MOM AS FAST AS I COULD, SO SHE COULD TELL ME ONE MORE TIME THAT EVERYTHING WOULD BE OKAY.
"I THINK DEEP DOWN I KNEW--"

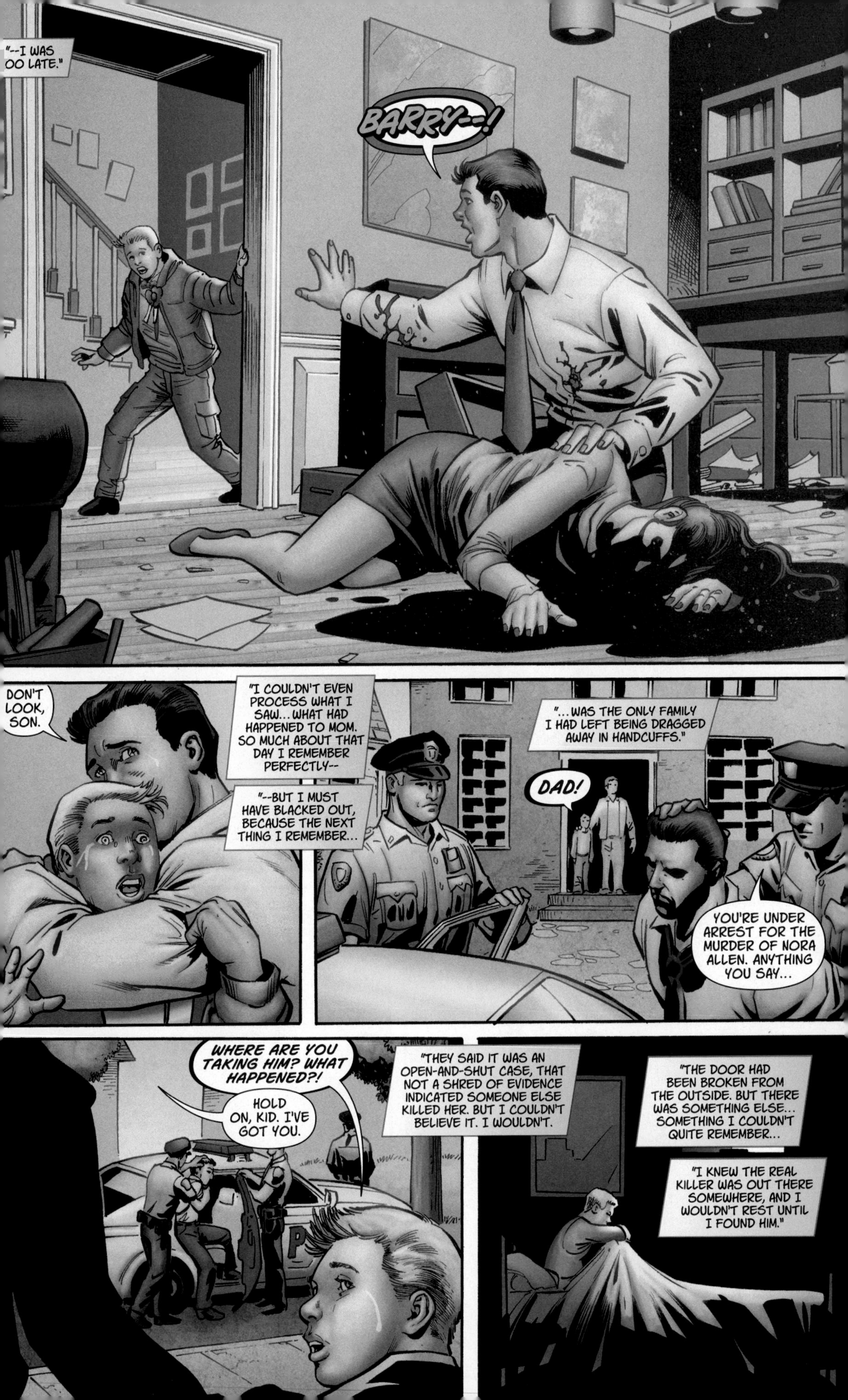
"--I WAS
OO LATE."
BARRY--!
DON'T LOOK, SON.
"I COULDN'T EVEN PROCESS WHAT I SAW... WHAT HAD HAPPENED TO MOM. SO MUCH ABOUT THAT DAY I REMEMBER PERFECTLY--
"--BUT I MUST HAVE BLACKED OUT, BECAUSE THE NEXT THING I REMEMBER...
"...WAS THE ONLY FAMILY I HAD LEFT BEING DRAGGED AWAY IN HANDCUFFS."
DAD!
YOU'RE UNDER ARREST FOR THE MURDER OF NORA ALLEN. ANYTHING YOU SAY...
WHERE ARE YOU TAKING HIM? WHAT HAPPENED?!
HOLD ON, KID. I'VE GOT YOU.
"THEY SAID IT WAS AN OPEN-AND-SHUT CASE, THAT NOT A SHRED OF EVIDENCE INDICATED SOMEONE ELSE KILLED HER. BUT I COULDN'T BELIEVE IT. I WOULDN'T.
"THE DOOR HAD BEEN BROKEN FROM THE OUTSIDE. BUT THERE WAS SOMETHING ELSE... SOMETHING I COULDN'T QUITE REMEMBER...
"I KNEW THE REAL KILLER WAS OUT THERE SOMEWHERE, AND I WOULDN'T REST UNTIL I FOUND HIM."

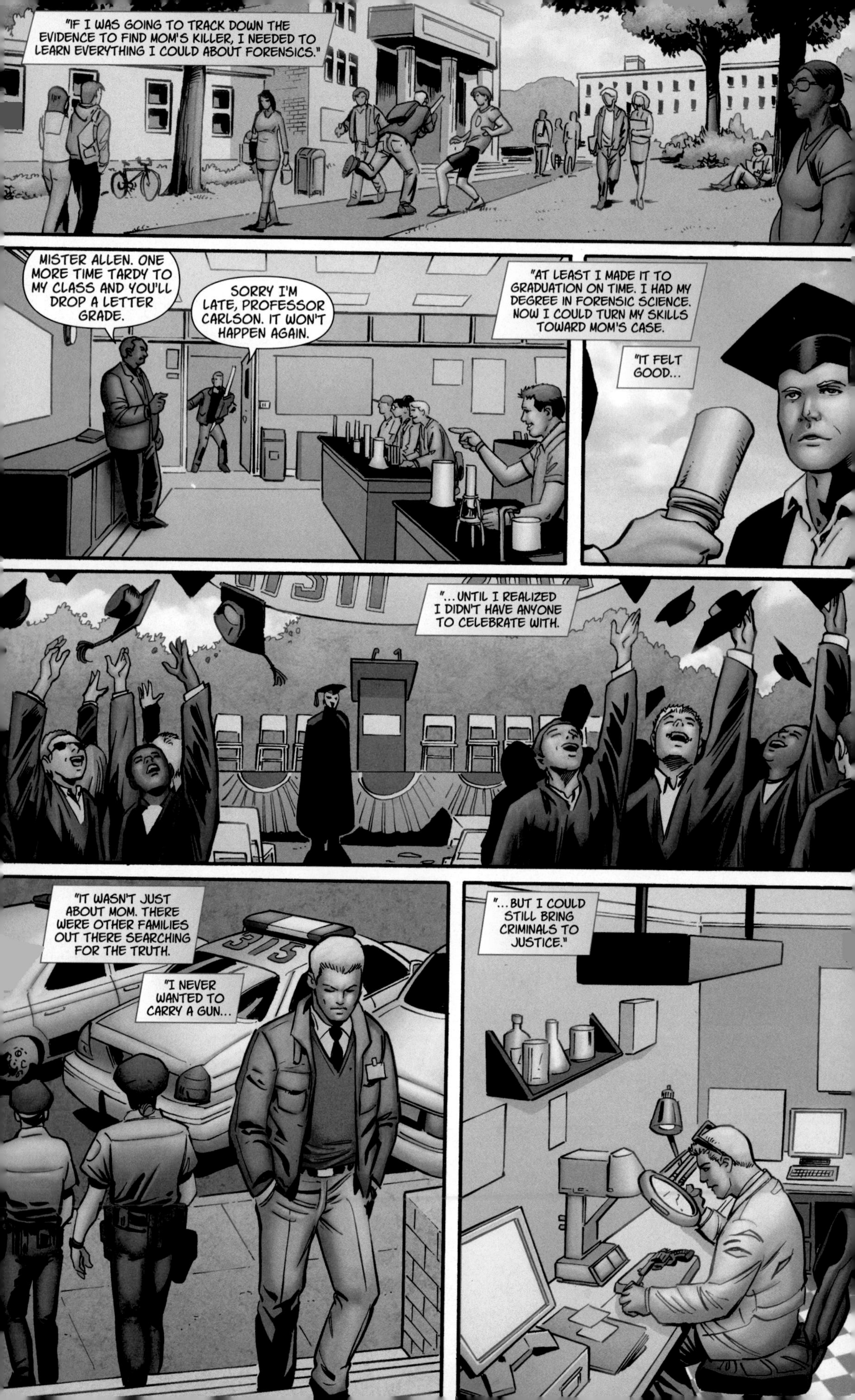
"IF I WAS GOING TO TRACK DOWN THE EVIDENCE TO FIND MOM'S KILLER, I NEEDED TO LEARN EVERYTHING I COULD ABOUT FORENSICS."
MISTER ALLEN. ONE MORE TIME TARDY TO MY CLASS AND YOU'LL DROP A LETTER GRADE.
SORRY I'M LATE, PROFESSOR CARLSON. IT WON'T HAPPEN AGAIN.
"AT LEAST I MADE IT TO GRADUATION ON TIME. I HAD MY DEGREE IN FORENSIC SCIENCE. NOW I COULD TURN MY SKILLS TOWARD MOM'S CASE.
"IT FELT GOOD...
"...UNTIL I REALIZED I DIDN'T HAVE ANYONE TO CELEBRATE WITH.
"IT WASN'T JUST ABOUT MOM. THERE WERE OTHER FAMILIES OUT THERE SEARCHING FOR THE TRUTH.
"I NEVER WANTED TO CARRY A GUN...
"...BUT I COULD STILL BRING CRIMINALS TO JUSTICE."

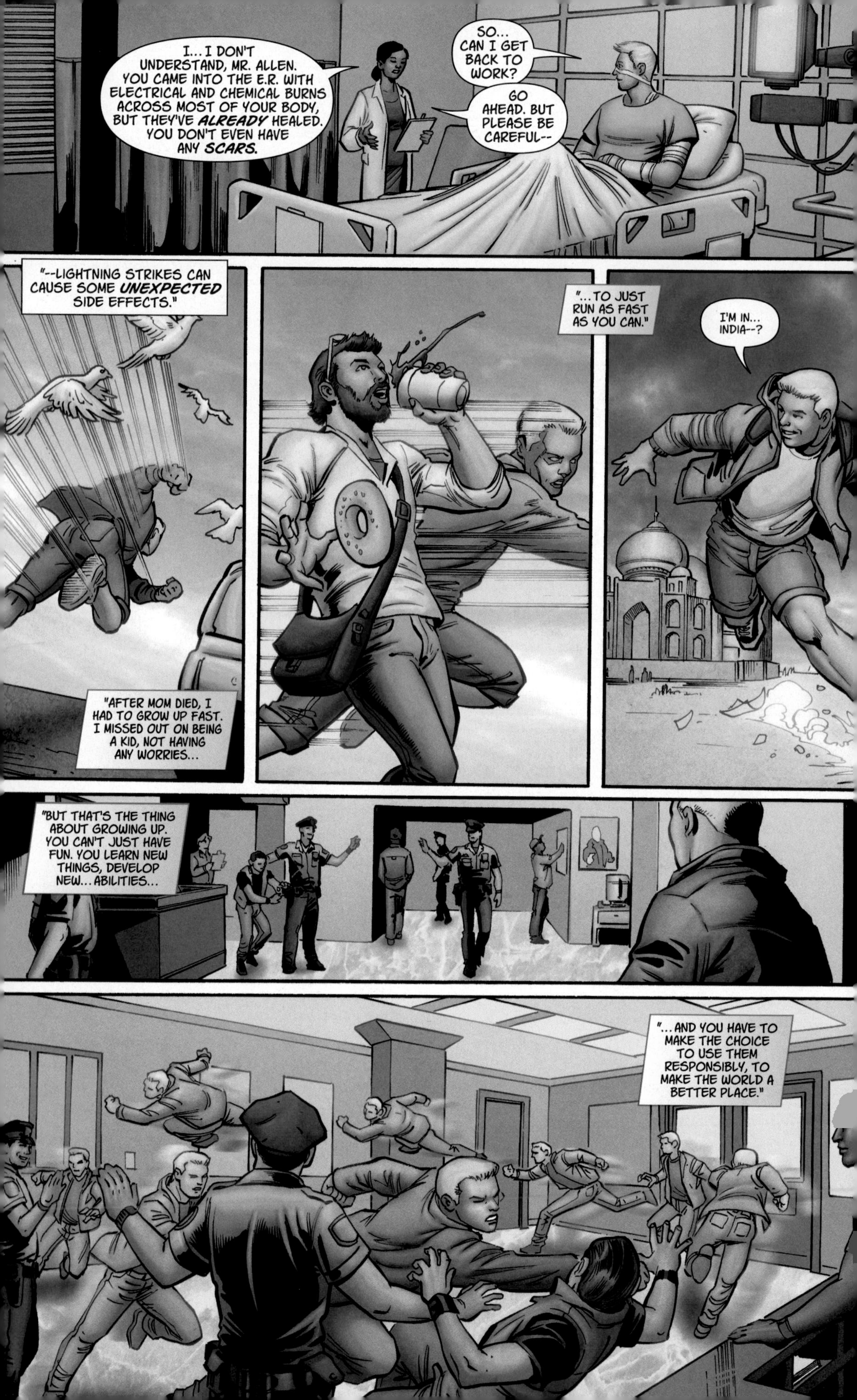
I... I DON'T UNDERSTAND, MR. ALLEN. YOU CAME INTO THE E.R. WITH ELECTRICAL AND CHEMICAL BURNS ACROSS MOST OF YOUR BODY, BUT THEY'VE ALREADY HEALED. YOU DON'T EVEN HAVE ANY SCARS.
SO... CAN I GET BACK TO WORK?
GO AHEAD. BUT PLEASE BE CAREFUL--
"--LIGHTNING STRIKES CAN CAUSE SOME UNEXPECTED SIDE EFFECTS."
"AFTER MOM DIED, I HAD TO GROW UP FAST. I MISSED OUT ON BEING A KID, NOT HAVING ANY WORRIES...
"...TO JUST RUN AS FAST AS YOU CAN."
I'M IN... INDIA--?
"BUT THAT'S THE THING ABOUT GROWING UP. YOU CAN'T JUST HAVE FUN. YOU LEARN NEW THINGS, DEVELOP NEW... ABILITIES...
"...AND YOU HAVE TO MAKE THE CHOICE TO USE THEM RESPONSIBLY, TO MAKE THE WORLD A BETTER PLACE."

TALKING ABOUT IT OUT LOUD MAKES ME REALIZE...I DIDN'T DECIDE TO FIGHT CRIME JUST BECAUSE OF MOM.

IT WAS BECAUSE OF WHAT A LIFE OF SERVICE MEANS TO THE *GREATER GOOD.*

"LOOK AT A POLICE OFFICER, AND WHAT ARE THE FIRST THINGS YOU NOTICE?

"THE BADGE.

"THE UNIFORM.

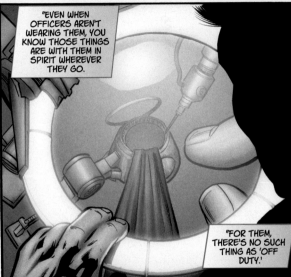

"EVEN WHEN OFFICERS AREN'T WEARING THEM, YOU KNOW THOSE THINGS ARE WITH THEM IN SPIRIT WHEREVER THEY GO.

"FOR THEM, THERE'S NO SUCH THING AS 'OFF DUTY.'

"AND WHEN THEY'RE *ON* DUTY--"

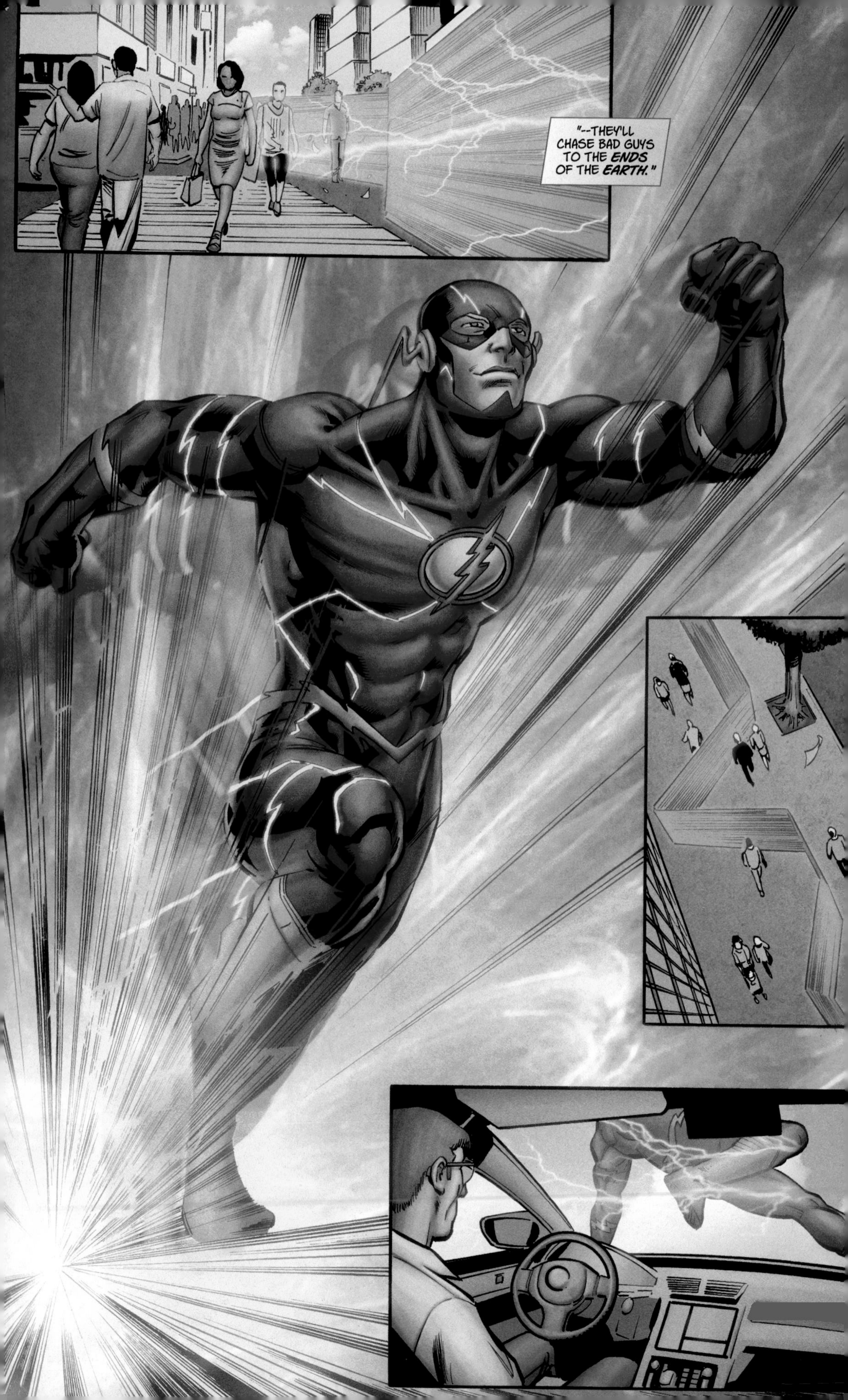
"--THEY'LL CHASE BAD GUYS TO THE ENDS OF THE EARTH."

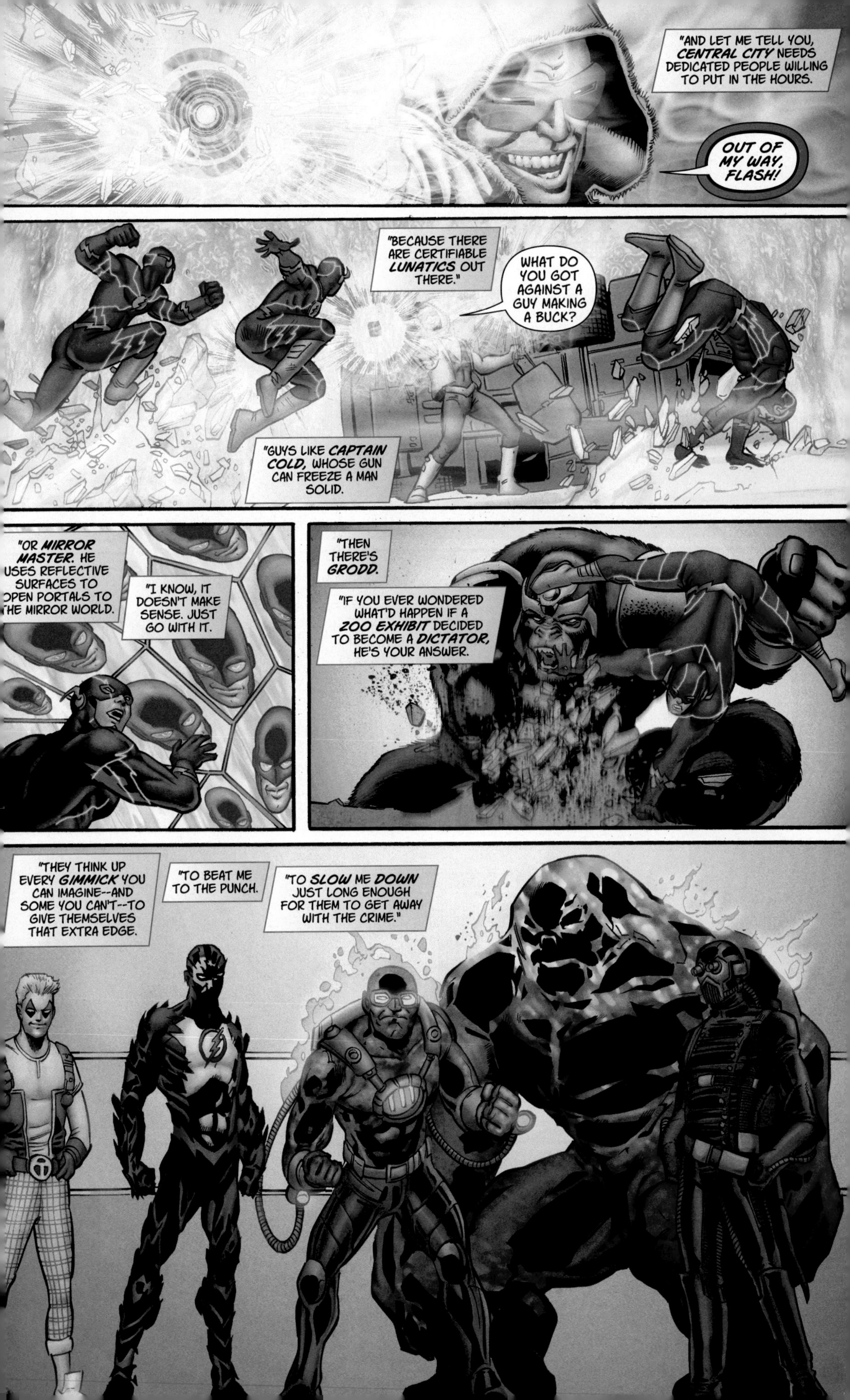
"AND LET ME TELL YOU, CENTRAL CITY NEEDS DEDICATED PEOPLE WILLING TO PUT IN THE HOURS.
OUT OF MY WAY, FLASH!
"BECAUSE THERE ARE CERTIFIABLE LUNATICS OUT THERE."
WHAT DO YOU GOT AGAINST A GUY MAKING A BUCK?
"GUYS LIKE CAPTAIN COLD, WHOSE GUN CAN FREEZE A MAN SOLID.
"OR MIRROR MASTER. HE USES REFLECTIVE SURFACES TO OPEN PORTALS TO THE MIRROR WORLD.
"I KNOW, IT DOESN'T MAKE SENSE. JUST GO WITH IT.
"THEN THERE'S GRODD.
"IF YOU EVER WONDERED WHAT'D HAPPEN IF A ZOO EXHIBIT DECIDED TO BECOME A DICTATOR, HE'S YOUR ANSWER.
"THEY THINK UP EVERY GIMMICK YOU CAN IMAGINE--AND SOME YOU CAN'T--TO GIVE THEMSELVES THAT EXTRA EDGE.
"TO BEAT ME TO THE PUNCH.
"TO SLOW ME DOWN JUST LONG ENOUGH FOR THEM TO GET AWAY WITH THE CRIME."

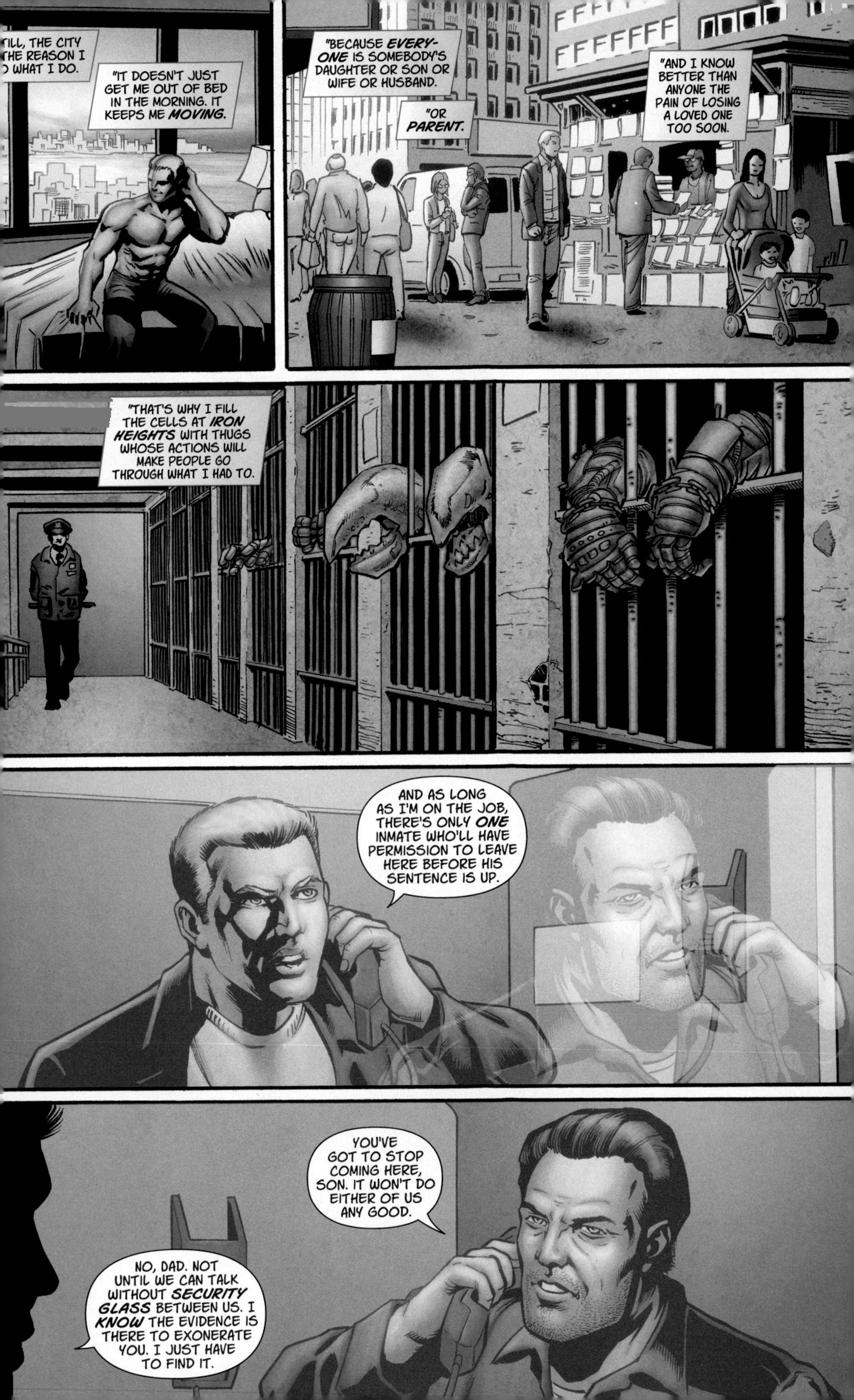

TILL, THE CITY THE REASON I WHAT I DO.
"IT DOESN'T JUST GET ME OUT OF BED IN THE MORNING. IT KEEPS ME *MOVING*.
"BECAUSE *EVERY-ONE* IS SOMEBODY'S DAUGHTER OR SON OR WIFE OR HUSBAND.
"OR *PARENT*.
"AND I KNOW BETTER THAN ANYONE THE PAIN OF LOSING A LOVED ONE TOO SOON.
"THAT'S WHY I FILL THE CELLS AT *IRON HEIGHTS* WITH THUGS WHOSE ACTIONS WILL MAKE PEOPLE GO THROUGH WHAT I HAD TO.
AND AS LONG AS I'M ON THE JOB, THERE'S ONLY *ONE* INMATE WHO'LL HAVE PERMISSION TO LEAVE HERE BEFORE HIS SENTENCE IS UP.
YOU'VE GOT TO STOP COMING HERE, SON. IT WON'T DO EITHER OF US ANY GOOD.
NO, DAD. NOT UNTIL WE CAN TALK WITHOUT *SECURITY GLASS* BETWEEN US. I *KNOW* THE EVIDENCE IS THERE TO EXONERATE YOU. I JUST HAVE TO FIND IT.

VARIANT COVER GALLERY

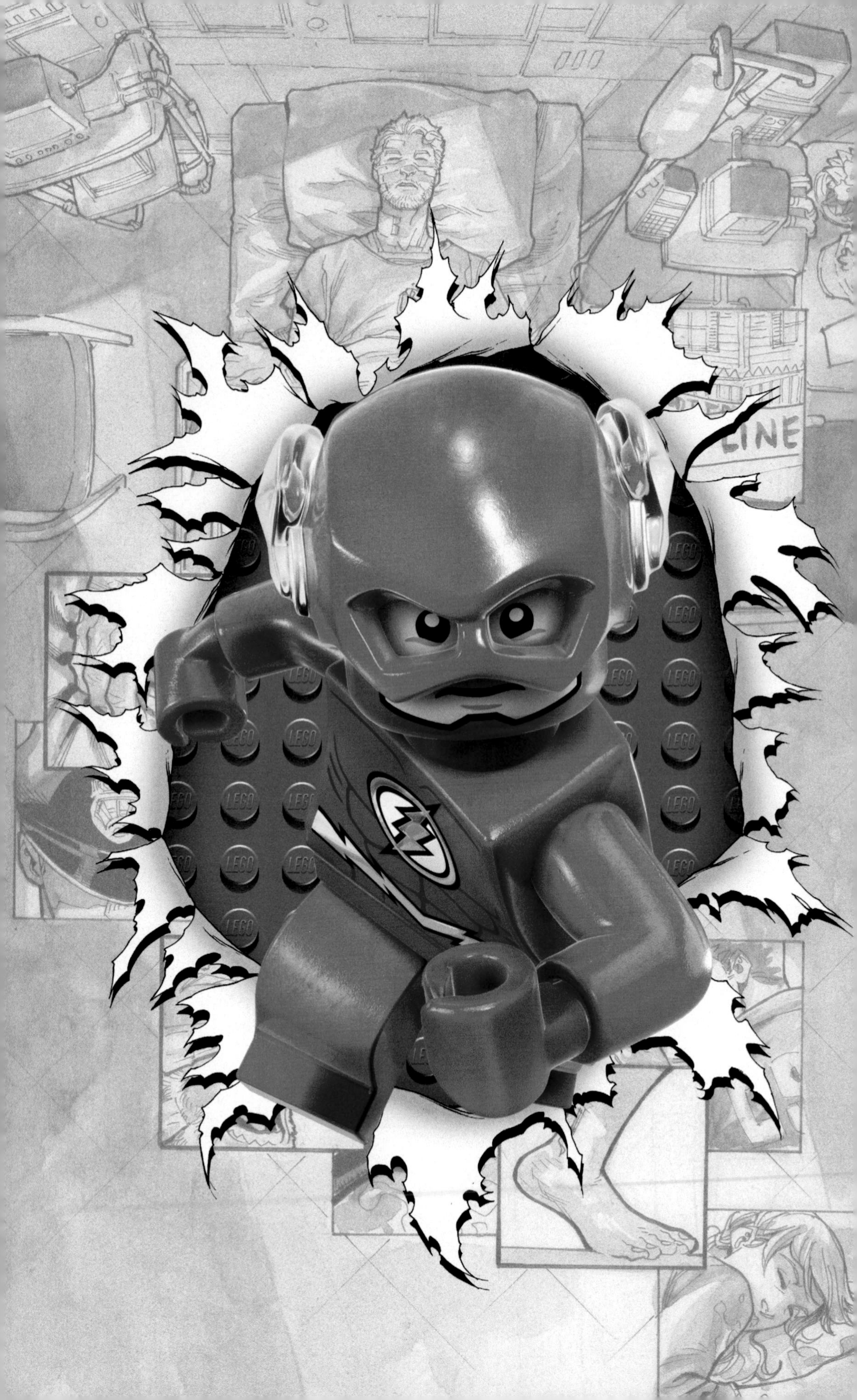

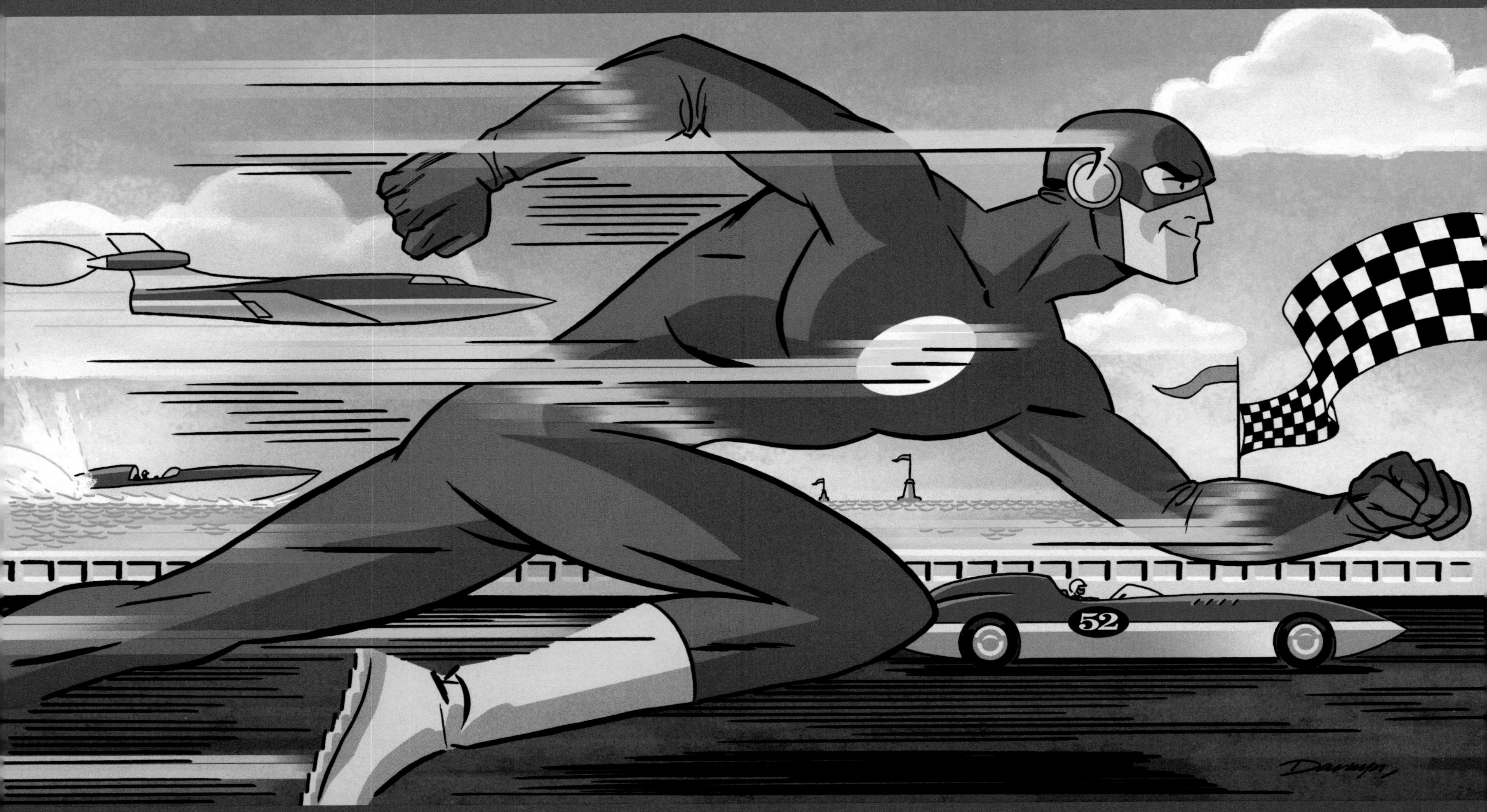
52
Darwyn

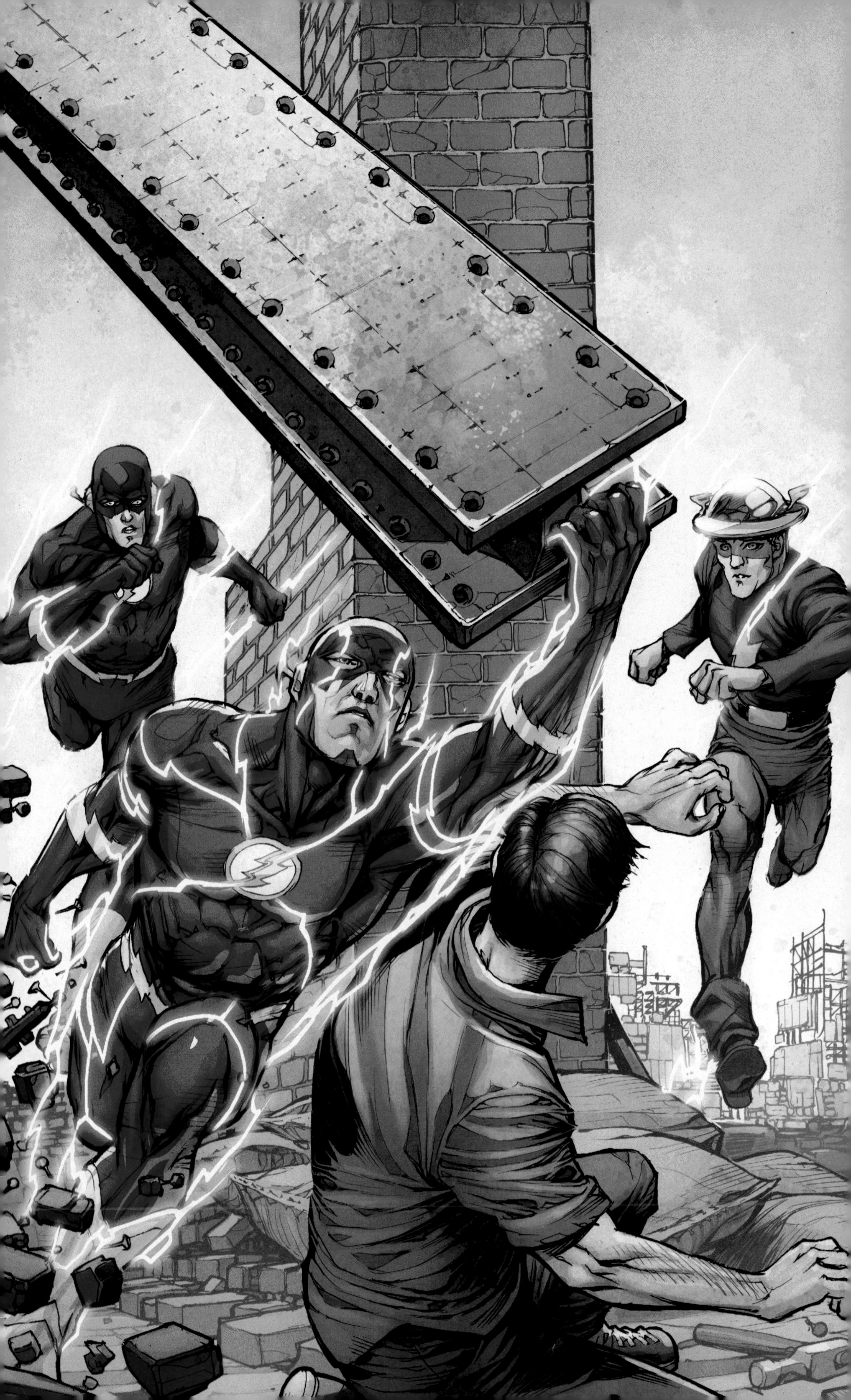

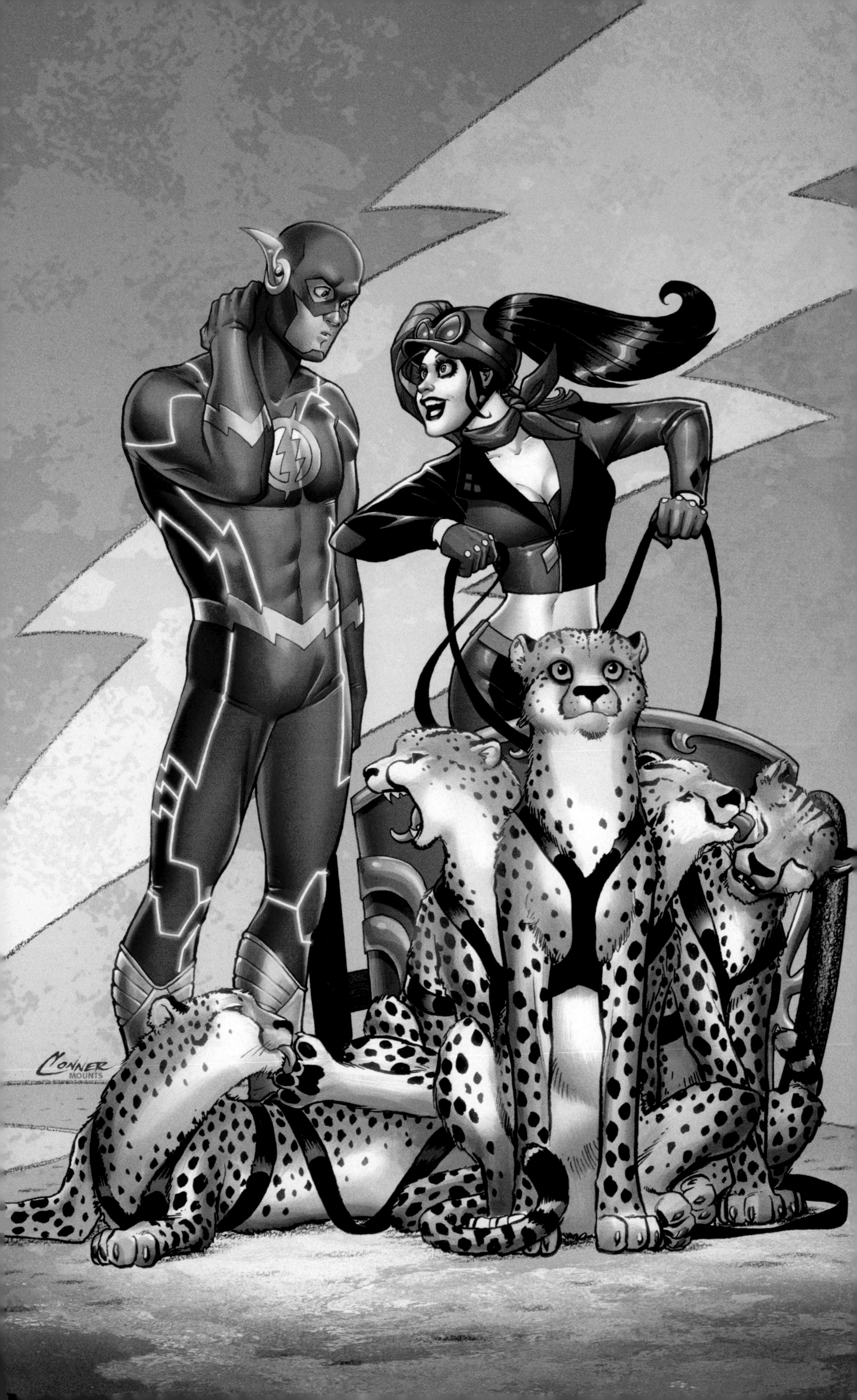
CONNER
MOUNTS

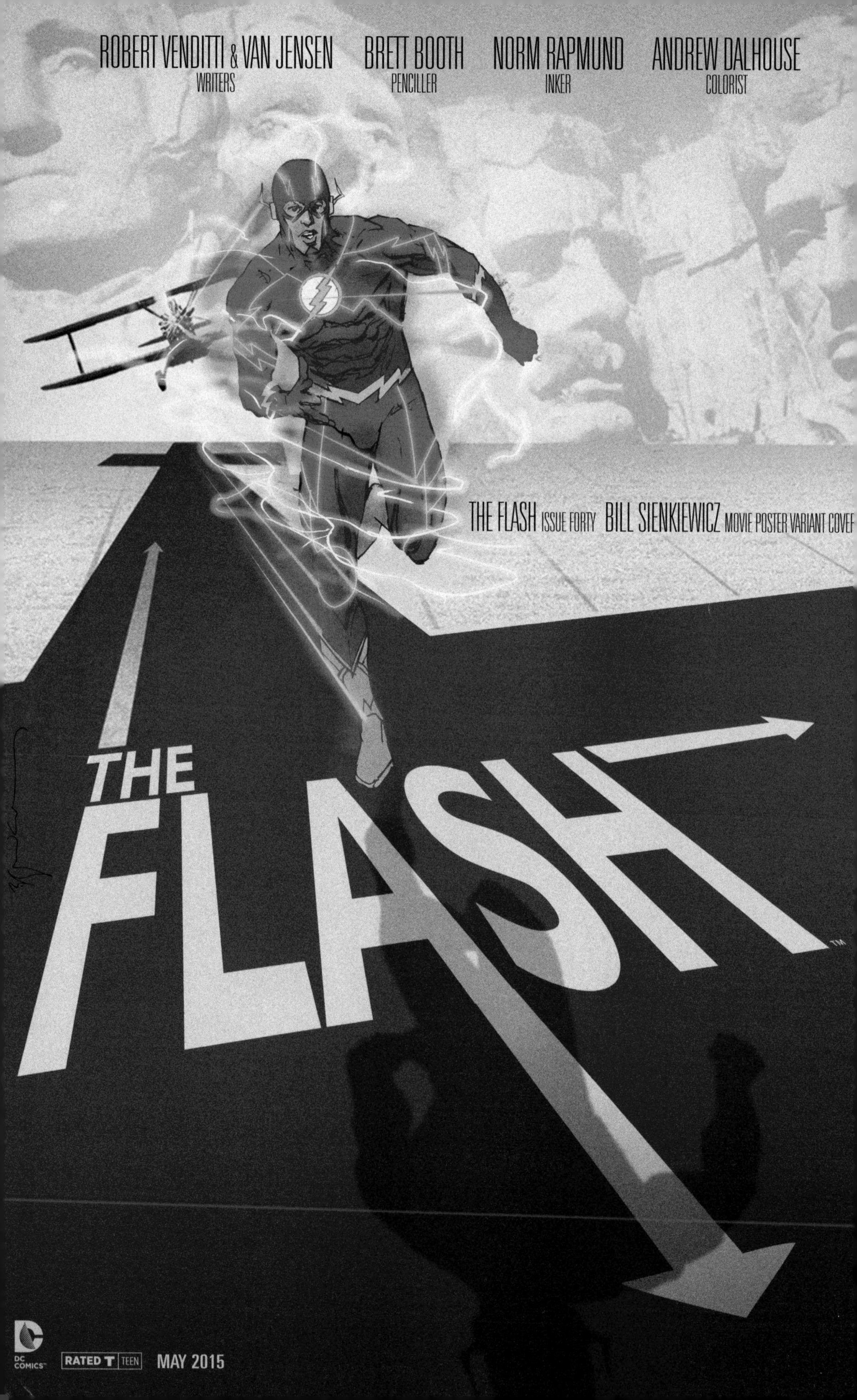

ROBERT VENDITTI & VAN JENSEN
WRITERS
BRETT BOOTH
PENCILLER
NORM RAPMUND
INKER
ANDREW DALHOUSE
COLORIST
THE FLASH ISSUE FORTY BILL SIENKIEWICZ MOVIE POSTER VARIANT COVEF
THE FLASH™
DC COMICS™
RATED T TEEN
MAY 2015

NAPALM CHARACTER SKETCH BY
BRETT BOOTH

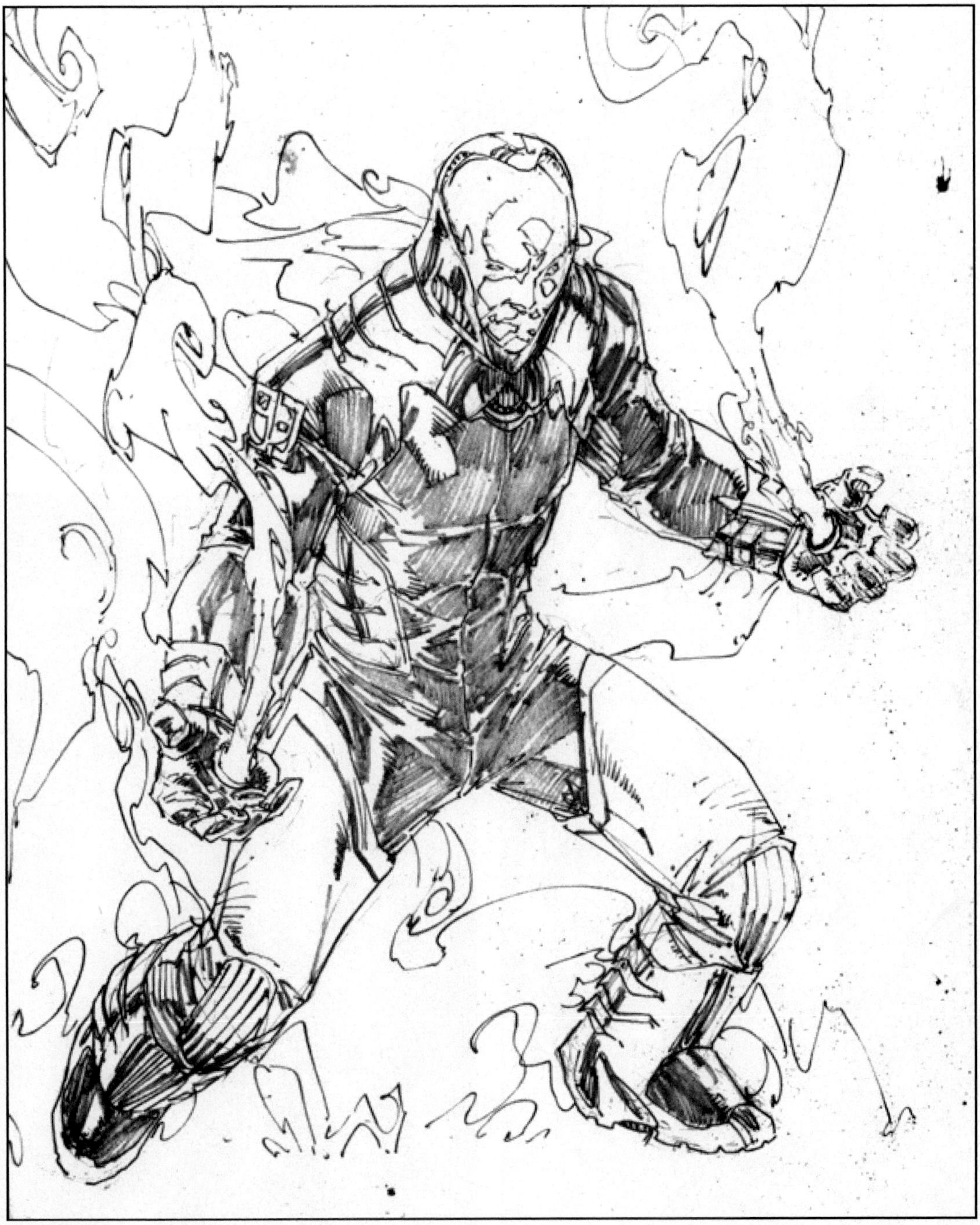

THE FLASH #36
COVER ROUGH LAYOUTS TO PENCILS TO FINAL

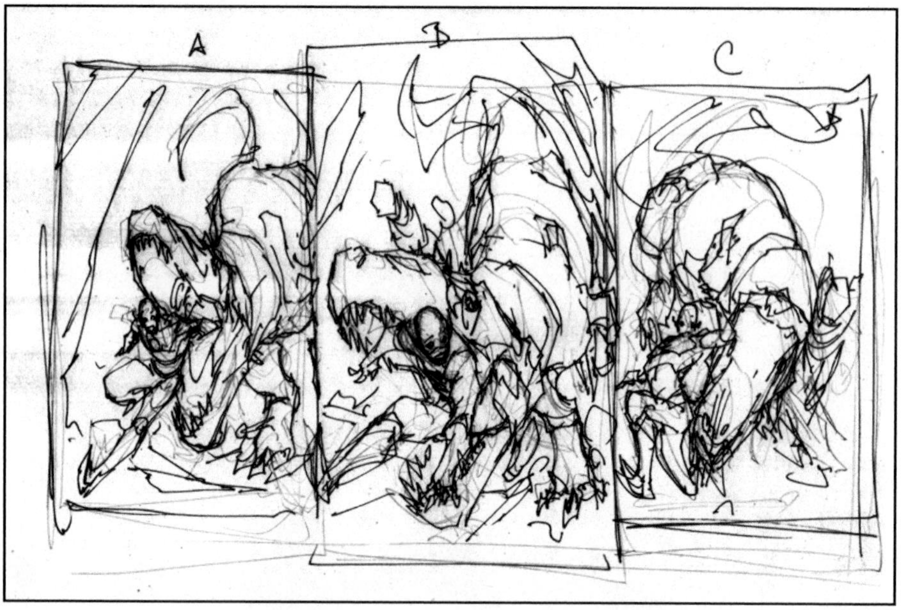
A
B
C

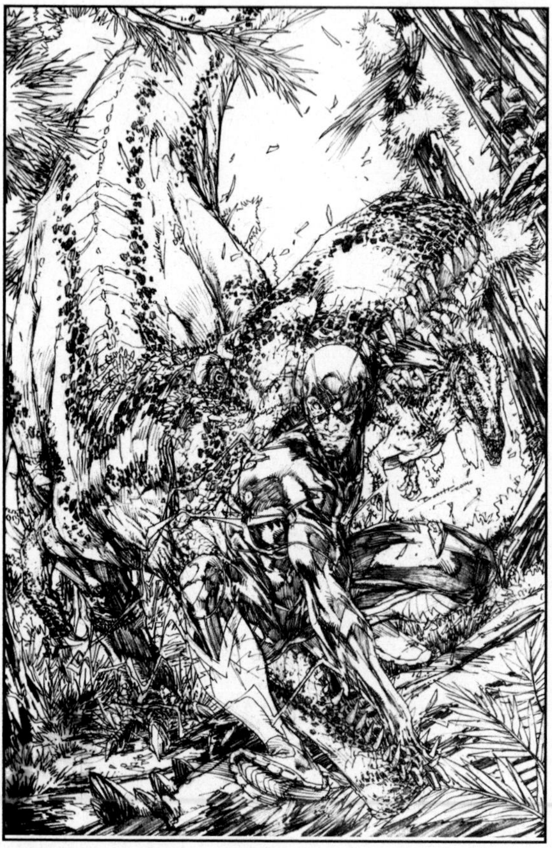

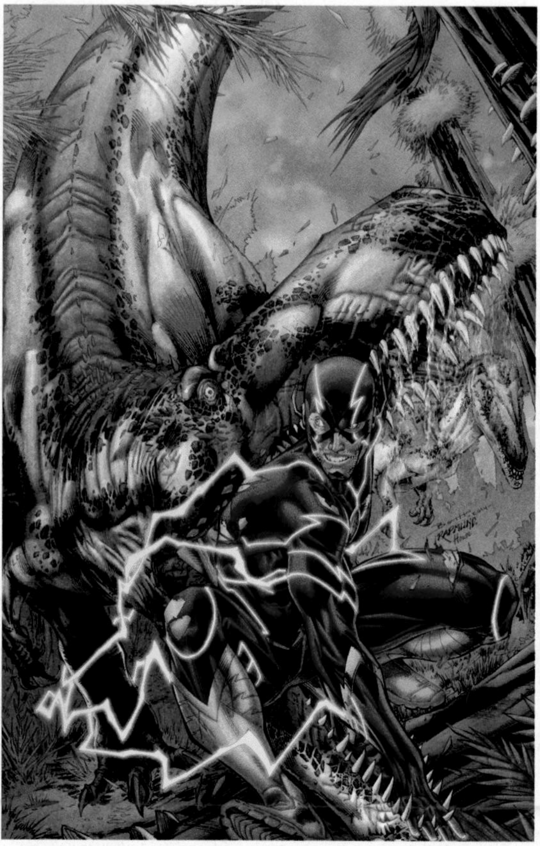

THE FLASH #38
COVER ROUGH LAYOUTS TO PENCILS TO FINAL

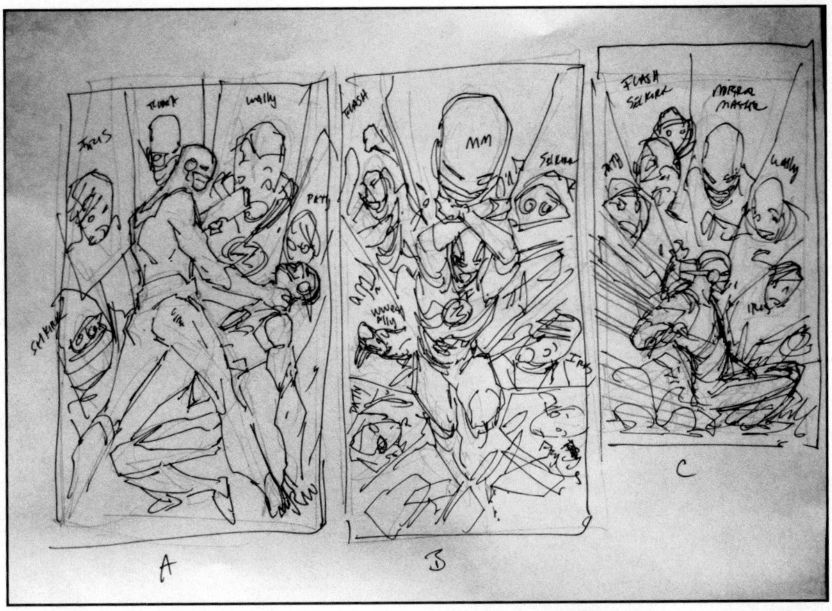
FLASH
Wally
MM
A
C

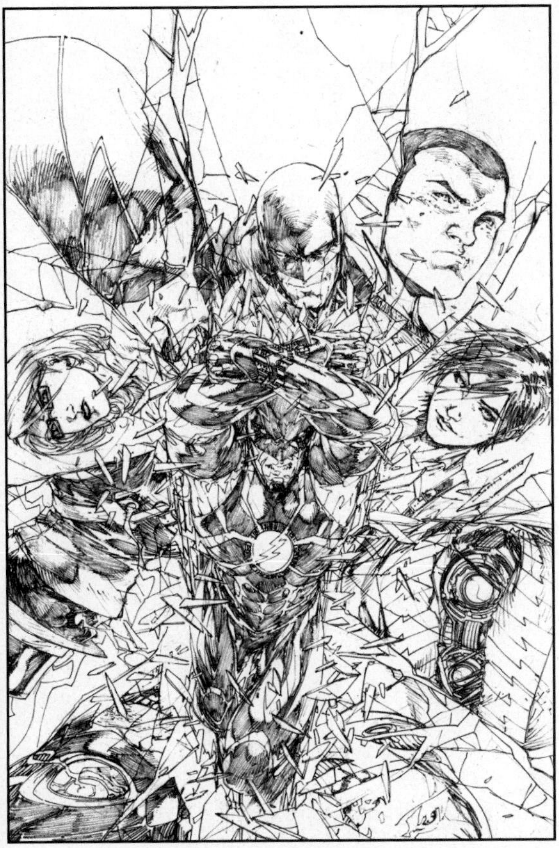

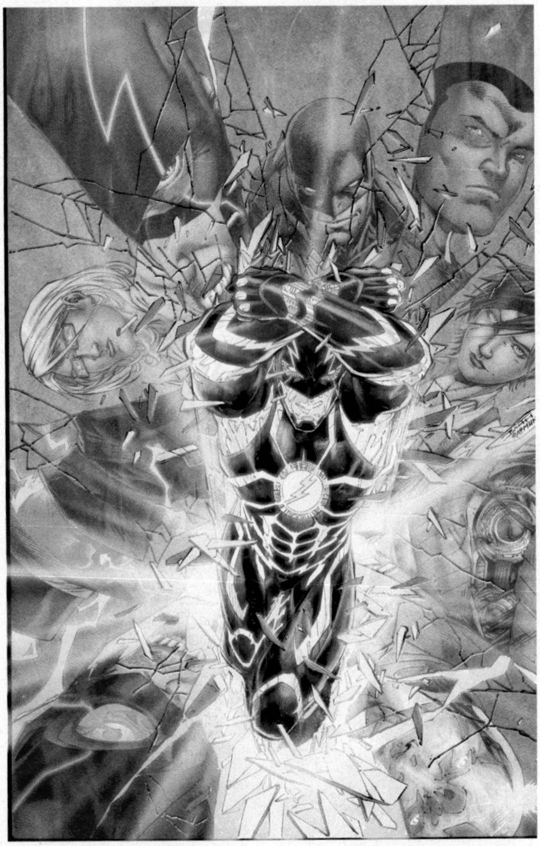

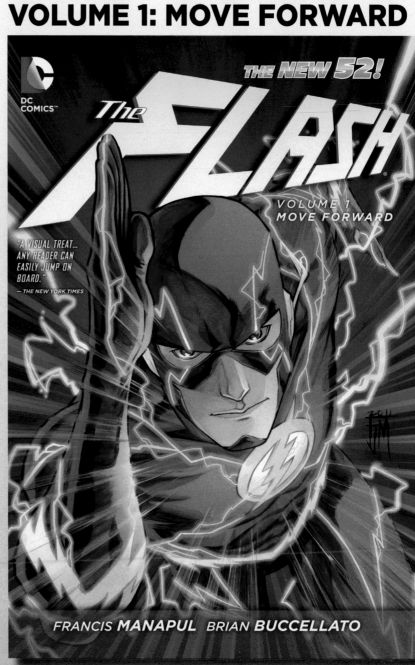